Spark of Independence

THE INDEPENDENCE TRILOGY

Spark of Independence:
The American Revolution in the Northern Colonies, 1775–1776

United for Independence:
The American Revolution in the Middle Colonies, 1775–1776

March to Independence:
The American Revolution in the Southern Colonies, 1775–1776

A JOURNAL OF THE AMERICAN REVOLUTION BOOK

SPARK

OF

INDEPENDENCE

THE REVOLUTIONARY WAR IN THE NORTHERN COLONIES, 1775–1776

MICHAEL CECERE

WESTHOLME
Yardley

© 2024 Michael Cecere

Maps by Tracy Dungan. © 2024 Westholme Publishing

Westholme Publishing, LLC

904 Edgewood Road

Yardley, Pennsylvania 19067

Visit our Web site at www.westholmepublishing.com

ISBN: 978-1-59416-432-3

Also available as an eBook.

Printed in the United States of America.

CONTENTS

Contents

Maps

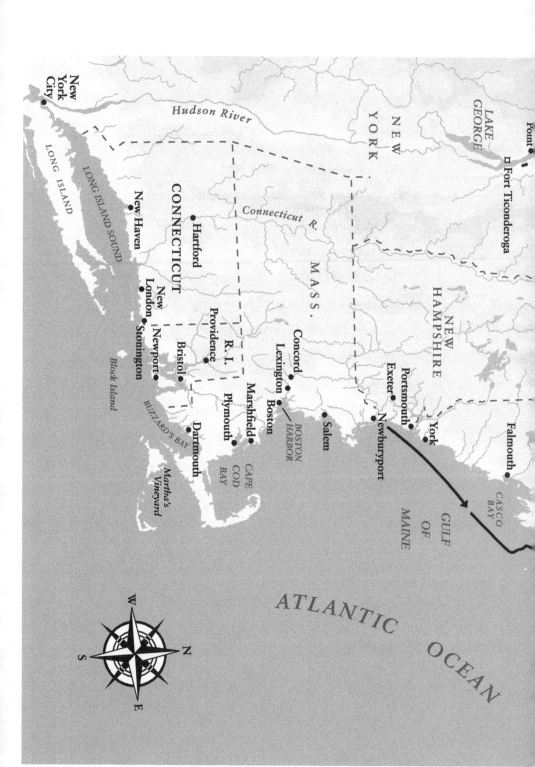

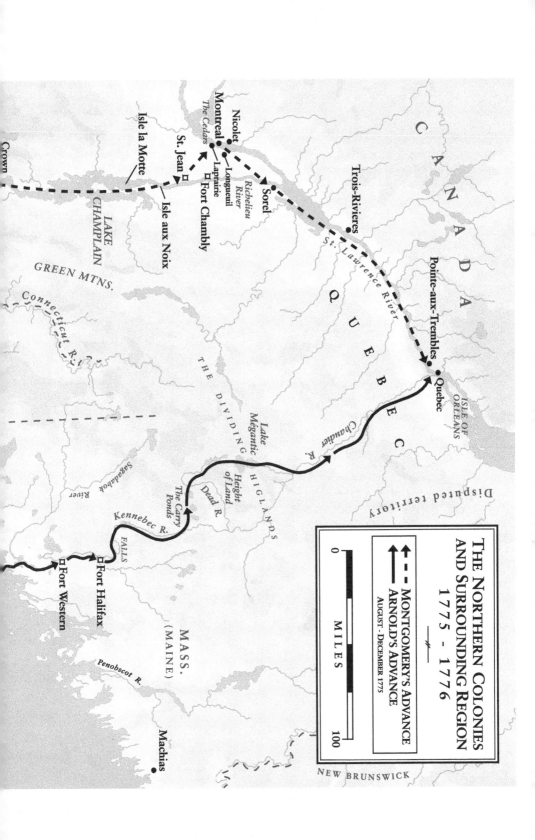

THE NORTHERN COLONIES
AND SURROUNDING REGION
1775 - 1776

MILES
0   100

- - - MONTGOMERY'S ADVANCE
━━━ ARNOLD'S ADVANCE
AUGUST - DECEMBER 1775

C A N A D A

Q U E B E C

Montreal
Nicolet
The Cedars
Longueuil
Laprairie
Fort Chambly
St. Jean
Sorel
Richelieu River
Trois-Rivières
St. Lawrence River
Pointe-aux-Trembles
Quebec
ISLE OF ORLEANS

Isle la Motte
Isle aux Noix
LAKE CHAMPLAIN
Crown
GREEN MTNS.
Connecticut R.

THE DIVIDING HIGHLANDS

Lake Mégantic
Height of Land
Chaudière R.

Disputed territory

The Carry Ponds
Dead R.
Kennebec R.
Sagadahoc River
FALLS
Fort Western
Fort Halifax

MASS.
(MAINE)

Penobscot R.
Machias

NEW BRUNSWICK

INTRODUCTION

The Northern Colonies on the Eve of the Revolution

THE COMMENCEMENT OF HOSTILITIES IN MASSACHUSETTS BETWEEN British troops and Massachusetts militia in April 1775 was the culmination of a decade of political tension and dispute between Great Britain and her American colonies. Prior to the bloodshed at Lexington and Concord, colonial opposition to the British Parliament's attempts to exert more authority over the colonies came mostly in the form of nonviolent protests. Letters and petitions full of declarations of loyalty to the British Crown urged Parliament to repeal its offending colonial polices. Incidents of violence against British officials did occur, but they were limited and largely condemned by most colonists.

Parliament's harsh crack down on Boston after the Tea Party in 1773 compelled most of the American colonies to unite behind Massachusetts to oppose Parliament's Intolerable Acts (Parliament's reaction to the Boston Tea Party). That decision, made separately in each colony over the summer of 1774, set in motion a chain of events that led to bloodshed in Massachusetts less than a year later.

This book completes a trilogy seeking to answer one simple question: What happened in the colonies after the battle at Lexington and Concord in April 1775? We are taught that the American colonies rallied forces to Massachusetts and in fact some of them did. New Hampshire, Rhode Island, and Connecticut sent troops to Boston upon the first reports of fighting and joined an Army of Observation proposed by Massachusetts. Within two months of Lexington, the Continental Congress, representing all thirteen colonies, assumed authority over that army, placed General George Washington, a Virginian, in command, and sent riflemen from Pennsylvania, Maryland, and Virginia to reinforce it. Newspapers throughout the colonies reported on events in Massachusetts on a weekly basis and it was undoubtedly a topic of regular conversation from Maine to East Florida.

But for most of the colonists in the other colonies, once the shock of the first reports of bloodshed in Massachusetts faded, events in their own communities took precedence. The actions of British officials in each colony, and especially the British navy, dominated the attention of colonists and led to confrontation after confrontation.

These incidents in the other colonies outside of Massachusetts have largely been overshadowed in historical accounts of the American Revolution by our focus on Boston and Philadelphia. At the time they occurred, however, these local clashes and incidents were probably more influential upon the inhabitants of the colony in which they occurred than were events in Massachusetts.

So, the purpose of this book, like the two that came before, is to highlight the events that occurred in the northern colonies of New Hampshire, Massachusetts, Rhode Island, and Connecticut between the start of the Revolutionary War at Lexington in April 1775 and the Declaration of Independence in July 1776. Readers will discover that although the New England colonies were indeed united in their fight against the British in Boston, a fight that is rightfully considered the spark for American independence, each colony also had their own particular concerns and crises to address during the fifteen months between Lexington and Concord and independence.

MASSACHUSETTS
The largest of the four colonies of New England and the second English colony established in America, the population of Massachusetts in 1774, some 338,667 inhabitants, was second only to Virginia on

the eve of the Revolutionary War.[1] Included in this count were nearly 50,000 settlers spread along the coast of what is now Maine, separated from Massachusetts by land but connected to the colony by sea. Predominately white (98 percent) and of English origin, the population of Massachusetts exceeded the populations of New Hampshire, Rhode Island, and Connecticut combined.

The city of Boston, with its fifteen thousand inhabitants, was the hub of most social, economic, and political activity in Massachusetts and had been a hotbed of political and social unrest since the Stamp Act of 1765. Occupied by thousands of British troops in 1774 as part of Britain's Intolerable Acts, the city seethed with resentment and tension.

General Thomas Gage assumed the reigns of colonial government in Massachusetts in May 1774, backed by British warships anchored in the harbor and British troops posted throughout Boston. Such an imposing show of force was likely meant to intimidate Massachusetts and the other colonies into obedience, but it had the opposite effect.

Representatives from twelve colonies met in Philadelphia in the fall of 1774 at the First Continental Congress. John Adams, Samuel Adams, Thomas Cushing, Robert Treat Paine, and James Bowdoin (who declined to serve) were selected by the Massachusetts House of Representatives to attend the Congress.[2] Gage dissolved the Massachusetts Assembly in response to its action, but he could not stop the delegation from attending the Congress in early September.

While the First Continental Congress gathered in Philadelphia, the seizure of gunpowder just outside of Boston by British troops on September 1 nearly sparked bloodshed in Massachusetts. Gage had sent troops into the countryside to remove gunpowder stored in a powder magazine near the towns of Cambridge and Charlestown. The redcoats carried out their orders without incident, but when reports of their action spread, many included claims that the British killed several colonists while removing the powder.

Thousands of militiamen in New England, inflamed by the false reports of bloodshed, prepared to march upon Boston. Some were enroute before the rumors were corrected. Although direct confrontation was avoided, the willingness of colonists to confront the British Army with armed force in 1774 was noteworthy.

Several days after this uproar, the leaders of Suffolk County, which included the town of Boston, adopted a series of resolutions that called for civil disobedience against the Coercive Acts and those who enforced it. The resolves also called for frequent militia drills to better prepare for possible conflict with the British Army.[3]

News of the powder raid (which first arrived in Philadelphia as a report that Boston had been bombarded by the British navy) and the Suffolk Resolves united the First Continental Congress in support of Massachusetts. John Adams expressed much pleasure in the Congress's unanimous support of the Suffolk Resolves:

> The Esteem, the Affection, the Admiration, for the People of Boston and the Massachusetts, which were expressed Yesterday, And the fixed Determination that they should be supported, were enough to melt a Heart of Stone. I saw the Tears gush into the Eyes of the old, grave, pacifist Quakers of Pennsylvania.[4]

Encouraged by such strong support for Boston in Congress, Adams proposed a resolution calling for all the colonies to better organize and train their colonial militia. Richard Henry Lee of Virginia proposed a similar resolution.[5] Both men overestimated the readiness of their fellow colonists in Congress to militarily confront Great Britain and their proposals were rejected as too extreme; the representatives instead agreed to support a nonimportation and nonexportation agreement, to take effect on December 1, 1774, and September 10, 1775. It was left to each colony to manage its own militia as it saw fit without guidance from the Continental Congress.

In early October, representatives from most of the towns in Massachusetts met in Salem as a Provincial Congress, much to the chagrin of General Gage, who did nothing to stop the meeting despite the Coercive Acts, which outlawed such meetings. The representatives had first arrived to attend a scheduled legislative assembly meeting, but Gage cancelled it. Not to be deterred, they met anyway and proclaimed themselves a Provincial Congress.[6]

After several weeks of deliberation, the Provincial Congress adopted a plan to better equip and organize the Massachusetts militia. The purchase of twenty cannons, five thousand muskets, one thousand barrels of gunpowder, five tons of lead ball (for the muskets), and twenty tons of round and grape shot (for the cannons) were all authorized by the Massachusetts Provincial Congress.[7]

A Committee of Safety, with the power to call out the militia, was also formed to serve when the Provincial Congress was not in session.[8] The Provincial Congress called on militias throughout Massachusetts to better organize themselves into companies and regiments and enlist at least one-quarter of their men into minute companies "who shall equip and hold themselves in readiness, on the shortest notice from the said Committee of Safety, to march to the place of rendezvous."[9]

The Provincial Congress adjourned for a few weeks in early November and then reconvened at the end of the month to approve the actions of the Continental Congress and appoint delegates to the next Congress in Philadelphia that was scheduled to meet in May 1775. John Hancock, Thomas Cushing, Samuel Adams, John Adams, and Robert Treat Paine were selected to represent Massachusetts in the Second Continental Congress.[10]

Throughout the countryside, communities heeded the Provincial Congress's call to better organize their militia. An unidentified colonist described the widespread militant spirit found throughout Massachusetts and the region in January 1775:

> The state of this Province is a great curiosity. . . . Four hundred thousand people are in a state of nature, and yet as still and peaceable at present as ever they were when Government was in full vigour. We have neither Legislators, nor Magistrates, nor Executive Officers. We have no officers but [militia] ones. Of these we have a multitude, chosen by the people, and exercising them with more authority and spirit than ever any did who had commissions from a Governor. . . . The neighbouring Colonies in New-Hampshire, Rode-Island, and Connecticut, are arming and training themselves with great spirit.[11]

Not every colonist in Massachusetts supported such activity. Some of the inhabitants of the coastal towns of Marshfield and Scituate, about twenty miles south of Boston, proclaimed their loyalty to the

British government and refused to abide by the Continental Association, much less arm themselves for possible conflict with the British
Army. Concerned for their safety because their Loyalist views were
unpopular among the general population, they petitioned General
Gage for protection in late January:

> Being insulted, our persons and property threatened by many ill
> disposed people, who declare their intention of Assembling in
> great Numbers to Attack & destroy us and many others among
> us who are determined . . . to Support the Laws of the Realm, and
> repel by force every unlawful Attempt to destroy his Majesty's
> good Government over us, [we] Desire [that] we may be Assisted
> with One Hundred of his Majesty's troops to repair to
> Marshfield.[12]

Gage sent the requested troops to Marshfield by boat.

Six weeks later, Gage sent arms and ammunition to Colonel
Thomas Gilbert of Freetown, near the Rhode Island border.[13] Gilbert
was a staunch Loyalist and veteran of the French and Indian War.
He raised a company of Loyalists in Freetown who "train and exercise in the Kings name."[14]

In late March, Gilbert appealed to Captain James Wallace of the
HMS *Rose* (twenty guns, 130 men) posted nearby in Newport,
Rhode Island, to send an armed tender (small vessel) to Freetown
should "any of our People [be] obliged to Retreat [that] they may be
taken onboard."[15] Gilbert boldly proclaimed that "nothing but the
Last Extremity will oblige them to quit the Ground," but less than
three weeks later his Loyalist company was dispersed by a large body
of Massachusetts and Rhode Island militia and he was forced to take
refuge aboard the *Rose* in Newport Harbor.[16]

Although these instances of Tory opposition within the colony disappointed the Massachusetts Provincial Congress, they remained
much more concerned about the intentions of Gage and the British
Army in Boston. The Congress urged all inhabitants in mid-February
to "immediately prepare against every attempt that may be made to
attack them by surprise," and that the militia "spare neither time,
pains, or expense, at so critical a juncture, in perfecting themselves

forthwith in military discipline."[17] Jedediah Preble, Artemas Ward, Seth Pomery, John Thomas, and William Heath were appointed to serve as general officers for the Massachusetts militia.[18] Preble, who was sixty-eight years old, declined to serve, so the Provincial Congress added John Whitcomb as a general officer. Preble's refusal to serve meant that Ward, who was two decades Preble's junior, became the ranking officer of the Massachusetts militia.[19] Like most of the other officers chosen, Ward was a veteran of the French and Indian War and well respected.

On February 22, 1775, Gage sent two British officers "disguised like countrymen, in brown clothes" into the Massachusetts countryside to create maps and sketch the terrain.[20] Rivers, creeks, hills, and woods were all to be noted as was each town and village they passed on their way to Worcester. The two officers, accompanied by a servant, were nearly seized by suspicious colonists several times, but with the help of a few Loyalists, managed to complete their mission and return to Boston by early March.[21]

While preparations for a possible military expedition into the Massachusetts countryside were underway west of Boston, an actual British expedition sailed out of the city on February 26, to raid the town of Salem. Lieutenant Colonel Alexander Leslie landed with a strong detachment of British troops in Marblehead and marched rapidly toward Salem to seize cannons and military stores. The raid caught the inhabitants by surprise, but Leslie was forced to stop at a raised drawbridge before he reached the cannons. An account of the incident appeared in the *Essex Gazette*:

Last Sabbath the Peace of the Town was disturbed by the coming of a Regiment of the King's Troops. . . . A transport arrived at Marblehead . . . covered with Soldiers, who having loaded and fixed their Bayonets, landed with great Dispatch; and instantly marched off. Some of the Inhabitants suspecting they were bound for Salem, to seize some Materials there preparing for an Artillery, dispatched several Messengers to inform us of it. These Materials were on the North Side of the North River, and to come at them it was necessary to cross a Bridge, one part of which was made to draw up. . . . The Regiment marched off with a quick Pace, in a direct Course for the North Bridge; just before their Entrance upon which, the Draw-Bridge was pulled up. . . . The Colonel who led them expressed some Surprize; and then turning about, ordered an Officer to face his Company to a Body of Men standing on a Wharf on the other Side of the Draw-Bridge and fire. One of our Townsmen (who had kept along Side the Colonel) . . . instantly told him he had better not fire, that he had no Right to fire without further Orders, "and if you do fire (said he) you will be all dead Men." The company neither fired or faced.[22]

According to the newspaper account, Leslie consulted with his officers and informed the colonists that "he would maintain his Ground, and go over the Bridge before he returned, if it was a Month first."[23] The townspeople replied that they could stay as long as they liked, but the bridge would not be lowered. They then asked Leslie what his purpose was for crossing the bridge. He replied that he had orders to cross it and that he must comply with those orders. After a ninety-minute standoff, a compromise was reached:

Finally the Colonel said he must go over; and if the Draw-Bridge were let down so that he might pass, he pledged his Honour he would march not above thirty Rods beyond it, and then immediately return. The Regiment had now been on the Bridge about an Hour and a Half; and every Thing being secured, the Inhabitants directed the Draw-Bridge to be let down. The Regiment immediately passed over, marched a few Rods, returned, and with great Expedition went back to Marblehead, where they embarked on board the Transport without Delay.[24]

The British version of this incident was a bit different. Major John Pitcairn related an account of the affair that was likely told to him by Leslie himself:

The Colonel landed, and marched with great expedition to Salem; the people beat their drums, rung their alarm bells, but the Colonel saw none in arms but five, and those took care to get out of the way as fast as they could. The people behaved as I suppose

they will ever do, made a great noise when there is nobody to oppose them, but the moment they see us in arms and in earnest they
will talk very differently. The Colonel found no guns—it is supposed a false information. He marched back to Marblehead and
embarked for this place. The moment he left Salem, I am told the
people got arms and paraded about.[25]

Such tense confrontation, along with the constant scorn and con-
tempt leveled at the British troops in Boston, increased the animosity
they felt toward the colonists. Pitcairn expressed the view of many
British officers in early March:

Orders are anxiously expected from England to chastise those very
bad people. The General had some of the Great Wigs, as they are
called here, with him two days ago, when he took the opportunity
of telling them, and swore to it by the living God, that if there was
a single man of the King's troops killed in any of their towns he
would burn it to the ground. What fools you are, he said, to pretend to resist the power of Great Britain; she maintained [in the]
last war three hundred thousand men, and will do the same now
rather than suffer the ungrateful people of this country to continue
in their rebellion. This behavior of the General's gives great satisfaction to the friends of Government [Tories]. I am satisfied that
one active campaign, a smart action, and burning of two or three
of their towns, will set everything to rights. Nothing now, I am
afraid, but this will ever convince those foolish bad people that
England is in earnest. What a sad misfortune it was to this country, the repealing of the Stamp Act; every friend to Government
asserts in the strongest terms that this has been the cause of all
their misfortunes.[26]

The Provincial Congress reconvened in late March and urged
greater compliance to its militia resolves. It also drafted a letter to
the Stockbridge Indians, thanking them for their support and participation in several minuteman companies.[27] In early April, the Provincial Congress passed a series of regulations to govern an Army of
Observation should such a force be necessary to "prevent or repel

any further attempt to [enforce] the late cruel and oppressive Acts of the British parliament, which are evidently designed to subject us and the whole Continent to the most ignominious slavery."[28]

The need for such an army became evident just two weeks later.

NEW HAMPSHIRE

New Hampshire's population in 1775 of 81,300 was just under one-quarter of its neighbor, Massachusetts.[29] The inhabitants were predominately of English origin and the coastal town of Portsmouth was the focus of much of the colony's social, economic, and political activity.

John Wentworth had served as royal governor of New Hampshire for nearly a decade. It was a difficult balancing act to remain on good terms with both the British Ministry and the inhabitants of New Hampshire, a situation that Wentworth would not be able to maintain.

Like all the other colonies except Georgia, New Hampshire's Whig leaders (those who opposed Britain's new policies for the colonies) selected delegates in the summer of 1774 to attend the First Continental Congress in Philadelphia. Nathaniel Folsom and John Sullivan were chosen by a Provincial Congress that met in Exeter in August.

Although Governor Wentworth was troubled by New Hampshire's participation in the Continental Congress, he confidently informed Lord Dartmouth, the British secretary of state for the American colonies, that, "I think this Province is much more moderate than any other to the Southward, although the spirit of enthusiasm is spread, and requires the utmost vigilance and prudence to restrain it from violent excess."[30]

Two weeks later, in mid-September, Governor Wentworth repeated his belief of New Hampshire's moderate sentiments to Lord Dartmouth. He added a warning, however:

> Truth requires me to suggest that the union of the Colonies in sentiment is not divided or lost in New Hampshire, although they have hitherto been prevailed upon to abstain from acts of general violence and outrage.[31]

This avoidance of violence and outrage against British authority in New Hampshire ended in mid-December 1774 when Paul Revere rode into Portsmouth with news that the British had banned further export of military stores to the colonies.[32] By noon of the following day, December 14, four hundred angry men gathered in Portsmouth and marched upon Fort William and Mary, located near the entrance of Portsmouth Harbor.[33] The fort was manned by just a handful of soldiers and its commander, Captain John Cochran, described what happened when the angry crowd arrived:

> Having only five effective men with me, I prepared to make the best defence I could and pointed some Guns [cannons] to those places where I expected they would enter. About three o' clock the Fort was besieged on all sides by upwards of four hundred men. I told them on their peril not to enter; they replied they would; I immediately ordered three four-pounders to be fired on them, and then the small army, and before we could be ready to fire again, we were stormed on all quarters, and they immediately secured both me and my men, and kept us prisoners about one hour and a half, during which time they broke open the Powder House and took all the Powder away except one barrel.[34]

Although Captain Cochran described a valiant effort to hold the fort, the fact that no casualties occurred suggests that the small garrison either fired blanks or intentionally over the heads of the attackers. Governor Wentworth estimated that upward of one hundred barrels of gunpowder were taken from the fort, and the following day another armed party entered the fort and carried away several cannons and sixty muskets. "This Town is full of armed men, who refuse to disperse, but appear determined to complete the dismantling of the Fortress entirely," lamented Wentworth in a letter describing the incident to Lord Dartmouth.[35]

The arrival of HMS *Canceaux* (eight guns, 45 men) and HMS *Scarborough* (20 guns, 130 men) on December 17, offered some relief for Wentworth, but there was little in the fort left to protect.[36]

At another Provincial Congress held in Exeter in late January 1775, John Sullivan and John Langdon were selected as New Hampshire's next delegates to the Second Continental Congress. The New Hampshire Congress also urged the colony's militia to better "acquaint yourselves with the manual exercise . . . and also improve, themselves in those evolutions which are necessary for infantry in time of engagement."[37]

Although the expectation of, and preparation for conflict with Britain was not as intense in New Hampshire as it was in Massachusetts, the actions that occurred in Portsmouth in late December and with the Convention in Exeter in January, must have alarmed Governor Wentworth and those in New Hampshire who still held Loyalist sentiments. Wentworth informed Lord Dartmouth in March that he had requested British troops from General Gage to "support the civil magistrates [so that] the ringleaders in the attack on the fort might be apprehended and confined."[38] Wentworth stressed, "There is an absolute necessity for the continuance of troops here until this service should be effected but the General does not at present think they can spare so long, and . . . in case matters should come to extremities in the Massachusetts province this place will be much exposed without the protection of some troops."[39]

While it is doubtful that the inhabitants of New Hampshire were aware of Wentworth's letter to Lord Dartmouth, his refusal to seat the New Hampshire legislature and his dismissal of civil officials and militia officers suspected of being involved with the storming of Fort William and Mary in December angered many in New Hampshire. Accusations leveled against Governor Wentworth in March 1775 that he had "risen up against your native Country, and done all in your power to enslave it," certainly did little to ease his anxiety; nor did a report that a company of militia volunteers in Portsmouth, "their numbers being so much increased," voted in early April to drill twice a week at dawn.[40]

RHODE ISLAND

The population of Rhode Island was just under sixty thousand inhabitants in 1774 with nearly 10 percent being people of color (people of African or Native American descent).[41] Like the other New England colonies, much of Rhode Island's commerce was tied to the sea, and the town of Newport was a center of social, economic, and political activity in the small colony.[42]

Rhode Island's royal charter granted the elected representatives of the colonial legislature the authority to annually select a governor. This meant that the governor of Rhode Island was not as accountable to the British Ministry as most of the other colonial governors were. Although this was a tremendous advantage for Rhode Island's Whigs who opposed Parliament's continued efforts to assert more control over the colonies, there was always the risk that King George III and Parliament could revoke Rhode Island's charter the way they did with Massachusetts following the Boston Tea Party. As a result, some of Rhode Island's leaders urged caution in their opposition to the British Parliament.

This caution did not extend, however, to abandoning Boston when news of the Intolerable Acts arrived in the spring of 1774. The Rhode Island General Assembly, meeting on June 13, 1774, in Newport, was the first colonial legislature to name delegates to a Continental Congress. Political rivals Stephen Hopkins and Samuel Ward were selected to represent Rhode Island in an expected congress of the colonies that had yet to be officially formed. The assembly declared that "a firm and inviolable union of all the colonies, in councils and measures, is absolutely necessary for the preservation of their rights and liberties."[43]

By late October 1774, the Rhode Island General Assembly had endorsed the formation of several independent militia companies in Newport, East Greenwich, Warwick, Coventry, and Providence.[44] Five weeks later, on December 5, the General Assembly, likely prompted by the same reports of a British embargo of gunpowder and arms on the colonies that prompted the storming of Fort William and Mary in New Hampshire, voted to remove all but three cannons and all the gunpowder, shot, and military stores held in Fort George, located on an island just off Newport.[45] The assembly also approved the actions of the Continental Congress in Philadelphia, made arrangements to enforce the nonimportation association adopted by that body, and reappointed Stephen Hopkins and Samuel Ward to represent Rhode Island at the next Congress in May.[46]

Unlike the removal of the cannons and gunpowder in Portsmouth, the removal of these items from Fort George was completed without incident or resistance. Reverend Ezra Stiles was in Newport when the cannon and military stores were removed and noted in his diary that,

> The Gen. Assembly have ordered & sent several Vessels to dismantle the Fort at Newport, & take all the Cannon & Stores & carry them to Providence. Two or three Packets [small ships] came down from Providence & arrived here at Ten O' Clock last Night [December 8] & worked all night at the Fort in removing the Cannon. Early this Morning, several Cannon were discharged, Drums beat up for Volunteers to assist, & thereupon Multitudes went over to the Fort to assist. At Noon three Vessels were loaded & sailed off.[47]

Although the removal of the cannon and gunpowder from Fort George occurred without incident, one appalled inhabitant of Newport who disapproved of this action likely captured the sentiment of many Tories in Rhode Island regarding the affair.

> The people here have, I think, openly declared themselves against Government, and in such a manner as surely must be pronounced rebellion. Is it possible that a people without Arms, Ammunition, Money, or Navy, should dare to brave a Nation dreaded and respected by all the Powers on earth? What black ingratitude to the parent state, who has nourished, protected, and supported them in their infancy. What can these things indicate but a civil war?[48]

The HMS *Rose* (twenty guns, 130 men) arrived off Newport just four days later, on December 12, and its captain, James Wallace, met with Governor Joseph Wanton to inquire why the cannons were removed from the fort. Captain Wallace reported that, "He [Governor Wanton] very frankly told me, they had done it to prevent their falling into the hands of the King, or any of his Servants; and that they meant to make use of them, to defend themselves against any power that shall offer to molest them."[49] Wallace added that the inhabitants of Rhode Island "intend to procure Powder and Ball and Military stores of all kinds, wherever they can get them."[50]

All indications suggested that Rhode Islanders, like their brethren in New England, were ready to fight for their rights if necessary. The Reverend Ezra Stiles noted as much in his diary in March 1775:

> Military Exercise universal thro New Engld. Connecticut Assembly about raising & equipping Ten Thousd Men for the Field—these to be Men from 20 to 30 [years old] & not above. But Everywhere thro the Country Men [aged] 60 take their places in the Ranks & assiduously learning the Exercise.[51]

CONNECTICUT

The population of Connecticut in 1774 was just under two hundred thousand inhabitants, 97 percent of whom were white and most of English descent.[52] The Long Island Sound and the Connecticut River were the two most influential geographical features of the colony. Unlike the other colonies of New England, Connecticut did not have a single town or city that dominated its affairs.

Like its neighbor Rhode Island, Connecticut did not have an appointed royal governor at the head of its government. The colony was established under a charter that granted the colonial legislature the authority to select governors annually. By 1774, Jonathan Trumbull had been governor of Connecticut for five years and his Whig sentiments, coupled with similar sentiments in the colonial legislature, meant that Connecticut did not suffer a disruption in governance the way so many other colonies did in 1774 and 1775.

The Connecticut Assembly met in May 1774 to handle routine business and adjourned in early June. Anticipating a call for a Continental Congress, the assembly authorized the Connecticut Committee of Correspondence to select delegates for such a meeting whenever it was determined to have it.[53] Six weeks later, Eliphalet Dyer, Silas Deane, and Roger Sherman were selected by the Committee to represent Connecticut in the First Continental Congress.[54]

Silas Deane commented on the sentiment of his fellow colonists in Connecticut in the summer of 1774 regarding Parliament's actions against Massachusetts (the Intolerable Acts):

The inhabitants of this Colony are unanimous in the common Cause, and have their Attention fixed on the result of the expected Congress, which they trust will be, the [formation of] such a Union, of the American Colonies, and the devising, and Recommending those Firm, but Just, Constitutional and Spirited Measures in which, all the Inhabitants of these extensive Colonies will unite, & by Union & Perseverance effect not only the Salvation of British America, but of Great Britain itself.[55]

Samuel Blachley Webb reported on his return to Connecticut from Philadelphia in early October that,

The Spirit of Liberty which has so long been buried in silence [along Long Island Sound in southwestern Connecticut] seems now to rear its head. Fairfield has had a meeting and entered into good and spirited resolves, and are now collecting grain for Boston. Greenwich, I am informed, and Stratford are doing the same.[56]

When word of the Continental Association (boycott) adopted by the Continental Congress reached Connecticut in November, several communities passed resolves in support of the measure.[57] The inhabitants of the Town of Danbury added their endorsement for the second article of the association passed by the Continental Congress:

It is with singular pleasure we notice the second Article of the Association, in which it is agreed to import no more Negro Slaves, as we cannot but think it a palpable absurdity so loudly to complain of attempts to enslave us, while we are actually enslaving others; and that we have great reason to apprehend the enslaving the Africans is one of the crying sins of our land, for which Heaven is now chastising us. . . . We could also wish that something further might be done for the relief of such as are now in a state of slavery in the Colonies, and such as may hereafter be born of parents in that unhappy condition.[58]

Sadly, colonial unity superseded principle on the issue of slavery and when another chance to address the issue of slavery appeared in July 1776, it was deferred at the insistence of the southern states.

By the end of 1774, much of Connecticut had adopted the mindset of the other New England colonies; it was time to prepare for armed conflict with Great Britain. Joseph Trumbull acknowledged this widespread sentiment in a letter to his father, Governor John Trumbull, in late December: "It seems to be the universal opinion of all here," wrote the younger Trumbull, "that a supply of Ammunition should be procured at the Colony's expense as soon as possible."[59] Less than a month later, an unknown observer in Connecticut reported to a friend in New York that,

> Every body among us seems determined not to [allow] the loss of their civil and religious liberties. We have favourable sentiments of the justice and clemency of our Sovereign [the King] but are preparing against the worst. . . . By fresh returns from various parts of the Government, we find that a park of forty pieces of Cannon may be formed in the Spring, should there be occasion, (which may God forbid) and our Army will be pretty expert at most of the maneuvers; will have in the first Grand Division about ten thousand men, that need not blush to encounter an equal number of foreign Troops from any quarter of the globe.[60]

Not every community in Connecticut agreed with the Continental Congress or believed it was necessary to prepare for armed conflict. At a town meeting held at the end of January the inhabitants of Ridgefield refused to conform with the Continental Association adopted by the Continental Congress the previous fall:

> It would be dangerous and hurtful to the inhabitants of this Town to adopt [the] Congress's measures; and we hereby publickly disapprove of, and protest against said Congress, and the measures by them directed, as unconstitutional, as subversive of our real liberties, and as countenancing licentiousness.[61]

The inhabitants of Newtown followed suit a week later.[62] The opposition of these two towns sparked a response in mid-February from the rest of Fairfield County. At a meeting of town delegates from the county, it was resolved that "the good people of this County, and throughout the Colony, [will] withdraw and withhold all commerce, dealings, and connection from the inhabitants," of Ridgefield and Newtown.[63] In other words, those who refused to abide by the Continental Association passed by the Continental Congress the previous fall would be punished for their noncompliance. This measure did not apply to those inhabitants of the rogue towns who pledged to support the Continental Association.[64]

Undeterred by such measures, some of the inhabitants of the town of Reading formed their own association and proclaimed their opposition to the Continental Congress.[65] Loyalist James Rivington, who published a newspaper in New York, reported this news on February 23 but did not include the names of those involved (reportedly over 140 inhabitants). Rivington announced that a list of names could be viewed at his place of business in New York.[66]

The Reading Committee of Observation, angry at this embarrassing development, obtained the names and had them printed in several other newspapers. The Committee noted that only forty-two freeholders from Reading were on the list. That number climbed to seventy-four when minors (those under twenty-one years old) were included in the count.[67] Although their opposition was still a concern, the smaller number was a relief to the Reading Committee.

When the Connecticut General Assembly met in early March 1775, it ordered an investigation into whether opponents to the Continental Association were officers in the colonial militia.[68] The assembly also urged inhabitants to continue to aid their suffering brethren in Boston and granted nearly 150 military commissions ranging in rank from colonel to ensign for the numerous militia units that had formed over the winter.[69]

Like the rest of New England, much of Connecticut spent the winter preparing to fight.

Part I
1775

One

Spring

P REPARATIONS FOR ARMED CONFLICT AMONG THE INHABITANTS OF
  Massachusetts did not go unnoticed by General Thomas Gage
in Boston. He reported to Lord Dartmouth in London in late February that committees of safety and war organized by the Massachusetts Provincial Congress had taken measures throughout the colony
to collect military stores. The committees also called for updated militia rolls from each town in case it was necessary to use force to resist
the British Army.[1]

The British monarch and Ministry had already determined that
force was necessary. Lord Dartmouth wrote to Gage to inform him
of such in late January, three weeks prior to the general's report on
the Massachusetts committees. Noting that Gage's earlier dispatches
to London in 1774 described a situation in Massachusetts "that
amount to actual revolt and show a determination in the people to
commit themselves at all events in open rebellion," Dartmouth asserted that "the King's dignity and the honour and safety of the empire
require that in such a situation force should be repelled by force."[2]

Declaring that "there is a strong appearance that the body of the
people in at least three of the New England governments are determined to cast off their dependence upon the government of this king-

dom, the only consideration that remains is in what manner the force under your command may be exerted to defend the constitution and to restore the vigour of government."[3]

Reinforcements were on their way, added Dartmouth, and it was expected that Gage would use them to "take a more active and determined part" to suppress the rebellion in Massachusetts.

"The first and essential step to be taken towards reestablishing government," continued Dartmouth, "would be to arrest and imprison the principal actors and abettors in the Provincial Congress."[4] The British minister acknowledged that such action might provoke violent resistance, but he dismissed it with the observation that "any effort of the people unprepared to encounter with a regular force cannot be very formidable."[5] Dartmouth added, perhaps as a precaution against any blame directed toward him should his assumption be wrong, that Gage was to act at his own discretion.

Gage responded to the British Ministry's pressure in mid-April. On the evening of April 18, he ordered the flank companies (light and grenadier) of his army to assemble with one day's rations on the shore of Boston's Back Bay.[6] Ten light infantry companies and eleven grenadier companies, totaling approximately eight hundred troops, assembled at 10:00 p.m.; their preparation and movement was observed by much of the town.[7] Commanded by Lieutenant Colonel Francis Smith of the 10th Regiment and Major John Pitcairn of the British Marines, the troops were transported across the bay to Cambridge in longboats, unaware of their ultimate destination.

Paul Revere and other alarm riders, however, realized that this force could be headed for only one place, Concord, where a large cache of military stores and provisions was hidden and where until recently, the Provincial Congress had met. While the British troops assembled on the other side of Back Bay and prepared to march (it took several trips to bring them all across), Revere and the other riders spread the alarm.

Word reached the small village of Lexington, just six miles from Concord and twelve miles from Boston, around midnight, delivered by Revere himself. Colonel Smith and his British troops had yet to begin their march inland, delayed by an insufficient number of boats to ferry the troops across the bay.

Militia gathered on the village common, or green, the designated muster place. Captain John Parker, forty-five and in poor health, commanded the men who assembled. He sent riders toward Cambridge to locate the British Army and report back, but when one of them returned after 3:00 a.m. and reported no British Army was in sight, Parker dismissed his men with orders to remain nearby.[8] Their respite was disturbed about an hour later by the arrival of a second rider with news that the British Army was very near. Captain Parker mustered his men upon the green to await their arrival.

Approximately seventy-five militia were assembled in two lines upon Lexington Green when the advance element of the British column arrived at dawn. They were positioned on the green, between the road to Concord and another road to Bedford, blocking neither, but covering both. Parker reportedly ordered, "Stand your ground! Don't fire unless fired upon! But if they want to have a war let it begin here!"[9]

Similar orders were issued by Major Pitcairn upon the arrival of the British vanguard in Lexington. Two companies of light infantry formed a battleline on Lexington Green. They stood directly in front of the militia just seventy yards away.[10] The rest of the British advance guard marched on the Concord Road and deployed to face the right flank of the militia.

Pitcairn rode between the two lines of troops on the green and ordered the militia to lay down their arms and disperse. Parker, no doubt rattled by the overwhelming force arrayed against him, paused for a moment, then partially complied, ordering his men to disperse. He did not, however, instruct them to lay down their arms. As the militia broke formation, a shot rang out, the origin of which remains a mystery to this day.

The shot had an electric effect upon the British troops; many fired and then charged at the militiamen. Months of pent-up rage at the colonists was unleashed at that moment upon the militia and for a few moments the British officers lost control of their men. Seventeen colonists were killed or wounded in the clash before the officers restored order. One British soldier was shot in the thigh by one of the few militiamen that managed to return fire.[11]

Colonel Smith, who arrived with the main body of British troops moments after the fighting began, was displeased by the incident but

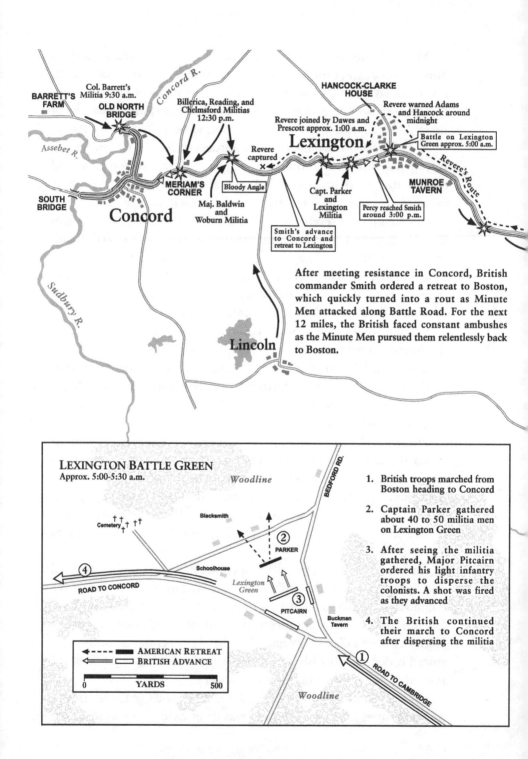

Col. Barrett's
BARRETT'S   Militia 9:30 a.m.
FARM   OLD NORTH
           BRIDGE

Concord R.

Billerica, Reading, and
Chelmsford Militias
12:30 p.m.

HANCOCK-CLARKE
HOUSE

Revere warned Adams
and Hancock around
midnight

Revere joined by Dawes and
Prescott approx. 1:00 a.m.

Lexington

Battle on Lexington
Green approx. 5:00 a.m.

Assebet R.

Revere
captured
×

Revere's Route

MERIAM'S
CORNER

Bloody Angle

Capt. Parker
and
Lexington
Militia

MUNROE
TAVERN

SOUTH
BRIDGE

Concord

Maj. Baldwin
and
Woburn Militia

Percy reached Smith
around 3:00 p.m.

Smith's advance
to Concord and
retreat to Lexington

Sudbury R.

Lincoln

After meeting resistance in Concord, British
commander Smith ordered a retreat to Boston,
which quickly turned into a rout as Minute
Men attacked along Battle Road. For the next
12 miles, the British faced constant ambushes
as the Minute Men pursued them relentlessly back
to Boston.

LEXINGTON BATTLE GREEN
Approx. 5:00-5:30 a.m.

Woodline

BEDFORD RD.

Cemetery † † ††
           †

Blacksmith

② PARKER

Schoolhouse

*Lexington
Green*

④
ROAD TO CONCORD

③ PITCAIRN

Buckman
Tavern

AMERICAN RETREAT
BRITISH ADVANCE

0   YARDS   500

Woodline

① ROAD TO CAMBRIDGE

1. British troops marched from
   Boston heading to Concord

2. Captain Parker gathered
   about 40 to 50 militia men
   on Lexington Green

3. After seeing the militia
   gathered, Major Pitcairn
   ordered his light infantry
   troops to disperse the
   colonists. A shot was fired
   as they advanced

4. The British continued
   their march to Concord
   after dispersing the militia

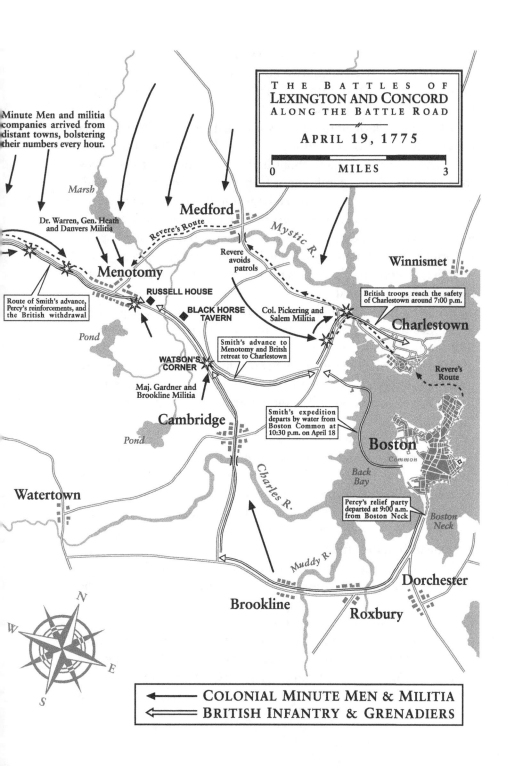

determined to complete his mission to Concord, so the British pushed on. When they arrived about two hours later, they found little of military value there. Most of the military stores had been removed and there were no militia in town.

While the bulk of Smith's troops searched the town, detachments marched beyond Concord to inspect several sites. One of these detachments secured a bridge about half a mile from the town. They soon faced hundreds of militiamen from Concord and the surrounding area who had gathered upon a large hill, determined to cross the bridge and march to Concord. When they proceeded to do so, they were met with musket fire from the outnumbered British troops at the bridge. The militia responded in kind and continued to advance, inflicting several casualties upon the redcoats and prompting the rest to flee back to Concord.

Realizing that he and his troops were in significant danger, deep in the Massachusetts countryside, Smith commenced a return march to Boston. The redcoats retraced their route, but this time hundreds of militiamen from the surrounding area, hidden behind stone walls, trees, and buildings, ambushed them along the route. The intense militia fire took a heavy toll upon the British, especially among the officers. By the time Smith's troops reached Lexington, nearly all order had broken down among his troops.

His force was saved by the timely arrival of one thousand reinforcements under Lord Hugh Percy. Gage sent General Percy from Boston with British reinforcements when he learned that the countryside was alarmed by Smith's march. Percy and his troops marched via Boston Neck at daylight and met Smith and his mauled column at Lexington in the afternoon.

Percy's men joined the fight and the combined British force continued toward Boston, harassed by the Massachusetts militia all the way to Charlestown, where the terrain finally protected them from further attack. It was a momentous and bloody day for both sides. Gage reported 272 total casualties with 65 officers and men killed, 180 wounded, and 27 missing.[12] Historian David Hackett Fischer concludes that militia casualties numbered 50 officers and men killed, 39 wounded, and 5 missing. He also notes that these losses came from twenty-three different Massachusetts towns.[13]

MASSACHUSETTS

The Massachusetts Committee of Safety in Watertown learned of the early morning clash at Lexington about the same time the first British soldiers fell at the North Bridge in Concord several hours later. Estimating the British force at Lexington to be between 1,000 and 1,200 strong, the committee drafted a dispatch at 10:00 a.m. announcing that the redcoats "found a Company of our Colony Militia in arms whom they fired upon without provocation, killed six men and wounded four others."[14]

Isaac Bessel carried this official dispatch on horseback from town to town all the way to Connecticut. Scores of other riders took to the road in all directions, spreading the news verbally of bloodshed at Lexington.[15] Although the details were often exaggerated and inaccurate, the core of the message remained the same—British soldiers had killed and wounded militia at Lexington in an unprovoked attack.

With the Massachusetts Provincial Congress not in session, the Committee of Safety temporarily took charge. The minute companies performed as planned on April 19, but the situation outside Boston required an organized army, so the Committee called for the recruitment of eight thousand soldiers, approximately double the number of redcoats in Boston, to serve in the field through November.[16] The Committee looked to General Artemas Ward and the other general officers appointed in February to provide them with a list of officers to command the regiments formed from these new provincial soldiers.[17]

Dr. Joseph Warren, president of the Committee of Safety, addressed another concern created by the onset of hostilities. In a letter to Gage the day after the fighting at Lexington and Concord, Warren requested that those who wished to enter and leave Boston be allowed to do so.[18] The Boston Committee of Selectmen, in essence the city council, also approached Gage on this issue and an agreement was reached between Gage, the selectmen, and the Committee of Safety. Inhabitants of Boston were free to leave the town with their effects, provided they first lodge whatever firearms they possessed in Faneuil Hall under the care of the selectmen.[19] With less than four thousand soldiers in Boston fit for duty, Gage was concerned that many of the town's residents might join the rebels in a coordinated attack gathered outside of town.[20] Allowing those in Boston with

Whig sentiments to leave, without their weapons of course, reduced the threat from within. Gage assured the selectmen that the weapons would be returned to their owners "at a suitable time." In return for this arrangement, the Committee of Safety agreed to allow those outside of Boston who wished to move into the city with their effects, presumably Loyalists, to do so without interference.[21]

Within days of the agreement over 1,775 firearms, 630 pistols, 38 blunderbusses, and nearly 1,000 bayonets were delivered to the selectmen at Faneuil Hall as the first set of refugees left Boston.[22] The agreement soon fell apart, however. Pressured by Loyalists within Boston who argued that the continued presence of Whigs within town prevented the rebels surrounding Boston from attacking, General Gage halted further departures. These unfortunate detainees became in essence hostages for the British and their Loyalist supporters.

To prevent a similar situation in reverse from developing with a detachment of one hundred British troops who were posted forty miles south of Boston in the town of Marshfield, Gage ordered their evacuation, along with one hundred Loyalist residents.[23] The British navy retrieved them without incident on April 20.

When the Massachusetts Provincial Congress reassembled in Watertown on April 22, they assumed authority over the crisis. The Congress immediately formed a committee to investigate and report in detail what transpired on April 19, and then replaced the Committee of Safety's call for 8,000 troops with a resolution to raise a 30,000-man Army of Observation made up of troops from all four New England colonies.[24] Massachusetts was to raise the largest portion of the army, 13,600, and the other three New England colonies were to raise the remainder, 16,400 men.[25] The Committee of Safety remained involved in affairs; it was instructed to devise a specific plan for the establishment of this new army.

In a letter to the Continental Congress in Philadelphia dated May 3, the Massachusetts Provincial Congress justified its call for a larger army, hinting that such a force should include all the colonies:

> With the greatest deference, we beg leave to suggest, that a powerful army, on the side of America, hath been considered by this Congress as the only means left to stem the rapid progress of a tyrannical

ministry. Without a superior force to our enemies, we must reasonably expect to become the victims of their relentless fury.[26]

General Ward was at his home in Shrewsbury (about thirty-five miles west of Cambridge) and suffering from kidney stones when he learned of the bloodshed at Lexington. He was tasked with organizing the thousands of militiamen that had voluntarily remained outside Boston.[27] Generals John Thomas and John Whitcomb joined Ward in Cambridge in a war council on April 20 to begin the process.[28]

Ward initially concentrated the troops outside Boston in two locations: Cambridge, which lay across the Charles River just a few miles west of Boston, and Roxbury, which lay just south of Boston Neck, the only land access to and from Boston. Holding these two positions and the adjoining countryside largely isolated Boston and its British occupiers by land.

Thomas, aged fifty-one and second in command of the Massachusetts forces, was placed in charge of the troops at Roxbury while Ward maintained command of the troops at Cambridge. A third post in Chelsea, which lay across the Mystic River and Chelsea Creek, north of Boston, was guarded by New Hampshire militia under Colonel John Stark upon their arrival on April 22.[29] Providing provision and shelter for the thousands of troops in the three posts was an enormous challenge.

Ironically, this challenge eased when many of the troops left the field in late April to return to their homes. It was planting time on their farms, and many believed that since the immediate crisis of British redcoats in the countryside had subsided, they were free to go home. General William Heath, who commanded troops at Roxbury under General Thomas, recalled that "The camps became very weak; that at Roxbury did not exceed 1,000 men. Had the British sallied at that time, there would have been but few to oppose them on that side."[30] It was therefore critical to raise the provincial troops authorized by the Provincial Congress as quickly as possible.

Falmouth Incident
While the focus of most of those in New England was upon the situation outside of Boston, a dispute in Cumberland County (present-

day Maine) that began three weeks prior to the fighting in Lexington, grew into a crisis of its own in early May. On April 2, a ship loaded with rigging, sails, and other ship stores arrived in Falmouth (present-day Portland, Maine). The gear was intended for a new ship that Thomas Coulson had nearly completed, but the Falmouth Committee of Inspection ruled that its cargo violated the Non-Importation Agreement implemented by the Continental Congress in the fall of 1774 and ordered that the cargo be returned to England.[31]

Coulson turned to the British navy for help and on April 11, the HMS *Canceaux* (eight guns, forty-five men), under the command of Lieutenant Henry Mowat, arrived to protect Coulson and oversee the transfer of the disputed cargo to the incomplete ship.[32] Falmouth's leaders, fearful of provoking violence, refused to intercede to stop the transfer and it was completed without incident.

Colonel Samuel Thompson of Brunswick was not so hesitant to act, however. When an opportunity arose a month later in early May to seize the commander of the *Canceaux* while he was ashore in Falmouth, Thompson acted.[33] Thompson hoped to use Lieutenant Mowat as a hostage to gain control of the *Canceaux*.

Falmouth's leaders were horrified when Thompson seized Mowat. They feared retribution upon their coastal town from the British navy and demanded that Mowat be released. *Canceaux*'s crew threatened to bombard Falmouth unless their commander was released, and many of Falmouth's inhabitants fled in panic.[34] They passed hundreds of armed men marching toward Falmouth from the surrounding communities. By nightfall, six hundred militia were in Falmouth ready to fight. They were outraged to learn that Falmouth's leaders had already arranged for Mowat's release (on his promise that he would return the following day).[35]

When Mowat, who had returned to the *Canceaux*, failed to return to shore the next day, the militia turned their anger on Falmouth's leaders, whom they saw as weak and cowardly, and threatened to burn the town as a den of Tories. It did not help Falmouth's standing with the militia when they learned that the town's leaders had apologized profusely to Mowat for his treatment. After a day of venting their anger, the disgruntled militia spared Falmouth and returned to their homes, but the seed of Falmouth's destruction had been planted.[36]

Two weeks after the incident in Falmouth, the British navy suffered its first casualties in an engagement with Massachusetts sailors in Buzzards Bay. The HMS *Falcon* (fourteen guns, one hundred crew) had seized several American vessels while patrolling off the southern coast of Massachusetts. Captain John Linzee of the *Falcon* placed eight of his sailors, three marines, a gunner, a surgeon's mate, and a midshipman in one of the captured sloops.[37] Armed with several muskets and swivel guns (small cannons used to blast the crew of opposing ships with clusters of lead bullets), the sloop proceeded to Dartmouth (present-day Fairhaven) where it seized another sloop docked in port and returned to sea with it.

The owner of the seized vessel in Dartmouth, Jesse Barlow, and thirty men manned the whaling sloop *Success*, commanded to Captain Daniel Egery, and gave pursuit a few hours later. Armed with two swivel guns and muskets of their own, the *Success* caught up to the two British vessels off Martha's Vineyard.[38] An account of what occurred appeared in the newspapers in late May:

> [The British vessels] lay at anchor at about a league's distance from each other, the first surrendered without firing a gun, our people after putting a number of hands on board, bore down upon the other, which by this time had got under sail, but the people in the Dartmouth sloop coming up with her, the pirates [British] fired upon them; the fire was immediately returned, by which three of the pirates were wounded, among whom was the commanding officer; our people boarded her immediately and have taken both sloops [back to] Dartmouth.[39]

In what many view as the first naval engagement of the Revolutionary War, the patriots emerged victorious. The British prisoners were taken to Cambridge and then Worcester.[40]

NEW HAMPSHIRE
The news of bloodshed at Lexington and Concord reached New Hampshire before a full day had passed, arriving in Portsmouth early in the morning of April 20.[41] It likely reached towns like Nashua,

Plaistow, and Hampton hours earlier. Hundreds of New Hampshire's minutemen, reported one observer in the colony, "fired with Zeal in the Common Cause, and Resentment at the inhumane Cruelty, and Savage Barbarity of the Action, instantly flew to [Massachusetts's] Assistance, and vast Numbers more were on the march."[42]

New Hampshire's Andrew McClary rushed to Massachusetts upon word of the bloodshed. He informed the Third New Hampshire Provincial Congress on April 23 that "there are now about two thousand brave and hearty resolute New Hampshire men, full of vigour and blood" in the militia camp at Cambridge.[43] He added that there was a great need for officers to establish better order among the men.

Such a strong display of support in the immediate days following Lexington overwhelmed militia leaders gathered outside of Boston. The day before McClary wrote to New Hampshire's leaders, the Massachusetts Committee of Safety informed the Committee of Correspondence in Hampton, New Hampshire, that "they have a sufficient number of men . . . and therefore would not have any more [militia] come from the Northward for the present, but think it needful they should be ready to guard the sea-coast in their own neighborhood."[44]

The enthusiastic support for Massachusetts, displayed by thousands of New Hampshire men at the news of Lexington and Concord, was not replicated with the same urgency by some of New Hampshire's political leaders. When the New Hampshire Committee of Safety learned about Lexington and Concord, it called for a special convention of delegates to meet in Exeter. The hastily assembled Third Provincial Congress was comprised primarily of representatives from the towns surrounding Exeter. Troubled by its limited representation, the delegates in Exeter deferred a decision on joining the proposed New England Army of Observation, leaving it to the next Provincial Congress, previously scheduled to convene on May 17, to decide.[45] The delegates were confident that the next Provincial Congress "will readily concur and co-operate with their brethren in New England in all such measures as shall be thought most conducive for the common safety."[46]

The inaction of the Third Congress left the approximately two thousand New Hampshire militia in Massachusetts in limbo.[47] Many were willing to serve for the remainder of the year and enlisted into the ranks of Massachusetts units with the understanding that they could transfer to New Hampshire units once the New Hampshire Provincial Congress met to organize the colony's provincial forces.[48]

When New Hampshire's Fourth Provincial Congress finally convened in mid-May, it fulfilled the earlier Congress's prediction, authorizing the recruitment of two thousand provincial troops to serve for the remainder of the year in three regiments.[49] Forty-nine-year-old Nathaniel Folsom, a respected merchant who served as one of New Hampshire's delegates to the First Continental Congress in 1774 and a veteran of the French and Indian War, was appointed brigadier general over New Hampshire's provincial troops.[50]

Colonel John Stark, a forty-seven-year-old veteran of the French and Indian War, was placed in command of the First New Hampshire Regiment.[51] Stark had been in Massachusetts since the Lexington alarm, commanding the New Hampshire militia that first marched to Boston, and many of these men formed the core of his new regiment.

Another veteran of the previous war, thirty-nine-year-old Enoch Poor, was placed in command of New Hampshire's 2nd Regiment and yet another veteran, fifty-three-year-old James Reed, commanded the 3rd Regiment.[52]

Governor John Wentworth, a royal appointee who had served as New Hampshire's governor for nearly a decade, was powerless to stop these actions. He admitted as much in a letter to Lord Dartmouth in London on May 17:

> It is difficult to describe how exceedingly this part of the country had been agitated and disturbed since the unhappy affair happened between the troops and country people near Boston. Bodies of armed men in motion in the country and constant reports circulating of their intentions to come to Portsmouth to execute their designs on particular persons [Loyalists]. . . . This is the dismal situation we are now reduced to, without any government power to remedy and without any place of strength or security in the province for any person to take shelter in, there being only one frigate [HMS *Scarborough*, twenty guns, 130 men] near the entrance of the harbour to cover the fort.[53]

Despite Wentworth's concern for mob violence in New Hampshire, he remained at his residence in Portsmouth until mid-June, assured by the residents at a town meeting that he and the other royal officials in the colony would be preserved from injury or insult.[54] However, when Wentworth's home was "Beset by great bodies of armed men who proceeded to such length of violence as to bring a cannon directly before my house, and point it at my door, threatening fire and destruction unless Mr. Fenton [a Loyalist member of the legislature who was visiting the governor] . . . should instantly deliver himself [which he did], the governor had had enough.[55] He left his home and took up residence in Fort William and Mary, where he hoped the small garrison and the HMS *Scarborough* anchored offshore could offer him some protection. Wentworth explained his decision to Lord Dartmouth:

> Finding every idea of the respect due to His Majesty's commission so far lost in the frantic rage and fury of the people as to find them proceed to such daring violence, and not being able to get any assistance . . . I thought it no longer advisable to remain in town and therefore have withdrawn to Fort William and Mary.[56]

It is likely that a letter from the New Hampshire Provincial Congress, meeting in Exeter on June 8, also influenced Wentworth's decision. Informed by Whig supporters in Britain that the governor had requested two regiments of troops from Gage, the Congress wrote Wentworth to seek an explanation:

> As we humbly conceive it as your Excellency's duty, in your official capacity, to guard and defend the lives, liberty, and properties of the inhabitants of this Province, your Excellency sending for Troops to destroy the lives, liberty and properties you have solemnly engaged to defend and protect, conveys in our minds such shocking ideas.[57]

The Congress desired an explanation, expressing hope that the reports from London concerning the governor's troop request "to be farce."[58] They were of course, not so, and Wentworth likely factored the discovery of his request for British troops into his decision to leave his home for the relative safety of Fort William and Mary.

Like Governor Wentworth, Captain Andrew Barkley, commander of the HMS *Scarborough*, was also concerned about the insurrectionary conduct of New Hampshire's colonists. He informed Admiral Graves in Boston two weeks prior to Wentworth's flight to that fort, that his recent seizure of vessels off Portsmouth loaded with corn, flour, pork, and bread meant for the town has "been the cause of great Commotions."[59] Barkley added that threats for "two or three thousand people to come down and destroy the *Scarboroh*" were made, following which he assured the admiral that "the King's Ship will be defended."[60] Barkley concluded his letter with support for the new policy to halt all provision from reaching New Hampshire:

> I don't know any other Scheme, that will have a great effect in bringing the People of this Province to a due sense of the Duty they own to the Mother Country than that of stopping their Provisions, I therefore think it an Object worthy of Attention.[61]

If the British army was unable to crush the rebellion militarily, perhaps the British navy could do it with a blockade and starve the inhabitants into submission.

RHODE ISLAND

The news of bloodshed in Massachusetts reached Providence, Rhode Island, on the evening of April 19. Like the first reports sent throughout New England, the details were uncertain and inaccurate, but the theme remained the same: British troops had fired on and killed militia in Lexington.[62] The militia of Providence assembled upon the news, but waited for verification before they proceeded north. One correspondent to the *Newport Mercury* reported, "One thousand Rhode Island militia stood ready to march to Boston. Some began to march but halted when an express arrived informing them that they would be notified . . . if their assistance should be necessary."[63]

Rhode Island's Assembly also acted, authorizing on April 25, that 1,500 provincial troops be raised to join the Army of Observation proposed by the Massachusetts Provincial Congress just two days earlier.[64] In their haste, the assembly adjourned without appointing officers for these troops and the ensuing confusion delayed their recruitment. James Angell, brigadier general of militia in the county of Providence, sheepishly informed the Massachusetts Congress of the recruitment delay as well as the loss of three hundred barrels of flour to the HMS *Rose*. The loss of the flour added to the delay of forming the troops because it left them "destitute of provisions."[65] General Angell assured the Massachusetts Congress, however, that "As Brigadier of the three battalions [of militia] under my command in the County of Providence, I will furnish you upon any alarm 600 men."[66]

The delay in raising the 1,500 provincial troops for the Army of Observation was resolved in early May when the Rhode Island Assembly reconvened and passed the necessary ordinances to recruit three regiments to serve in the field for the remainder of the year.[67] The speaker of the assembly, Metcalf Bowler, assured leaders in Massachusetts on May 6, that Rhode Island was doing its part to assist its sister colony:

> We are now pursuing every method in our power to have our men in readiness to take the field as early as possible; and you may rest assured that we will exert ourselves upon this important occasion; and that the Army we have voted to be raised, which is to consist of fifteen hundred men, will be supplied with all necessary stores and ammunition; and one company is to be furnished with six three-pounders.[68]

Governor Joseph Wanton, who had just been reelected as governor, but not sworn in for his next term, harboring strong Loyalist sympathy, refused to approve the resolution on troops or sign military commissions. In response, the assembly ordered that the oath of office not be administered to him, effectively removing him from office.[69] Deputy Governor Nicholas Cooke assumed the duties of Rhode Island's chief executive.

The assembly's choice to command the colony's three new regiments of provincial troops was a surprise. Thirty-two-year-old Nathanael Greene had not seen war and had served just eight months as a private in a company of militia that he helped form in 1774. Passed over among his peers for consideration as an officer in this company because of a limp, Greene undertook an intensive study of military affairs over the winter of 1774–1775.[70]

Although there were more experienced military men with better political connections to choose as commander of Rhode Island's provincial troops, the Rhode Island Assembly, apparently impressed by Greene's newly acquired military expertise, selected him as brigadier general of the Rhode Island troops.[71] Greene rode to Cambridge ahead of his troops in late May and learned that the Rhode Island troops were to be attached to General Thomas's division at Roxbury. Greene surveyed and selected a location on Jamaica Plain for his brigade to camp, then returned to Rhode Island to hurry along the recruitment process.[72] Greene's three regiments were commanded by forty-eight-year-old Thomas Church, thirty-four-year-old Daniel Hitchcock, and twenty-seven-year-old James Varnum.[73]

While Rhode Island's patriots went about the business of providing troops for the Army of Observation outside Boston, two British warships, the HMS *Rose* and HMS *Swan* (14 guns, 125 crew) sat anchored off Newport. At the start of May, a small party of Newport Tories informed Captain Wallace on the *Rose* of the efforts of the Rhode Island Assembly to raise troops, but he was powerless to interfere.[74] Wallace did, however, convey the news to Admiral Graves in Boston. Graves informed London in mid-May, based on additional reports from Captain Wallace, that Newport could be "brought over to the King," provided the Tories there were supported by the British. Graves proposed to the British admiralty that the possession of Newport would allow the navy to "cut off any Supplies that could be sent from the Southern to the Northern Colonies," and he "most heartily wish[ed] it was established as a Kings Post and fortified accordingly."[75]

Tory sentiment was apparently so prevalent in Newport that Captain Wallace and his officers felt comfortable enough to dine ashore in Tory households. This nearly led to a confrontation on May 23, when a recruiting party for Rhode Island's provincial troops marched "from the Courthouse down the Parade & then thro' the main street, beating up for Volunteers. . . ."[76] The Tories in Newport had claimed that Wallace would fire upon the town if any such military demonstration occurred, yet when nearly one hundred new recruits passed

where the British officers were dining, the officers did not respond.
Nor were the British officers and their Tory hosts challenged by the
newly raised rebel troops.[77] Just a week later, however, a dispute over
flour nearly led to bloodshed in Newport.

Wallace had made it a point to secure as much provisions as he
could for both his sailors and the British Army in Boston. When he
was not seizing ships that unwittingly sailed into his sight, he purchased provisions locally through contractors. This led to a shortage
of basic foodstuffs in Newport. When a delivery of eighty barrels of
flour meant for the Newport market was purchased by George Rome
on behalf of Wallace, a large crowd gathered at Rome's home to demand the flour. Reverend Stiles recalled what happened in his journal:

> The Patience of the people was exhausted. A Body arose & de-
> manded the Flour. Rome at first promised to deliver it up; but
> Capt. Wallace soon landed about 100 Marines and Sailors armed
> & stationed them around Rome's House & Stores to protect him.
> Upon which the people beat to arms, & about 90 Resolute Men
> appeared under Arms. There was the utmost Danger of Hostilities
> & a bloody scene. However, all was at length settled—the Flour
> delivered up & instantly removed & lodged in the Grainery—the
> Marines retired on board—& so the Tumult subsided.[78]

Captain Wallace shared his own account of the incident with Admiral Graves in Boston:

> On the 3d [of June] An Insurrection happened here. The People
> took it in their heads, A Merchant (Mr. Rome) had bought some
> Provisions for the Use of Government. They stopped the Carts,
> threw about the Flour, flew to Arms with an avowed intent to de-
> stroy the Merchant's House and Stores crying out through the
> Streets now was the time to kill the Tories. . . . I went on Shore,
> saw the Rebels coming in Shoals, Armed with Musquets, Bayo-
> nets, Sticks and Stones etc. . . . . . I got a hundred Men and More
> ashore well [armed]. Stopt them . . . told them upon the first Act
> of Hostility We would rush on and put every Man to the Sword,
> and at the same time order the Ships to fire the Town in every

quarter. This together with the prayers and entreaties of Several of their principal Men . . . put a Stop to an Affair wherein the lives of hundreds were concerned.[79]

The dispute's resolution differed somewhat in each account. Reverend Stiles claimed the decision to release the flour for public sale defused the situation while Wallace claimed it was his show of force and the "entreaties" of several leading colonists that finally calmed things down. He never mentioned what became of the flour. Violence had been averted in Newport, but tensions remained high and other Rhode Island troops were on the march to Massachusetts to join the siege of Boston.

CONNECTICUT

It took less than a day for the news of Lexington and Concord to reach Connecticut, but when it did, the reaction of its inhabitants was the same as the rest of New England. "Every Preparation is making to support your Province," wrote Connecticut's Committee of Safety to John Hancock on April 21; "The Ardour of our People is such that they can't be kept back."[80] The committee added that militia officers were ordered to "forward part of the best men and most ready" to Massachusetts as soon as possible. A resident of Weathersfield, just south of Hartford, noted on April 23 that,

> We are all in motion here, and equipt from the Town, yesterday, one hundred young men, who cheerfully offered their service; twenty days provision, and sixty-four rounds per man. They are all well armed, and in high spirits. . . . Our neighboring Towns are all arming and moving. . . . We shall, by night, have several thousands from this Colony on their march.[81]

The *Connecticut Courant* described a similar situation:

> This engagement occasions a universal muster of the troops in Connecticut; great numbers of whom, completely equipped with arms, ammunition and provision, are gone to the relief of their distressed brethren.[82]

The Connecticut Assembly acted almost as quickly as their con-stituents did to support Massachusetts, decreeing on April 26 that one-quarter of the militia (six thousand men) be enlisted into six reg-iments for the "special defence and safety of this Colony."[83] The troops were to serve no more than seven months and were to be pro-vided with everything necessary to take the field (or be compensated for any gear they provided themselves).[84]

Sixty-four-year-old David Wooster was a Connecticut native who had served in two previous wars (King George's War, 1744–1748, and the French and Indian War, 1754–1763). Wooster held a cap-tain's commission in the British Army during the first war and com-manded colonial militia, first a regiment and then a brigade, during the latter war. Such extensive military service along with his commit-ment to the patriot cause made Wooster the natural choice for major general of Connecticut's forces.

Sixty-one-year-old Joseph Spencer and fifty-seven-year-old Israel Putnam, two other veterans of the French and Indian War, were se-lected to serve as brigadier generals.[85] Putnam arrived in Cambridge five days before the Connecticut Assembly appointed him as a field officer and just two days after the fighting at Lexington and Concord. When news of the bloodshed reached Putnam at his farm in Pomfret, he reportedly unyoked his oxen, abandoned his plow in the field, and rode off toward Boston, some seventy miles away.[86] He arrived in time to attend a war council on April 21, and in his honor the parole or watchword for the army that evening was "Putnam."[87] With no troops from Connecticut to command, but possessing a stellar military reputation from his service in the French and Indian War, Putnam was placed in command of Massachusetts troops at Cambridge.[88] His own troops from Connecticut did not join him until June.

Although Wooster was the overall commander of Connecticut's provincial troops, he was also the commander of the 1st Connecticut Regiment. Spencer also had the authority to command multiple reg-iments, but he had direct command over the 2nd Connecticut Regi-ment. Likewise for Putnam, who had direct command over the 3rd Regiment.

Colonels Benjamin Hinman, aged fifty-six, and David Waterbury, aged fifty-three, veteran officers of the French and Indian War, were placed in command of the 4th and 5th Regiments, respectively. Thirty-eight-year-old Samuel Holden Parsons had no experience at war, but his ardent support for the Whig cause led to his appointment as colonel of the 6th Regiment.[89]

The assembly ordered in late April that the 2nd, 3rd, 4th, and 5th Connecticut Regiments prepare to march to Boston.[90] When reports circulated that New York City could be a target of British forces, Connecticut militia from the western part of the colony marched to Manhattan to offer their assistance.[91] It appears that only the 2nd and 3rd Regiments marched to Boston in late May. Colonel Hinman's 4th Regiment was diverted to Upstate New York and Colonel Waterbury's 5th Regiment remained in Connecticut.

Not all of Connecticut's actions, however, were military oriented. Governor Trumbull, writing to General Gage in Boston in late April on behalf of the Connecticut Assembly, asked for an explanation of the actions of Gage's troops and whether "you have it in command and intention to ravage and desolate the country."[92] Trumbull went further, alarming leaders in Massachusetts who were made aware of the letter, when he asked Gage, "Is there no way to prevent this unhappy dispute from coming to extremities?"[93]

The letter was to be delivered to Gage by a small delegation. They stopped in Watertown to inform the Massachusetts Provincial Congress of their purpose. The Massachusetts Congress was shocked and expressed great concern that Connecticut's action threatened colonial unity:

> Any interruptions of that happy union of the colonies which has taken place would prove of the most fatal tendency, and we cannot but view every kind of negotiation between any colony and the chief instrument of ministerial vengeance here [General Gage] as being likely to operate towards such an interruption. We apprehend that things are now reduced to such a state that nothing but an immediate recourse to arms, and a steady and persevering exertion in military operations, can possibly prevent our destruction, and that a recourse to any other method is, at best, nugatory and vain. Any proposals, either to parliament, to the ministry, or to their agents here, made separately by a single colony, may pro-

duce most tremendous events with regard to America; and we apprehend nothing could be more pleasing to our enemies than the
making of such proposals.[94]

The rebuke of the Massachusetts Congress and unfavorable reply
of Gage ended any possibility of further negotiations. The Massachusetts Congress appeared to be correct, "Nothing but an immediate recourse to arms," seemed the only choice for Connecticut and
its sister colonies in New England.[95]

Fort Ticonderoga

One notable inhabitant of Connecticut, who was fully convinced
that a recourse to arms was necessary after Lexington, sprang into
action to assist neighboring Massachusetts. Thirty-four year-old
Benedict Arnold, a New Haven merchant and captain of militia,
formed a fifty-man volunteer company of independent militia and
marched to Cambridge ahead of the provincial troops being raised.[96]
When he arrived in Cambridge, he approached the Massachusetts
Committee of Safety with a solution to the shortage of cannons and
other military stores in the New England army: seize Fort Ticonderoga in New York, urged Arnold, and bring its cannons and ordnance to Boston.

Originally built by the French in 1755 on the western bank of
Lake Champlain to defend a strategic portage connecting Lake
Champlain with Lake George, Fort Carillon was captured by the
British in 1759 and renamed Fort Ticonderoga. Although its strategic
importance diminished when Britain gained control of Canada from
France in 1763, the fort remained a powerful frontier outpost, bris-
tling with a significant number of heavy cannons and military ord-
nance.

Captain Arnold estimated that there were over one hundred cannons ranging in size from 4-pounders to 18-pounders, and ten to
twelve large mortars at Fort Ticonderoga.[97] There was also a considerable amount of gunpowder and shot at the fort, which, he claimed,
was in "a ruinous condition," guarded by not more than fifty men.[98]

The Massachusetts Committee of Safety sent a dispatch to the
New York Committee of Safety on the same day of Arnold's report,
seeking permission to move against Fort Ticonderoga. Connecticut's

leaders, unbeknownst to the Massachusetts Committee, had settled upon a similar plan the day before, recruiting Ethan Allen of the New Hampshire grants (present-day Vermont) to lead a force to seize Fort Ticonderoga.[99]

Thirty-seven-year-old Allen, a veteran of the French and Indian War, was well respected in the New Hampshire grants and well despised by New York officials for his leadership of the Green Mountain Boys. Formed in 1770 to resist the claims of New York for land they had already received from New Hampshire, they drove settlers from New York away and threatened the lives of New York officials, who in turned took out warrants of arrest for Allen and several other Green Mountain Boys. This dispute, which eventually grew bloody, was superseded by the Revolution and flight of New York's governor in 1775.

Colonel Allen raised his force for Ticonderoga while on the march there. One hundred and forty Green Mountain Boys joined him along with sixteen men from Connecticut and seventy men from Western Massachusetts.[100]

Benedict Arnold had just begun the process of recruiting four hundred men in Western Massachusetts when he learned of Allen's intention to seize the fort.[101] Despite the fact that not a single man had joined him, Arnold rushed to take command of Allen's force. His claim of command, which one officer with Allen observed, "bred such mutiny among the soldiers [that it] nearly frustrated the whole [attack]," was ridiculed and dismissed by Allen and his men.[102]

Before sunrise the next morning, Allen proceeded across Lake Champlain with less than ninety men (all that his boats could carry in one trip). Arnold accompanied Allen, much to the chagrin of Allen and his men. They surprised a lone sentry at the main gate, which was open, and rushed into the fort unopposed.[103] Allen and Arnold seized the fort's startled commander, Captain William Delaplace, from his quarters. He grudgingly surrendered the garrison and fort without a shot. Two days later, Captain Seth Warner with just fifty Green Mountain Boys, captured the small British garrison at Crown Point, ten miles north of Ticonderoga. In two daring raids, two powerful British forts on Lake Champlain had fallen without bloodshed. More importantly, nearly two hundred cannons were now in the possession of troops from New England.[104]

Siege of Boston

Outside Boston, General Ward and his fellow officers quickly discovered that maintaining a siege upon Boston while simultaneously
raising a new Army of Observation required a Herculean effort. The
Massachusetts Committee of Safety, acknowledging in late April that
"many of the persons now in camp, came from their respective
towns, without any expectation of [staying], and are now under the
necessity of returning [to their homes]," sent a circular letter on April
29 to nearby towns requesting them to "send other persons to supply
their places, for a few days, until the enlistments are completed."[105]
This was a temporary solution to the steady departure of troops outside of Boston.

A better solution was to quickly raise the 13,600 troops authorized by the Provincial Congress to serve for seven months. Doing so,
however, went slowly. To encourage the militia still in the field to enlist as provincial troops, the Massachusetts Congress announced that
"the utmost care will be taken to make every soldier happy in being
under good officers."[106] Determining those officers, however, proved
to be a challenge.

Thirteen regiments of Massachusetts militia were in the field outside Boston on May 8.[107] Colonel John Stark also commanded nearly
six hundred militia from New Hampshire.[108] Most of these troops
were not part of the Army of Observation in early May because Massachusetts had not yet finalized its organization and New Hampshire
had yet to even commit to such an army.

Ward, frustrated by the delay, pleaded with the Massachusetts
Congress a month after Lexington and Concord to act faster, writing,
"It appears to me absolutely necessary, that the Regiments be immediately settled; the officers commissioned; the soldiers numbered and
paid . . . if we would save our Country."[109]

The Massachusetts Congress addressed some of Ward's concerns that
same day, first drafting his own overdue officer's commission naming
him commander in chief of the Massachusetts troops.[110] The Provincial
Congress also granted the Committee of Safety powers to organize the
Massachusetts troops and settle the issue of rank among the officers.

An issue that remained unresolved, however, was that of command of the entire Army of Observation. In late May, New Hamp-

shire agreed to place its provincial troops in Massachusetts under the command of Ward, but Rhode Island and Connecticut had yet to formally do so. As the first Rhode Island and Connecticut troops arrived in camp in late May and early June, a voluntary obedience to Ward was practiced, but this held the potential of rupturing upon the first disagreement among the general officers.[111]

Supplying the growing army outside of Boston with provision, ammunition, and equipment was also a significant challenge because each colony assumed responsibility for just their troops. When General Greene, who had returned to Rhode Island in May to supervise the recruitment of troops, joined his men in Roxbury in early June, he noted, "I arrived in camp . . . and found it in great commotion. . . . The want of government and of a certainty of supplies, had thrown every thing into disorder."[112] Two of Rhode Island's three regiments were encamped at Roxbury and Greene reported that several companies were so frustrated by their treatment that they "had clubbed their muskets [pointed them straight down] in order to march home."[113] Greene persuaded the disgruntled men to stay and brought better order to his camp.

The New Hampshire troops, encamped in Medford under Colonel Stark, also suffered for a want of supplies, particularly blankets, medicine, and money. Stark urged New Hampshire's Provincial Congress in late May to address the shortages:

> A great part of the Regiment or Army here, are destitute of blankets, and cannot be supplied by their Towns, and are very much exposed, some of whom, for the want thereof, are much indisposed, and thereby rendered unfit for duty.[114]

Although it appears that Connecticut's provincial troops had yet to reach Boston before June, Israel Putnam commanded some of the Massachusetts troops posted at Cambridge. Ever the energetic commander, he found himself in a heated skirmish with the British in late May, the first such engagement since Lexington and Concord.

Skirmish at Hog and Noodle Islands

General Gage and his troops in Boston had remained surprisingly docile in the weeks following Lexington and Concord, content, like their rebel adversaries outside of Boston, to build earthworks and stand guard. The need for supplies, particularly hay for their horses and bedding for the troops, prompted Gage in mid-May to send a foraging party to one of the islands off Boston. The militia of Weymouth skirmished with British foragers on Grape Island and eventually chased them away before they could secure the bulk of the hay they desired. Although there was much gunfire, little damage was done to either side.[115]

Wishing to prevent further raids upon the other islands near Boston, Ward sent several hundred troops to Hog and Noodle Islands to collect or destroy the livestock and hay on there. Noodle Island was just one-quarter of a mile northwest of Boston and Hog Island a mile and a half further away. The latter was separated from the mainland near Chelsea by a narrow passage of water that was easily fordable at low tide. One could also cross from Hog Island to Noodle Island in knee-high water at low tide as well.[116]

A small detachment of Ward's force, just twenty to thirty men, crossed onto Hog Island late in the morning of May 27; the rest remained on the mainland. According to Private Amos Farnsworth who was part of the detachment sent to Hog Island, they successfully brought off 6 horses, 27 cattle, and 411 sheep.[117] They then crossed over to Noodle Island in midafternoon, burned a house and barn, and killed several horses and cattle.[118]

This drew the notice of the British navy. A party of British marines were landed upon Noodle Island while the schooner *Diana* (six guns, thirty men), commanded by Admiral Samuel Graves's nephew, Lieutenant Thomas Graves, attempted to sail around the north side of the island and cut off the rebel retreat to Hog Island.[119] The small rebel party raced back toward Hog Island and successfully crossed under fire from the schooner. Private Farnsworth recalled that,

> About fifteen of us Squatted Down in a Ditch in the marsh and Stood our ground. And there Came a Company of Regulars [British marines] on the marsh [on Hog Island] and the Schooner; And we had a hot fire until the Regulars retreated. But notwithstanding the Bullets flew very thick yet there was not a Man of us killed.[120]

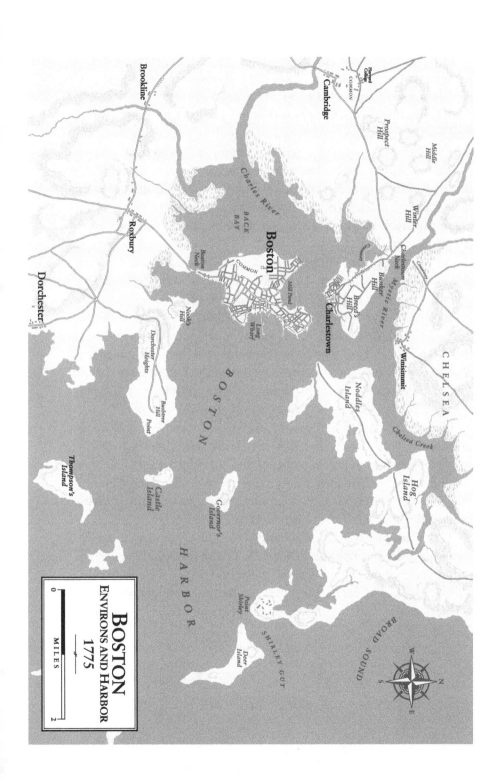

BOSTON
ENVIRONS AND HARBOR
1775

Farnsworth did not comment on the damage his ambush did to the enemy, but another account of the skirmish claimed that two British marines were killed and two were wounded.[121]

Attention now turned to the schooner *Diana*, which had moved well up Chelsea Creek past Hog Island with the incoming tide. Realizing his ship was in danger of grounding, Lieutenant Graves sought to return down the creek into the deeper water of Boston Harbor. With little wind and the tide still rising (pushing the schooner further up the creek), Graves used several longboats to tow his ship down the creek against the tide, all the while under heavy musket fire from shore.[122]

Putnam arrived at 9:00 p.m. with several hundred reinforcements and two 4-pound cannons. He hailed the *Diana* from shore, calling upon Graves to surrender. Graves replied with two cannon shots that prompted a fierce reply from the Provincials.[123] Sometime before midnight, the *Diana* grounded off the town of Winnisimmet and with the tide ebbing, there was little chance to free her. Still under fire from shore, Graves and his crew abandoned the *Diana* around 3:00 a.m. and fled to the sloop *Britannia*, which continued to fire upon the Provincials to keep them away from the stricken *Diana*.[124]

Their efforts failed and cost several casualties inflicted by rebel musket fire from shore. The stricken *Diana* was plundered by the rebels for its cannons and swivel guns and gear and then was set afire around dawn.[125] British marines manning two 12-pound cannons that were landed on Hog Island continued to fire upon the Provincials on the mainland, but to no effect.

At the cost of a handful of wounded men, the Provincials had destroyed a British schooner, damaged a British sloop, killed several sailors and marines, wounded even more, and denied the enemy valuable livestock. The engagement also boosted the confidence of what was already a very confident New England army surrounding Boston.

Two

Summer

ONE OF THE CURIOUS ASPECTS OF THE OUTBREAK OF ARMED conflict between the military forces of Great Britain and the American colonists is that in many ways, life went on as it always did. For instance, for most of 1775, British naval commanders expected continued access to fresh water and provision for their ships in any port in the colonies. Commanders were often befuddled when resistance to their requests for provision (which they offered to pay for) occurred. Time and again they expressed their desire to pay for such provisions, but also asserted that they would obtain such necessities by force if necessary. Such force became necessary in all the New England colonies by the summer of 1775.

MASSACHUSETTS

While events in and around Boston captured most of the attention of the inhabitants of New England and the other colonies, smaller clashes far away from Boston also occurred in the summer of 1775. One such clash occurred in the small coastal Massachusetts village of Machias (along the coast of present-day Maine). Approximately one hundred families lived in Machias in 1775 and they were heavily dependent on trade to supplement their food stocks.[1] Parliament's closure of Boston Harbor and the Continental Congress's response of a nonimportation association, which prevented the inhabitants of Machias from sending lumber and firewood to the British in Boston in exchange for provisions and supplies, placed these isolated colonists in a precarious situation that was made even worse by a recent drought. In desperation, they petitioned the Massachusetts Provincial Congress in early June for relief:[2]

> We, the distressed inhabitants of Machias, beg leave to approach your presence, and to spread our grievances at your feet. We dare not say we are the foremost in supporting the glorious cause of American liberty; but this we can truly affirm, that we have done our utmost to encourage and strengthen the hands of all the advocates for America with whom we have been connected; that we have not even purchased any goods of those persons, whom we suspected to be [hostile] to our country, except when constrained by necessity. . . . We must now inform your honors that the inhabitants of this place exceed one hundred families, some of which are very numerous, and that divine Providence has cut off all our usual resources. A very severe drought last fall prevented our laying in sufficient stores; and had no vessels visited us in the winter, we must have suffered; nor have we this spring been able to procure provisions sufficient for carrying on our business. . . . We must add we have no country behind us to lean upon, nor can we make an escape by flight; the wilderness is impervious and vessels we have none. To you therefore, honored gentlemen, we humbly apply for relief. You are our last, our only resource. . . . We Cannot take a denial, for, under God, you are all our dependence and if you neglect us, we are ruined.[3]

The Provincial Congress barely had time to consider the petition when stunning news of a naval engagement between a British warship and the settlers of Machias arrived. The clash stemmed from a commercial arrangement between a Machias merchant, Ichabod Jones, and the British in Boston. Firewood and lumber were the primary commodities of Machias, and the British garrison in Boston needed both. Jones embraced this business opportunity and reached an agreement with General Gage (in violation of the Non-Importation Association) to ship firewood and lumber from Machias to Boston in exchange for much needed food and supplies that he planned to sell to the inhabitants there.

On June 2, two sloops loaded with provisions from Boston arrived at Machias escorted by the HMS *Margaretta* (a lightly armed British tender). The town's freeholders were split on whether they should allow the exchange and debated the issue for days. The Reverend James Lyons, the chairman of the Machias Committee, recounted what happened:

> On the 2d instant Capt. Ichabod Jones arrived in this River with two sloops, accompanied with one of the Kings Tenders; On the 3d instant, a paper was handed about for the people to sign, as a prerequisite to their obtaining any provisions, of which we were in great want. The contents of this paper, required the signers to indulge Capt. Jones in carrying Lumber to Boston, & protect him and his property, at all events. . . . On the 6th the people generally assembled at the place appointed, and seemed so averse to the measures proposed, that Capt. Jones privately went down to the Tender & caused her to move up so near the Town that her Guns would reach the Houses. . . . The people . . . considering themselves nearly as prisoners of war . . . passed a Vote, that Capt. Jones might proceed in his Business as usual without molestation, that they would purchase the provisions he brought into the place and pay him according to Contract. After obtaining this Vote, Capt. Jones immediately ordered his Vessels to the Wharf & distributed his provisions among those only who voted in favour of his carrying Lumber to Boston. This gave such offence to the aggrieved party, that they determined to take Capt. Jones, if possible, & put a final stop to his supplying the Kings troops with any.[4]

Colonel Benjamin Foster was one of those determined to prevent this violation of the Non-Importation Association. He hatched a plan to seize Jones and the British officers of the *Margaretta* while they attended church in Machias on June 11. The attempt failed when

Foster's armed party was spotted approaching the Meeting House.[5] The British officers escaped to their ship while Captain Jones scurried off into the woods where he was eventually apprehended.

Midshipman James Moore commanded the *Margaretta* and vowed to protect Jones and his vessels and threatened to burn the town if necessary.[6] This threat was ignored and both of Jones's sloops were seized. Reverend Lyons described what happened next:

> Upon this, a party of our men went directly to stripping the sloop that lay at the wharf and another party went off to take possession of the other sloop which lay below & brought her up nigh a Wharf, and anchored her in the stream. The tender did not fire but weighed her anchors as privately as possible, and in the dusk of the evening fell down & came . . . within Musket shott of the [second] sloop, which obliged our people to slip their Cable, & run the sloop aground. In the mean time a considerable number of our people went down in boats and canoes, lined the shore directly opposite to the Tender, and having demanded her to surrender to America, received for answer, "fire and be damn'd." They immediately fired in upon her, which she returned, and a smart engagement ensued.[7]

Nathaniel Godfrey, a local pilot aboard the *Margaretta* who was pressed into service by the British, described the clash in more detail:

> Mr. Moore . . . was hailed on Shore by the Rebels, once more desiring him to strike to the Sons of Liberty, threatening him with Death if he resisted, upon Mr. Moore's replying he was not yet ready, they fired a Volley of small Arms, which was returned from the Schooner with Swivels and Small Arms. The Firing continued about an hour and a half, Mr. Moore then cut the Cable, drop't down Half a Mile lower, & anchored near a Sloop laden with Boards. In the Night they [the rebels] endeavoured to Board us with a Number of Boats & Canoes, but were beat off by a brisk fire from the Swivels & obliged to quit their Boats, four of which in the Morning were left upon the Flats full of holes.[8]

By daybreak, the British commander, having reassessed his situation, abandoned Machias (and Captain Jones) and set sail for the open sea. The *Margaretta* was peppered by musket fire from the shore, but gradually made its way toward Machias Bay with the tide.[9] The incident may have ended there, but the determination of Foster and Captain Jeremiah O' Brien to capture the *Margaretta* led them to pursue the British tender in one of the captured sloops and a schooner. Reverend Lyons recalled:

Our people, seeing [the *Margaretta*] go off in the morning, determined to follow her. About forty men, armed with guns, swords, axes & pick forks, went in Capt. Jones's sloop under the command of Capt. Jeremiah O Brien; about Twenty, armed in the same manner, & under the command of Capt. Benjamin Foster, went in a small Schooner. During the Chase, our people built them a breast works of pine boards, and anything they could find in the Vessels, that would screen them from the enemy's fire. The [*Margaretta*], upon the first appearance of our people, cut her boats from the stern, & made all the sail she could—but being a very dull sailor, they soon came up with her and a most obstinate engagement ensued, both sides being determined to conquer or die; but the [*Margaretta*] was obliged to yield, her Captain was wounded in the breast with two balls, of which wounds he died next morning. . . . The Battle was fought at the entrance of our harbour, & lasted for over the space of one hour.[10]

Godfrey also described the engagement from his position aboard the *Margaretta*:

A Sloop & Schooner appeared, we immediately weighed Anchor & stood out for the Sea, they coming up with us very fast, we began to fire our Stern Swivels, & small Arms as soon as within reach. When within hail, they again desired us to strike to the Sons of Liberty, promising to treat us well, but if we made any resistance they [would] put us to Death. Mr. Moore seeing there was no possibility of getting clear, [swung] the Vessel too and gave them a Broadside with Swivels & Small Arms in the best manner he was able, and likewise, threw some Hand Grenadoes into them; they immediately laid us Onboard, [mortally wounded Mr. Moore and] took possession of the Schooner [carrying] her up to Mechias, in great triumph.[11]

The bold actions of the people of Machias, which resulted in the loss of a handful of men on both sides and the capture of a British warship and two other vessels, garnered the thanks of the Massachusetts Provincial Congress in late June.[12] Appreciation was also extended for the efforts of two young ladies from nearby Jonesborough, sixteen-year-old Hannah Weston and her sister-in-law Rebecca, who gathered lead, pewter, and powder from the surrounding communities and traveled sixteen miles over rough terrain to deliver their much needed military supplies to Machias.[13]

In July, Captain O'Brien attracted more attention for Machias when he surprised the British schooner *Diligent* along the Maine coast and captured it without loss.[14] Admiral Graves in Boston undoubtedly wished to retaliate for these humiliating developments, but he and General Gage had their hands full in Boston.

Bunker Hill

The bold actions of the inhabitants of Machias in June may have received more attention had not a much bigger clash occurred just five days later outside Boston. Gage, reinforced by detachments of cavalry, marines, and artillery, but most notably three British generals, William Howe, John Burgoyne, and Henry Clinton, decided at about the same time the *Margaretta* was seized that he would take possession of high ground overlooking Boston at Dorchester Heights and Bunker Hill, across the Charles River. Both areas had remained unoccupied, a sort of a no-man's-land between the two armies, yet both were strategically important to the defense of Boston. Gage decided to launch his operation to seize and fortify the hills on June 18.[15]

The Massachusetts Committee of Safety learned of Gage's plans and voted on June 15 to seize and fortify Bunker Hill. There was not enough gunpowder or cannons to risk doing the same to Dorchester Heights, so it would have to wait.[16] The next evening, June 16, hundreds of Massachusetts troops, led by Colonel William Prescott, marched from their camp in Cambridge to the Charlestown peninsula. Their mission was to fortify Bunker Hill, depriving the British from doing so, and threatening the British in Boston with cannon fire. Although Bunker Hill was the highest point on the peninsula, Prescott decided to fortify Breed's Hill, about six hundred yards closer to the city. His troops began work on an earthen redoubt and breastwork around midnight.

British sailors noticed the activity in the predawn light and sounded an alarm with cannon fire. Their fire increased in intensity with daylight and continued all morning. As noon approached, Prescott's exhausted men wondered where their relief and reinforcements were. One soldier recalled,

[At about eleven oClock . . . they] began to fire as brisk as ever, which caus'd many of our young Country people to desert, apprehending the danger in a clearer manner than others who were more diligent in digging, & fortifying ourselves against them. We began to be almost beat out, being fatigued by our Labour, having no sleep the night before, very little to eat, no drink but rum, but what we hazarded our lives to get, we grew faint, Thirsty, hungry, and weary.[17]

The absence of cannon to respond to the British bombardment and impending attack also weighed heavy on the minds of Prescott's men. "Our Officers sent time after time for Cannon from Cambridge in the Morning & could get but four, the Captn of which fir'd a few times then swung his Hat three times round to the enemy and ceas'd to fire."[18]

Although the lack of effective artillery support disappointed Prescott and his men, infantry reinforcements arrived before the British launched an assault. Two hundred Connecticut troops under Captain Thomas Knowlton took post to the left but downhill, several hundred yards further back of Prescott's men. A short stone wall and rail fence offered some protection to these troops. They were joined by Colonel John Stark in the early afternoon with hundreds of troops from New Hampshire. Stark reinforced Knowlton and extended the American line left to the shore.[19]

Erosion at the shoreline created an eight-foot drop that shielded the beach, prompting Stark to post sixty men there to defend against a British flank attack. These men hastily erected a barrier of stones and driftwood to screen them from the British, should they attempt to use the beach to flank the Americans.[20]

A gap between the redoubt on Breed's Hill and the line of troops under Knowlton and Stark was covered by three fleches (V-shaped breastworks) positioned at right angles between the redoubt and line of Connecticut and New Hampshire men. Prescott also sent men into Charlestown, on the opposite side of Breed's Hill, to screen the American right flank. The total American force that stretched across Charlestown peninsula by the afternoon of June 17 was around 1,200 men from Massachusetts, New Hampshire, and Connecticut.[21] They were tired, hungry, and low on ammunition, but determined to make a stand.

Approximately 2,600 British redcoats were ferried from Boston to Charlestown peninsula in the early afternoon while British cannons from both the navy and army in Boston shelled the American redoubt as well as the town of Charlestown.[22] General Howe commanded the attack. He hoped to break through the American left with a direct assault upon Knowlton and Stark at the rail fence and beach while General Robert Pigot feigned an assault on the redoubt. The beach attack had the most promise, but it was stopped cold by Stark's New Hampshire men, who inflicted nearly one hundred casualties upon the advancing British.[23] A similar outcome occurred with Howe's attack on the rail fence; his troops were repulsed with heavy losses. The rebels displayed outstanding fire discipline and waited until the British were within point-blank range before they leveled devastating volleys into their ranks. The stunned redcoats were forced to withdraw.

They soon returned, bloodied but resolved to break the American line. Howe abandoned his effort to break through at the beach and used the troops there to reinforce his right wing. They advanced toward the Connecticut and New Hampshire men who once again displayed amazing discipline, holding their fire until the British were within thirty-five yards. More devastating volleys tore into the exposed British troops from behind the rail fence. One British officer described the carnage that was caused by such close, accurate fire:

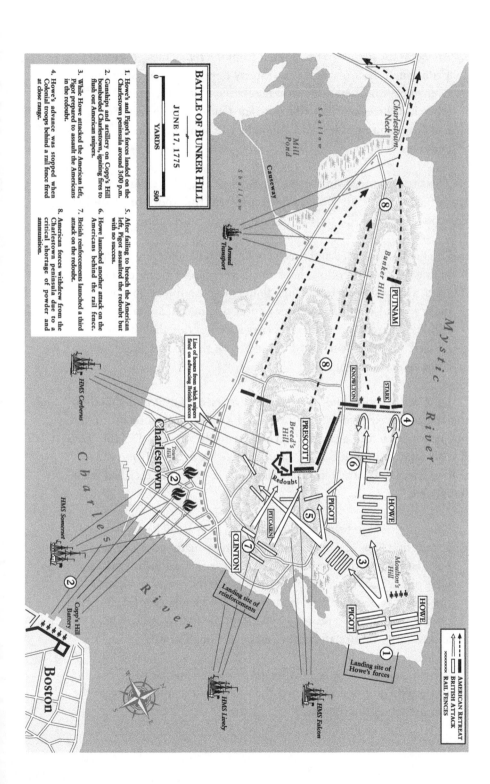

BATTLE OF BUNKER HILL

JUNE 17, 1775

YARDS
0   500

1. Howe's and Pigot's forces landed on the Charlestown peninsula around 3:00 p.m.

2. Gunships and artillery on Copp's Hill bombarded Charlestown, igniting fires to flush out American snipers.

3. While Howe attacked the American left, Pigot prepared to assault the Americans in the redoubt.

4. Howe's advance was stopped when Colonial troops behind a rail fence fired at close range.

5. After failing to breach the American left, Pigot assaulted the redoubt but with no success.

6. Howe launched another attack on the Americans behind the rail fence.

7. British reinforcements launched a third attack on the redoubt.

8. American forces withdrew from the Charlestown peninsula due to a critical shortage of powder and ammunition.

AMERICAN RETREAT
BRITISH ATTACK
RAIL FENCES

Charlestown Neck

Shallow

Mill Pond

Shallow

Causeway

Armed Transport

Bunker Hill

PUTNAM

Mystic River

Line of houses from which snipers fired on advancing British forces

STARK
KNOWLTON

HMS Cerberus

PRESCOTT
Breed's Hill

Charlestown
Town Hill

Redoubt

PIGOT

HOWE

Moulton's Hill

Charles River

HMS Somerset

PITCAIRN

CLINTON

Landing site of reinforcements

HOWE

PIGOT

Landing site of Howe's forces

Copp's Hill Battery

Boston

HMS Lively

HMS Falcon

An incessant stream of fire poured from the rebel lines; it seemed a continued sheet of fire for near thirty minutes. . . . Most of our Grenadiers and Light-infantry, the moment of presenting themselves lost three-fourths, and many nine-tenths, of their men. Some had only eight or nine men a company left; some only three, four, and five.[24]

The situation was similar on the British left, where Pigot and his troops advanced up Breed's Hill toward the redoubt. Colonel Prescott described this part of the battle to John Adams:

The Enemy advanced and fired very hotly on the Fort and meeting with a Warm Reception there was a very smart firing on both sides, after a considerable Time finding our Ammunition was almost spent I commanded a cessation till the Enemy advanced within 30 yards when we gave them such a hot fire, that they were obliged to retire nearly 150 yards before they could Rally and come again to the Attack.[25]

Despite the enormous losses, Howe refused to quit and called up the last of his reserve troops for a final assault. It was to be an all-out bayonet charge against Prescott's redoubt on Breed's Hill. The British attacked the hill from three directions and this time did not stop to fire. Desperately low on ammunition, Prescott described what happened:

Our Ammunition being nearly exhausted [we] could keep up only a scattering Fire. The Enemy being numerous surrounded our little Fort, begun to mount our Lines and enter with their Bayonets, we were obliged to retreat through them while they kept up as hot a fire as it was possible for them to make. We having very few Bayonets could make no resistance. We kept the fort about one hour and twenty Minutes after the Attack with small arms.[26]

British lieutenant John Waller participated in the third assault upon the redoubt and described the scene within the fort once the British breached the rebel walls:

I cannot pretend to describe the Horror of the Scene within the Redoubt when we enter'd it, 'twas streaming with Blood & strew'd with dead & dying Men, the Soldiers stabbing some and dashing out the Brains of others was a sight too dreadful for me to dwell any longer on.[27]

Joseph Warren, president of the Massachusetts Provincial Congress but just a volunteer private in the battle, was killed in the final assault as were scores of other Americans. Those that could fled to Bunker Hill and continued across narrow Charleston Neck. Knowlton and Stark realized their position at the rail fence was no longer tenable and joined in the retreat.

Howe's bloody and battered, yet determined, British troops controlled Charlestown peninsula and the high ground that overlooked Boston, but the cost to do so was enormous. Approximately 1,150 British soldiers were killed or wounded in the battle as compared to only 440 for the rebels.[28] The combined British losses from Concord and Bunker Hill accounted for nearly one-quarter of the British Army. Gage's public report to Lord Dartmouth in London about the battle said little about the British losses (aside from including a return of the killed and wounded) but in a private letter written the same day, Gage confessed,

I wish most sincerely that it had not cost us so dear. The number of the killed and wounded is greater than our force can afford to lose, the officers who were obliged to exert themselves have suffered very much, and we have lost some extraordinary good officers. The trials we have had show that the rebels are not the despicable rabble too many have supposed them to be.[29]

NEW HAMPSHIRE
Provincial troops from two New Hampshire regiments fought at Bunker Hill under John Stark and James Reed and suffered approximately one-quarter of the total patriot losses. Ninety-three officers and men from New Hampshire were killed, wounded, or missing.[30] Stark reported to the New Hampshire Congress that although the

losses were regrettable, "we remain in good spirits as yet, being well satisfied that where we have lost one, they have lost three."[31]

Posted at Medford and upon Winter Hill to guard one of the two roads out of Bunker Hill and the Charlestown peninsula, the New Hampshire troops fell under the command of General Nathaniel Folsom. He reported in late June to the New Hampshire Committee of Safety that he had managed to get the troops "into tolerable regulation" (despite initial resistance from Stark who bristled for a few days at becoming subordinate to Folsom). He suggested however, that members of the Committee of Supplies, responsible for provisioning and supplying the New Hampshire troops, should "constantly . . . attend the camp" in order to see for themselves the needs of the troops.[32]

Folsom was not the only one concerned about provisions. Much of New Hampshire felt the pinch of the British navy's blockade in the form of the HMS *Scarborough* anchored off Portsmouth. Two days before the battle at Bunker Hill, the New Hampshire Committee of Safety had ordered that two whale boats constantly cruise the New Hampshire coast to warn all vessels sailing to Portsmouth of the *Scarborough*'s orders to seize them. They should attempt to land at York, Newburyport, or Hampton instead.[33] Captain Barkley of the *Scarborough* was aware of these alternative ports and requested that another vessel join him to patrol the waters, but Admiral Graves in Boston had no available ships to send.[34] Barkley reported that he believed the inhabitants were making cannon carriages to mount the artillery in order to drive the *Scarborough* away, but added, "I am at present upon pretty good terms with the People of the Town, how long it may remain is very uncertain."[35]

The reports of Captain Barkley and those of Governor Wentworth convinced Admiral Graves in Boston that New Hampshire, like Massachusetts, was in full rebellion. "All legal authority in New Hampshire is entirely at an End," declared Graves on June 22 in a letter to Philip Stephens, secretary of the British Admiralty, and "the impoverished state of the Country alone prevent their taking a more active part of the Rebellion."[36] Graves defended his orders to seize all vessels sailing to New Hampshire because "It deprives the Rebels of the means to keep together, and supplies the King's Army, which in the present state of this Country must supersede all other Considerations."[37]

Although Graves may have viewed New Hampshire in full rebellion and two thousand New Hampshire troops posted outside Boston clearly supported that view, the colony avoided a direct clash within its borders with British forces until August. Governor Wentworth described the incident in a letter to Lord Dartmouth in London. He explained that Captain Barkley of the *Scarborough* had reached an accommodation with the residents of Portsmouth and the surrounding communities to allow them to fish, unmolested, provided a fresh supply of beef was delivered to the British warship weekly. When one of Barkley's sailors deserted in early August, however, the captain unwisely seized a fisherman, declaring that he would only release him when the deserter was returned. Wentworth noted that

> This occasioned murmurs and jealousies among the lower class of people in the town who are in general glad at a pretence to create uneasiness. . . . Captain Barkley in a few days thought proper to release the man. Nevertheless the spirit the populace got into did not immediately subside. . . .[38]

Despite the increased tension, Barkley unwisely sent a boat to town and when it docked, the coxswain was "seized upon [by] a number of armed men [who] came to the wharf and called out to the boat's crew to come on shore, and upon [their] refusal they began to fire on the boat. The men in the boat returned fire and immediately departed; several fires were exchanged but no person was hurt. This threw the town suddenly into great confusion."[39]

Captain Barkley withheld immediate retaliation and instead wrote to Wentworth at Fort William and Mary to inquire "whether the town of Portsmouth meant [this action] as a declaration of war against the King, and if so that immediate satisfaction would be demanded and the consequence most likely would be fatal to the town."[40]

Barkley was assured by Wentworth and his council that Portsmouth's leaders disapproved of the incident, but there was little chance to apprehend those responsible for seizing the British coxswain (who was released and returned to the *Scarborough*) or those who fired upon the boat.[41] Barkley restrained his anger and did not carry out his threat against Portsmouth, but all shipping in and out of the town was once again stopped and the Committee of Safety severed all communication with both the *Scarborough* and Fort William and Mary.[42]

The incident and its aftermath convinced Governor Wentworth that it was time to leave the fort and go aboard the *Scarborough*. He and his family did so on the morning of August 24, and Captain Barkley sailed for Boston in the afternoon. The end of summer brought a temporary end to the British presence in New Hampshire, both militarily and politically. Thousands of New Hampshire troops, however, remained in service with the Continental Army and everyone knew the British navy could return at any moment.

RHODE ISLAND

In Rhode Island, concern about the activities of the HMS *Rose* and HMS *Swan* posted off Newport drew the focus of the colony's leaders at the start of the summer. On June 12, the General Assembly directed the Committee of Safety to charter "two suitable vessels for the use of the colony . . . to protect the trade of this colony."[43] These were to be the start of Rhode Island's state navy, but before the committee even met to proceed, private colonists took the initiative to challenge the British navy.

Captain Wallace of the *Rose* aggressively executed his instructions to interrupt all trade in the colony and seized several vessels in mid-June, two of which he armed and turned into tenders. The additional vessels expanded his ability to interdict even more shipping in Narragansett Bay. Rhode Island's leaders considered Wallace's actions criminal, and Deputy Governor Nicholas Cooke demanded an explanation for them in a letter to Captain Wallace in mid-June:

> The acts of the British Parliament, already filled with restrictions of trade, oppressive in the highest degree, seem by you, to be thought too lenient. . . . You have detained the persons and taken away the properties of His Majesty's American subjects, without any warrant from the acts of trade; by which, you have greatly

impeded the intercourse between this and the other colonies as well as between the different parts of this colony. . . . I demand of you the reason of your conduct towards the inhabitants of this Colony, in stopping and detaining their vessels.[44]

Cooke demanded that Wallace return the seized vessels, which the British commander refused, and the day after Cooke's letter one of the newly converted British tenders, the *Diana*, with a crew of thirteen, armed with four swivel guns and small arms, was confronted by an armed rebel sloop with six cannons and "a great number of men aboard."[45] The *Diana*'s commander recalled that the rebels

Hail'd Us and told Us to bring to or she would sink Us immediately and directly fired a shot which we returned with our Small Arms and Swivels and kept a smart fire on both Sides for near half an hour, till by accident the Powder Chest with the remainder of the Swivel Cartridges blue up. . . . The Ammunition for the Small Arms being near expended and another Armed Vessel with Carriage Guns belonging to the Rebels joining and bringing Us between two fires, so that there was no possibility of saving the Vessel—I thought it prudent to run her ashore.[46]

The British crew managed to escape to shore with two sailors injured.

Captain Wallace aboard the *Rose* at Newport attempted to intercept the rebel vessels the following day, but in doing so, he left five seized ships full of provisions unprotected in Newport. He intended to send the ships to Boston to help feed the British troops there, but upon his return to Newport discovered that, "A great number of the Towns People had taken advantage of our absence, Arm'd a number of Boats and Vessels—taken the Victuallers [ships loaded with food], carried them to Town, dismantled and unloaded them, and this done in the space of two or three hours."[47]

Wallace declared to Admiral Graves that this action, along with the assistance offered to Massachusetts by Rhode Island, "all demonstrate they are as much in Rebellion, as [Israel] Putnam and his Camp."[48] Wallace also reported that both Rhode Island and Connecticut were arming vessels to challenge the British navy:

I had information of this Colony's fitting out arm'd Vessels from Providence to attack the King's Ships—Report says a Brig of 18 Carriage Guns, 200 Men, a Sloop of 14—80 Men and four or five other smaller, besides two fitting out at New London, and two at Dartmouth.[49]

In early July the HMS *King Fisher* (16 guns, 100 crew), arrived in Newport.[50] Deputy Governor Cooke in Providence complained that the three British warships at Newport "are constantly [robbing] and plundering almost all the Vessels that come in Especially those that belong to Providence none Escape that they can get in their power."[51] Cooke added that Tory sentiment in Newport was so strong that "nothing can be done in the colony but they [the British warships] have immediate intelligence of it, [Governor] Wanton appears Very open in opposition to the American measures and has Capt. Wallace often at his house to dine."[52] Cooke speculated that "the Tories will have the Rule of [Newport] Soon."[53]

Such speculation appeared a bit premature, at least to Wallace, who a week after Cooke's prediction, threatened to bombard Newport and moved his ships into position to do so. On the afternoon of July 18, the *Rose*, *Swan*, and *King Fisher* positioned themselves close to Newport as if to deliver broadsides into the town. An account in the *Newport Mercury* recalled that

All the apparent preparations [were] made for cannonading this town, which greatly terrified the women and children, especially those women who were with child. . . . About half past 9, a cannon was discharged from the *Rose*, when the women really thought the firing on the town was begun, many of whom fainted away, and went into fits. . . . However this gun was loaded with powder only, and the men of war gave out to a number of persons, whom they had stopped coming down the river, that they should not beat the town down till next morning, when they would certainly do it. In the morning the like terrific scene was opened by firing another cannon, and seizing on four ferry boats. . . . The *Swan* moved down to the south part of the town, where she anchored with her guns pointing diagonally across the wharfs, so as to rake from thence up to the Parade and Court-house. . . . Quantities of tar and other inflammatory and combustible matter were put into the ferry boats in order, as was said to set on fire, and send into the town to burn it, a more expeditious way of destroying the town than by cannon only. . . . Thus the most warlike and hostile parade was kept up to the highest degree, till near two o'-clock . . . when, all at once, the boats were discharged, the ships weighed anchor and stood up the river.[54]

The cause for Wallace's threatening actions that day is uncertain, but it likely had to do with the desertion, or seizure, of two British sailors in Newport. The *Newport Mercury* mentioned the incident as a possible explanation, albeit unjustified, for the British navy's actions that day:

The story about two of the *Swan*'s people being seized by a mob in town, gagged, carried to Bristol gaol, &ct. had it not been absolutely disproved, would have been a most wretched pretext for firing on a defenceless town, in which there were not less than six thousand women and children. It must have been well known to the commanders of those ships, that there was not a single cannon in this town mounted for its defence.[55]

Whatever the cause for the near destruction of Newport, it was clear that the British naval officers anchored off the town were not convinced that Newport was as Loyalist as Cooke believed. Wallace redirected his efforts over the next few weeks toward raiding islands off Connecticut to collect livestock and forage for the British Army in Boston.[56] They also continued to seize whatever civilian vessel strayed into their sight. Patriot leaders in Rhode Island and Connecticut scrambled to arm and man vessels to challenge the small British tenders that worked in conjunction with the larger British warships, but they could do little to stop the *Rose* and *Swan* from seizing whatever vessel they encountered.[57]

In mid-August the HMS *Glasgow* (20 guns, 130 crew) arrived in Newport to replace the *King Fisher*, which was sent to Virginia.[58] Frustrated by the continued presence of a powerful British squadron, the Rhode Island General Assembly called upon the Continental

Congress to build a continental fleet "of sufficient force, for the protection of these colonies, and for employing them in such a manner and places as will most effectually annoy our enemies, and contribute to the common defence of these colonies."[59] The Rhode Island delegates to Congress were also instructed to "use all their influence for carrying on the war in the most vigorous manner, until peace, liberty, and safety, are restored and secured to these Colonies upon an equitable and permanent basis."[60]

It seems the activities of Captain Wallace and the British navy, far from intimidating Rhode Island into submission, made the colony's leaders more determined than ever to resist.

CONNECTICUT

Unlike Rhode Island's troops, Provincial troops from Connecticut under Thomas Knowlton fought at Bunker Hill in mid-June. They defended a critical position in the American line and inflicted enormous casualties upon the British. In doing so they suffered just three casualties.[61] Only two of Connecticut's six Provincial regiments, the 2nd and 3rd Regiments, served in the Army of Observation outside of Boston at the start of summer. They were joined in late June by the 6th Connecticut Regiment under Colonel Samuel Holden Parsons. The 4th Connecticut had been sent to reinforce Fort Ticonderoga in May and in early June seven companies of the 1st Regiment and all the 5th Regiment were ordered to march to within five miles of New York City, where they were to place themselves under the authority of the Continental Congress and New York Provincial Congress.[62] General Wooster's two remaining companies in the 1st Regiment were posted in New London.

With all but these two companies of Provincial troops posted outside of the colony, Connecticut was left with just its militia to defend against British naval raids. The colonial legislature convened at the start of July and authorized two additional provincial regiments totaling 1,400 men to serve for five months.[63] Colonel Charles Webb commanded the 7th Regiment and Colonel Jedidiah Huntington commanded the 8th.[64] The General Assembly also ordered that two vessels "of a suitable burthen" be armed and fitted out to defend the coast against the British navy.[65]

This effort to enhance their defensive capabilities at home was again offset by a request from the recently appointed George Washington for the two additional Provincial regiments under Webb and Huntington. They were instructed by the Council of Safety to march to Boston in late July.[66]

In early August, however, British naval activity off Connecticut's coast prompted an alarm of the militia and the diversion of several of Webb's companies from Boston to New London and New Haven.[67] General Wooster, who was still in New York, also marched 450 men to the eastern end of Long Island in response to British activity in Long Island Sound.[68] At the end of August, a clash between the British navy and Connecticut militia posted at Stonington erupted.

British foraging raids upon several islands in Long Island Sound prompted an effort by Rhode Island to defend Block Island from such a raid. Two vessels carrying seventy-five troops attempted to sail to the island but were spotted and pursued by the HMS *Rose* and several tenders.[69] The two patriot transports fled to Stonington and unloaded the troops. An account of the engagement in the *Connecticut Gazette* described what happened next:

> [The men in the transports] had but just Time to get on shore, before [a] Tender came in, and after making a Tack they came close alongside Capt. Dennison's Wharf and discharged a full broadside into the stores, houses &ct. and sailed out again, and in a little Time returned with the *Rose* Man-of-War and another Tender, and as soon as the *Rose* could get her broadsides to bear on the Town, she began a very heavy fire, also the Tenders who were under sail.[70]

Joseph Stanton of nearby Charlestown, Rhode Island, described the scene in the town as told to him by witnesses:

> In the morning the ship *Rose* and her tenders came into [Stonington] harbour, [and] began a heavy fire on the town, which continued most of the day. The women and children abandoned the town, in the midst of a severe rain storm. It is surprising that we had only one man wounded. The tenders stretched off and on

within 60 yards of the wharves, and received the fire of our musketry, from behind the wharves, stores and rocks. We have reason
to believe we killed [a] number of the enemy.[71]

Another account from New London, where the gunfire at Stonington could be heard, reported that two patriots were killed in the
clash and speculated that several British sailors also died from musket
fire from shore.[72] Each side blamed the other for the commencement
of gunfire.

The Continental Army is Formed

While all four New England colonies clashed with the British navy
along their coastlines during the summer, the Army of Observation
continued its siege of Boston. The Continental Congress was initially
hesitant in the spring to thrust itself, and thus all the colonies, into
the conflict, but by June a consensus developed in Philadelphia that
colonial unity required more involvement by Congress. On June 14,
1775, the Continental Congress, at Massachusetts' request, assumed
authority over the Army of Observation outside of Boston, establishing the Continental Army. Ten companies of riflemen from Pennsylvania, Virginia, and Maryland were authorized by Congress and
ordered to march to Boston as soon as possible to join this new Continental Army.

To encourage greater support from the southern colonies, especially Virginia, which was the largest colony in British North America, Congress shrewdly appointed George Washington as commander
in chief of the enlarged army. Washington had served as commander
of Virginia's provincial forces during the French and Indian War for
part of the conflict but retired to his plantation at Mount Vernon in
1758 when he failed to receive a commission in the British Army.

When Washington arrived in Cambridge on July 3, 1775, to take
command, he faced a monumental task: turning thousands of citizen-
soldiers from seven different colonies into one united American army.
Accompanied by Major General Charles Lee, a former British army
officer who had retired to Virginia in 1773 and been appointed by
Congress because of his military experience, Washington assumed
command of the newly designated Continental Army from General
Ward (who Congress appointed as Washington's second in command).

Washington immediately sought to reorganize the army, calling for troop returns for every unit as well as exact returns for "all the provisions, Ordinance, Ordinance stores, Powder, Lead, working Tools of all kinds, Tents, Camp Kettles, and all other Stores . . . belonging to the Armies at Roxbury and Cambridge."[73] He learned that he had approximately 17,370 officers and men fit for duty in July, far less than the 30,000 that had been authorized.[74] Another 1,350 men were with the army but sick and unfit for duty. Twenty-six regiments from Massachusetts accounted for the bulk of the troops. New Hampshire, Rhode Island, and Connecticut contributed three regiments each, totaling just over 5,000 officers and men, or 29 percent of the Continental Army posted outside of Boston.[75]

A shortage of tents, clothing, tools, and most particularly, gunpowder, concerned Washington and he wrote to the Continental Congress frequently for assistance. Disputes over rank among the general officers, caused by the appointments Congress made in Philadelphia, also plagued Washington and caused several Massachusetts generals to retire from the army in protest.[76] While Washington expressed his concern about his troop strength and their lack of discipline, he also complimented the troops by observing, "I have a sincere Pleasure in observing that there are Materials for a good Army, a great Number of able-bodied Men, active [and] zealous in the Cause & of unquestionable Courage."[77]

Organizing these men into an effective army challenged Washington all summer. In early August, he informed Congress that they were operating on the flawed assumption that all the regiments taken upon continental establishment were structured the same. "They are different in different Provinces," wrote Washington, "& even vary in the same Province. . . . In Massachusetts, some Regiments have Ten Companies, others Eleven. The Establishment of the former is 590, Men and Officers included, of the latter 649. The Establishment of Rhode Island, & New Hampshire is 590 to a Regiment, Officers included. Connecticut has 1000 Men to a Regiment."[78]

Congress was not the only one misinformed. Washington discovered in early August that there was far less gunpowder available for the troops than he had been led to believe. He was told upon his arrival at Cambridge that over three hundred barrels of gunpowder were available to the army, but when he ordered musket cartridges made up in August, he discovered that there were only thirty-six barrels of gunpowder in the Massachusetts inventory, and less than ten thousand pounds of gunpowder in the entire army. Washington informed Congress that the available powder allowed for "not more than 9 Rounds a Man."[79] The difference in the amount was due to a misunderstanding; the Committee of Supplies had initially provided Washington with an account of all the gunpowder that had been collected since the beginning of the siege. The estimate included gunpowder that had been used in the two months before Washington's arrival.[80]

Washington's frustration with his situation in Massachusetts extended to his officers and troops. In mid-August he expressed his candid views of the New England troops to his cousin, Lund Washington, who served as caretaker to the general's Mount Vernon estate in his absence:

> The People of this Government have obtain'd a Character which they by no means deserved—their Officers generally speaking are the most indifferent kind of People I ever saw. I have already broke one Colo. and five Captain's for Cowardice, & drawing more Pay & Provision's than they had Men in their Companies, there [are] two more Colos. now under arrest, & to be tried for the same Offences. In short they are by no means such Troops, in any respect, as you are led to believe . . . but I need not make myself Enemies among them, by this declaration. . . . I daresay the Men would fight very well (if properly Officered) although they are an exceeding dirty & nasty people.[81]

A week later, Washington expressed much the same sentiment to Richard Henry Lee, a fellow Virginian in the Continental Congress. Informing Lee that the army's defensive lines were nearly complete and that they now had little to fear from the enemy, Washington added this qualifier: "Provided we can keep our men to their duty and make them watchful & vigilant."[82] The American commander, once again criticizing the New England troops in private, questioned whether it would be possible to keep such men on duty:

It is among the most difficult tasks I ever undertook in my life to induce these people to believe that there is, or can be, danger till the Bayonet is pushed at their Breasts, not that it proceeds from any uncommon prowess, but rather from an unaccountable kind of stupidity in the lower class of these people, which believe me prevails but too generally among the Officers of the Massachusetts part of the Army, who are nearly all the same [stock] with the Privates.[83]

Washington observed that a big part of the problem was the way the Massachusetts officers were selected:

There is no such thing as getting Officers of this stamp to exert themselves in carrying orders into execution—to curry favour with the men (by whom they were chosen, & on whose Smiles possibly they may think they may again rely) seems to be one of the principal objects of their attention.[84]

Washington asked Lee and the Congress to change the process of appointing regimental and company officers, which left such appointments to the individual colonies, or worse, to the troops from each colony. This frequently resulted in the selection of poorly qualified officers. Washington wanted authority to appoint officers based on merit, no matter what colony they were from, subject to Congress's approval. In essence, Washington sought a more American army rather than the regional one he commanded in 1775. Aside from a few specialized units later in the war, however, Congress refused to adopt Washington's request, and appointment of regimental and company officers remained the responsibility of each colony.

Although the army was now under continental authority, its structure remained very much regional. The three New Hampshire regiments were all posted on Winter Hill under the command of General John Sullivan.[85] This New Hampshire veteran of the French and Indian War had been in the Continental Congress when that body formed the new army and the delegates appointed him as one of eight continental brigadier generals.

This created a dilemma because New Hampshire's leaders had appointed General Folsom to command all of New Hampshire's troops.

Recognizing that the troops were no longer Provincial New Hampshire troops but Continental troops and that he did not hold a Continental commission, Folsom nobly stepped aside for Sullivan and returned to New Hampshire where he was placed in command of the colony's militia.[86]

General Putnam's Third Connecticut Regiment was posted on Prospect Hill. The other two Connecticut regiments, the 2nd and 6th Connecticut, were posted at Roxbury along with nine regiments from Massachusetts. They guarded the only land route from Boston at Boston Neck. The rest of the troops from Massachusetts were posted in and around Cambridge while two of Rhode Island's three regiments with the army were moved from Jamaica Plain to Sewell's Farm, closer to Cambridge. The other Rhode Island regiment was posted with the New Hampshire troops on Winter Hill.[87]

Washington altered this arrangement within weeks of his arrival. The three Rhode Island regiments, which totaled over 1,250 officers and men, were united into a brigade that also included four regiments from Massachusetts.[88] This combined brigade fell under Nathanael Greene's command and was posted on Prospect Hill, between Winter Hill and Cambridge. The three New Hampshire regiments, some 1,600 strong, continued to serve together under Sullivan, but three Massachusetts regiments were added to his brigade, all of whom remained on Winter Hill.[89] Greene's and Sullivan's brigades comprised the left division, or wing, of the American army at Boston, which fell under the command of Major General Charles Lee.

The center division of the American line was in Cambridge. Putnam's 3rd Connecticut Regiment remained there, detached from the other two Connecticut regiments. The bulk of troops from Massachusetts were posted at Cambridge in two brigades under General Heath and Colonel James Frye. Putnam commanded the American center division at Cambridge.[90]

General Spencer's and Colonel Parson's other two Connecticut regiments were attached to a brigade with three other Massachusetts regiments posted at Roxbury and commanded by Spencer. Another brigade of Massachusetts troops commanded by General John Thomas was also posted at Roxbury and together they formed the right division or wing of the American army under Major General

Artemas Ward.[91] At the end of July, the number of Connecticut troops with the army totaled over 2,700 in three regiments while the total for Massachusetts was just under 13,000 men.[92]

When the rifle companies from Pennsylvania, Virginia, and Maryland arrived in late July and early August, they were posted among the three divisions. The riflemen from Virginia and Maryland—two companies each—were attached to the right wing of the army at Roxbury, while the six companies of Pennsylvania riflemen (which grew to eight companies) were attached to the left wing and center of the line.

The arrival of the riflemen caused quite a stir in the army, and they were much esteemed, initially. One unidentified American officer wrote:

> You will think me vain should I tell you how much the Riflemen are esteemed. Their dress, their arms, their size, strength and activity, but above all their eagerness to attack the enemy, entitle them to the first rank. The hunting shirt is like a full suit at St. James [the British royal court]. A Rifleman in his dress may pass sentinels and go almost where he pleases, while officers of other Regiments are stopped.[93]

The extended range of their rifled barrel weapons cost several British officers and men their lives in August as riflemen picked them off from several hundred yards away. The British quickly adapted, however, and with the shortage of gunpowder in the American army still acute, Washington ordered an end to all unauthorized firing at the enemy within weeks of their arrival.[94]

Discipline among the Pennsylvania riflemen soon became a problem and led to a near mutiny of over thirty of them attached to Greene's brigade on September 10. They were part of Captain James Ross's company from Pennsylvania and were upset that one of their fellow riflemen had been arrested and confined to the guard house. Determined to free their comrade, a party of riflemen set out under arms for Cambridge. Lieutenant Jesse Lukins, a Pennsylvania rifle officer, recalled that

We stayed in camp and kept the others quiet; sent word to General Washington, who reinforced the guard to 500 men with fixed bayonets and loaded pieces. Col. Hitchcock's regiment (being the one next to us) was ordered under arms and some part of General Greene's brigade. . . . Generals Washington, Lee, and Greene came immediately and our 32 mutineers who had gone about half a mile towards Cambridge and taken possession of a hill and woods, beginning to be frightened by the proceedings, were not so hardened but upon the General's ordering them to ground their arms they did it immediately. The General then ordered another of our company's (Capt. Nagles) to surround them with their loaded guns, which was immediately done and . . . he ordered two of the ring leaders bound.[95]

The mutineers were treated leniently by Washington, most being fined twenty shillings for their conduct. The riflemen in general, however, lost much of their luster and found themselves assigned to all the normal camp duties that they had originally been excused from. Lukins likely approved of the new arrangement. He believed that the initial indulgence shown to the riflemen had "rendered the men rather insolent for good soldiers," and such special treatment had been a major factor behind the behavior of Captain Ross's mutineers.[96]

Despite the continued shortage of ammunition and other supplies and the challenge of commanding citizen-soldiers, Washington felt that the Continental Army outside Boston was stronger in September than it had been in July when he first arrived. He confidently described his situation to his brother, John Augustine, on September 10:

Being, in our own opinion at least, very securely Intrenched, and wishing for nothing more than to see the Enemy out of their strong holds, that the dispute may come to an Issue. The inactive state we lye in is exceedingly disagreeable especially as we can see no end to it. . . . Unless the Ministerial Troops in Boston are waiting for reinforcements, I cannot devise what they are staying there after—and why (as they affect to despise the Americans) they do not come forth, & put an end to the contest at once. They suffer greatly for want of fresh Provisions notwithstanding they have pillaged several Islands of a good many Sheep and Cattle —. They are also scarce of Fuel, unless (according to the acct. of one of their Deserters) they mean to pull down Houses for Firing. In short, they are from all accts. suffering all the Inconveniencies of a Siege.[97]

The next day the restless American commander held a war council to discuss the possibility of attacking Boston. It was unanimously agreed among the generals in attendance that such an attack was "not expedient" at that time, so the idea was dropped.[98] The siege was to continue, but for over one thousand American troops, a grueling expedition was about to begin—one that held great promise and great risk.

Three

Fall

Although Boston remained the focal point of both England and the colonies in the summer of 1775, the Continental Congress authorized a military expedition into Canada in June as a preemptive strike against the British. The goal was to eliminate the British strongholds at St. Jeans, Montreal, and most particularly Quebec, to prevent them from being used as staging areas against the American colonies. Major General Philip Schuyler of New York was authorized to lead troops into Canada should he find such an endeavor practicable.

Schuyler struggled mightily to prepare an expedition for Canada and in early August wrote to General Washington to inform him that he would start north from Fort Ticonderoga in a few days. Although he could little spare any men himself, General Washington decided to send troops from his army in Massachusetts to Canada as well. Their objective was to be Quebec. Washington wished Schuyler well in his reply on August 14, but a week later he informed Schuyler of a plan to send his own force to Canada by way of the Maine wilderness.

CANADA: ARNOLD'S EXPEDITION TO QUEBEC
Washington revealed his plan to Schuyler in a letter on August 21:

> The Design of this Express is to communicate to you a Plan of an
> Expedition, which has engrossed my Thoughts for several Days.
> It is to penetrate into Canada, by Way of Kennebeck River, and
> so to Quebec. . . . It would make a Diversion [for you] that would
> distract [the British Governor of Canada, Guy Carleton] and fa-
> cilitate your Views. He must either break up and follow this party
> to Quebec, by which he will leave you a free passage or suffer that
> important Place to fall into our Hands; an Event which would
> have a decisive Effect and Influence on the public Interests.[1]

Washington mulled over his plan for another week and set it in
motion in early September. He instructed Reuben Colburn, a sawmill
owner on the Kennebec River in Maine, to construct two hundred
batteaux to transport the troops and supplies for the expedition upriver. To get to the Kennebec River, Nathaniel Tracy, a merchant from
Newburyport on the coast of Massachusetts, was instructed to assemble a number of transport ships.[2] Washington then called for approximately 1,100 officers and men, "active Woodsmen, and well
acquainted with batteaus," to volunteer and muster on the common
in Cambridge on September 6.[3]

Ten of the thirteen companies that were formed for the expedition
comprised troops from New England; the other three were riflemen
from Virginia and Pennsylvania. Colonel Benedict Arnold was tapped
to command the expedition.

Eleven ships crowded with men and supplies left Newburyport on
September 19 and arrived safely at the mouth of the Kennebec River
the next day. With the help of local pilots, the fleet made its way upriver, past Merrymeeting Bay, the ruins of Fort Richmond, and Pow-
nalborough Courthouse. The transports reached Colburn's sawmill
late on September 21 and transferred the troops and supplies to the
two hundred freshly built batteaux waiting for them there.

From Colburn's, the expedition continued upriver by batteau to
Fort Western, a French and Indian-era fort that had become a trading
post. Teeming with men and supplies, there was not enough shelter

for all the men, so many spent a cold and rainy evening on the grounds of the fort.[4]

While Colonel Arnold organized his detachments for the next leg of the expedition, a small scouting party was sent forward on September 23 in two birch bark canoes. These lightweight craft were better suited for the shallow water of the Kennebec River than the heavy bateaux that Arnold's main force was to use. As a result, the scouting party advanced twenty miles a day.[5]

To avoid bottlenecks at the narrow portage passages of the river (carrying paths around shallow rapids and waterfalls), Arnold divided the main body into four divisions with four different departure times. The first division comprised the three rifle companies under Captain Daniel Morgan of Virginia. They departed on September 25.

The second division was commanded by Lieutenant Colonel Christopher Greene of Rhode Island, a cousin of Nathanael Greene. His detachment consisted of three musket companies. Four musket companies under Major Return Meigs of Connecticut made up the third division, and the last division of three musket companies under Lieutenant Colonel Roger Enos of Connecticut brought up the rear. They also carried the bulk of the food reserve and a party of carpenters to repair the bateaux when necessary.

As each division left Fort Western, the men struggled to move the heavy bateaux through the shallow water and rocky shoals of the river. Two days into the trip, Private Caleb Haskell of Massachusetts, attached to the third division, noted, "We begin to see that we have a scene of trouble to go through this river, the water is swift and the shoal full of rocks, ripples, and falls, which oblige us to wade a great part of the way."[6]

While the men in the bateaux battled the swift current and rocky shoals, the rest of the expedition marched alongside the river. They were frequently called upon to help dislodge and manhandle boats through the shoals. It took each division two days to travel the eighteen miles upriver to Fort Halifax. This French and Indian-era fort was within site of the Ticonic Falls, and the detachments had to leave the river and carry their boats around them in order to continue upriver. Local settlers assisted with oxen and carts, but the work was still difficult and exhausting. The falls of Skowhegan were even worse, requiring Arnold's men to scale a steep precipice in order to continue upriver. Abner Stocking of Connecticut was with the third division and recalled the two-day struggle to reach and overcome the second portage at Skowhegan:

> We proceeded 8 miles but with great difficulty. The stream was in some places very rapid and shoal, and in others so deep that those who dragged the boats were obliged to nearly swim. [The next day] we arrived to the second carrying place, called Skowhegan falls. Though this was only 60 rods over, it occasioned much delay and great fatigue. We had to ascend a ragged rock, near 100 feet in height and almost perpendicular. Though it seemed as though we could hardly ascend it without any burden, we succeeded in dragging our batteaus and baggage up it.[7]

The difficult terrain was not the only challenge for the men; weather conditions deteriorated making the trek miserable for all. Captain Simeon Thayer of Rhode Island with the second division, noted on September 30 that "Last night our clothes being wet, were frozen a pane of glass thick, which proved very disagreeable, being obliged to lie in them."[8]

The expedition pressed on to another difficult portage, where Private Stocking observed in early October that

> By this time, many of our batteaux were nothing but wrecks, some stove to pieces. The carpenters were employed in repairing them, while the rest of the army were busy in carrying over the provisions. A quantity of dry cod fish . . . [left] lying loose in the batteaux, and being continually washed with the fresh water running into the batteaux [became unwholesome]. The bread casks not being water-proof, admitted the water in plenty, swelled the bread, burst the casks, as well as soured the whole bread. The same fate attended a number of fine casks of peas. These with the others were condemned. . . . Our fare was now reduced to salt pork and flour. Beef we had once now and then, when we could purchase a fat creature, but that was seldom. A few barrels of salt beef remained on hand, but of so indifferent quality, as scarce to be

eaten, being killed in the heat of summer, took [such] damage after salting, that rendered it not only very unwholesome, but very un-palatable.[9]

Further upriver, the expedition arrived at its most challenging obstacle yet—the Great Carrying Place. This was a grueling twelve-mile portage between the Kennebec and Dead Rivers that required two weeks and a herculean effort to overcome.

MASSACHUSETTS
While Arnold and his expedition slowly made their way north toward Quebec, little changed for the American army outside of Boston. Neither side was confident enough to attack the other in force, so the stalemate continued. In October, a visitor to the American camps at Roxbury and Cambridge described the impressive American fortifications:

> The lines of both [American camps] are impregnable; with forts (many of which are bomb-proof) and redoubts . . . [extending] about twenty miles; the breastworks of a proper height, and in many places seventeen feet in thickness; the trenches wide and deep in proportion, before which lay forked impediments; and many of the forts, in every respect, are perfectly ready for battle. The whole, in a word, the admiration of every spectator, for verily their fortifications appear to be the works of seven years, instead of about as many months.[10]

Another visitor to Roxbury in October noted the impact of the fortification upon the town.

> Nothing struck me with more horror than the present condition of Roxbury; that once busy, crowded street is now occupied only by a picquet-guard. The houses are deserted, the windows taken out, and many shot-holes visible; some have been burnt, and others pulled down to make room for the fortifications. A wall of earth is carried across the street to Williams' old house, where there is a formidable fort mounted with cannon.[11]

With his earthworks largely completed by the fall, Washington turned his attention toward the future of the army. The enlistments of many of his men were to end in December and January. A new army thus had to be formed to replace those who would leave, and Washington wanted instructions from Congress on how to do so.

Informed by his subordinate officers that many of the men would reenlist if granted furloughs to visit their homes, Washington suggested this approach to Congress as one way of preventing the complete dissolution of the army: "Most of the General Officers are of the Opinion, the greater Part of them may be re-enlisted for the Winter, or another Campaign, with the Indulgence of a Furlough to visit their Friends which may be regulated so as not to endanger the Service."[12]

Washington was also concerned about the shortage of clothing, blankets, gunpowder, and money to pay and feed the troops. He described his critical situation to Congress in mid-September:

> The Military Chest is totally exhausted. The Paymaster has not a single Dollar in Hand. The Commissary General assures me, he has strained his Credit for the Subsistence of the Army to the utmost. The Quarter Master General is precisely in the same Situation. And the great Part of the Troops are in a State not far from Mutiny, upon the Deduction of their stated Allowance. I know not to whom I am to impute this Failure, but I am of Opinion, if the Evil is not immediately remedied & more punctuality observed in the future, the Army must absolutely break up.[13]

In mid-October, three members of Congress, Benjamin Franklin, Benjamin Harrison, and Thomas Lynch, arrived in camp and met with Washington as well as representatives from the four New England colonies to discuss the details for raising a new army. In early November, the Continental Congress debated the recommendations of the committee.

The new Continental Army to be posted outside Boston for 1776 was to consist of 20,372 officers and men who would serve for the entire year.[14] Other Continental battalions were authorized for South Carolina and Georgia.[15] Three weeks earlier, Congress authorized two

Continental battalions for New Jersey and one for Pennsylvania.[16] None of these new Continental regiments, however, were destined to serve in Massachusetts.

Although the actions of Congress offered some hope for improvement, the condition of Washington's army in late 1775 was grave. Benjamin Thompson noted the deplorable condition of the army in November:

> The army in general is not very badly accoutered, but most wretchedly clothed, and as dirty a set of mortals as ever disgraced the name of a soldier. . . . They have no women in the camp to do washing for the men, and they in general not being used to doing things of this sort, and thinking it rather a disparagement to them, choose rather to let their linen rot upon their backs than to be at the trouble of cleaning 'em themselves.[17]

Thompson added that illness was widespread due to a diet primarily of meat, and there was little discipline or subordination. He closed with the comment, "The soldiers in general are most heartily sick of the service."[18]

Washington was well aware of the low morale of his troops and lamented to Joseph Reed, one of his aides, in November about the troops and the difficulty of raising new recruits to replace his shrinking army:

> Such a dirty, mercenary Spirit pervades the whole, that I should not be at all surprised at any disaster that may happen. In short, after the last of this Month, our lines will be so weakened that the Minute Men and Militia must be call'd in for their defence—these being under no kind of Government themselves, will destroy the little subordination I have been labouring to establish, and run me into one evil, whilst I am endeavouring to avoid another. . . . Could I have foreseen what I have & am like to experience, no consideration upon Earth should have induced me to accept this Command.[19]

Washington was not completely crestfallen, however. He remained hopeful that the expeditionary force that he sent to Canada in September would meet with success and significantly alter the situation in North America.

CANADA: ARNOLD'S MARCH CONTINUES

Since their departure from Fort Western in late September, Arnold's expedition had made slow but steady progress up the Kennebec River. This progress stalled when they reached the Great Carrying Place, a twelve-mile portage connected by three ponds between the Kennebec and Dead Rivers. Established long ago by Native Americans who traversed it easily with lightweight birch bark canoes, Arnold's men had to haul their heavy bateaux and all of their supplies across it. A rifleman with one of the Pennsylvania companies described the trek, which had to be repeated several times in both directions in order to bring all the supplies forward:

> This morning we hauled out our Batteaux from the river and carried thro' brush and mire, over hills and swamps . . . to a pond which we crossed, and encamped for the night. This transportation occupied us three whole days, during which time we advanced but five miles. This was by far the most fatiguing movement that had yet befell us. The rains had rendered the earth a complete bog; insomuch that we were often half leg deep in the mud, stumbling over all fallen logs. . . . Our encampments these last two nights were almost insupportable, for the ground was so soaked with rain that the driest situation we could find was too wet to lay upon any length of time; so that we got but little rest. . . . The incessant toil we experienced in ascending the river, as well as the still more fatiguing method of carrying our boats, laden with the provisions, camp equipage, etc., from place to place, might have subdued the resolution of men less patient and less persevering than we were.[20]

Dr. Isaac Senter provided a similar account of the hardship the men faced at the Great Carrying Place: "The army was now much fatigued, being obliged to carry all the batteaus, barrels of provisions, warlike stores, &ct. over on their backs through a most terrible piece of woods conceived. Sometimes in the mud knee deep, then over ledgy hills."[21]

It took two weeks for Arnold's troops to completely cross the portage. When they reached the Dead River, which was deep and the current slow, their progress quickened. It came to a sudden halt, however, when a hurricane swept in and flooded the river and countryside. Dr. Senter recorded in his journal that "The wind increased to an almost hurricane the latter part of the day. The trees tumbling on all quarters that rendered our passage not only exceeding difficult, but very dangerous."[22]

After a difficult night, they resumed their journey but found that that the river had risen ten feet with a strong current. Dr. Senter observed that, "This sudden alteration in the river not only impeded our water carriage, but rendered the marching of the party by land of the utmost difficulty, as the river was no longer confined to her banks, but extended to many low, flat places, a mile or more each way."[23]

The expedition pressed on, hit next by snow upon which Dr. Senter noted that, "Every prospect of distress now came thundering on with a two fold rapidity. A storm of snow had covered the ground of nigh six inches deep, attended with very severe weather."[24]

Next came shocking news that Lieutenant Colonel Enos and his rear division of three companies had turned back. Arnold was with the lead elements of the expedition when Enos and his officers, many miles behind, decided to turn back. As the last of the four divisions, they had the reserve stocks of provision, but when they turned back, they left just two barrels of flour for the rest of the expedition. Captain Henry Dearborn of New Hampshire noted the impact the news of their departure had on the expedition:

> The unhappy News of Colo. Enos, and the three Company's in his Division, being so Imprudent as to return back . . . disheartened and discouraged our men very much, as they Carri'd Back more than their part, or quota of Provision and Ammunition, and our Detachment, before being but Small, indeed, to think of entering such a place as Quebec, But being now almost out of Provisions we were Sure to die if we attempted to Return Back. And we could be in no Worse Situation if we proceeded on our route. Our men made a General Prayer, that Colo. Enos and all his men, might die by the way, or meet with some disaster, Equal to the

Cowardly dastardly and unfriendly Spirit they discover'd in returning Back without orders, in such a manner as they had done, and then we proceeded forward.[25]

Struggling on, Arnold's troops reached the highest elevation of their trek, the Height of Land, at the end of October. With their provision expended, the troops made do with whatever they could find to eat. Dr. Senter reported in his journal that

> Our greatest luxuries now consisted in a little water, stiffened with flour, in imitation of shoemakers' paste. . . . We had now arrived . . . to almost the zenith of distress. Several had been entirely destitute of either meat or bread for many days. The voracious disposition many of us had now arrived at, rendered almost any thing admissible. Clean and unclean, were forms now little in use. In company was a poor dog, [who had] hitherto lived through all the tribulations. . . . This poor animal was instantly devoured, without leaving any vestige of the sacrifice. Nor did the shaving soap, pomatum, and even the lip salve, leather of the shoes, cartridge boxes &ct. share any better fate.[26]

Abandoning their damaged and leaky boats, the troops marched on, following the Chaudiere River toward Quebec. Caleb Haskell with the third division recalled that at this point they were, "Very much discouraged, having nothing to eat and no prospect of anything; we are so faint and weak we can scarcely walk, obliged to lighten our packs, having been upon a very short allowance for sixteen days."[27]

Haskell noted three days earlier that, "A great number of our men being much beat out with hunger and fatigue, were not able to keep up with the main body. It was thought best to leave them behind to the mercy of the woods, and to get along as fast as they could."[28]

Joseph Henry with the riflemen made a similar observation in his journal: "The men were told by the officers that order would not be required in the march—each one must put their best foot forward."[29] Arnold's expedition, which was spread out over twenty miles, was dissolving within a few days' march of its goal.

Most pressed on and were finally rewarded for their determination on November 3 when an advance party Arnold had sent ahead returned with a number of cattle. His famished men gorged themselves on fresh beef and other provisions and many, rejuvenated, returned into the wilderness to encourage and retrieve their exhausted comrades who had fallen behind.

Benedict Arnold's expeditionary force, reduced by three companies and the loss of scores of men to fatigue and illness, had made it through the Maine wilderness. It remained to be seen whether they were strong enough to capture their objective—Quebec.

The British Navy Attacks

While Arnold's expedition slowly made its way north to Quebec and Washington and his troops continued their siege of Boston, the British navy went on the offensive. Admiral Samuel Graves, noting in two letters in September that "The Rebels are fortifying their Sea Port Towns, and are endeavouring to equip a Naval Force [that] will . . . become formidable" and "The four New England Governments [are] absolutely at War with us," decided to flex the might of the British navy in September.[30] He informed Captain Wallace of the HMS *Rose*, still posted off Newport, Rhode Island, that

> Many Rebel armed Vessels infest the Coast of America particularly about Providence, Rhode Island, Long Island, Long Island Sound, Mechias, and the Bay of Fundy, who have already taken two of his Majestys Schooners and several Trading Vessels'. . . . You are therefore hereby required and directed to use every means in your power to take, burn, sink and destroy all and every Pirate or Rebel you meet in Arms whether on Shore or at Sea; And you are to do your utmost to lay waste and destroy every Town or Place from whence Pirates are fitted out, or shall presume to harbour or shelter them, altogether with all the Vessels of what kind soever.[31]

Not wishing to appear overly ruthless, Graves reminded Wallace to "endeavour to distinguish as much as possible his Majesty's loyal Subjects from his inveterate Enemies and Subverters of legal Authority and good Government."[32]

Three weeks passed before Wallace acted on these instructions and when he did so, it was prompted by his effort to collect provision for the navy rather than target and destroy suspected rebels and pirates.

Several British warships and transports arrived in Rhode Island in early October with the intention of gathering livestock and forage for the British Army in Boston. When the Committee of Safety in Providence learned of this, it ordered five companies of minutemen to Newport to reinforce the militia there. Esek Hopkins was placed in command of this force and instructed to "Use your utmost Endeavours . . . to prevent any Live-Stock from being taken off . . . for the Use of the Ministerial Army and Navy in America."[33] He was also instructed to "resist, expel, kill, and destroy" any British sailors or marines who attempted to land or attack the inhabitants.[34]

While this force assembled and marched, Captain Wallace collected and loaded livestock at Brenton's Neck on the southern tip of Rhode Island, two miles below Newport. He reported that

> I engaged the quantity of Stock necessary for the Transports and began taking it on board when intelligence flew thro' the Country. Expresses sent off for the Rebel Camp. The Rebel Governor Cooke of Providence raised the Country and sent 1500 Men to Newport to prevent us. However I got all that could be got notwithstanding their utmost efforts.[35]

Dr. Ezra Stiles recorded a different outcome in his diary. A number of livestock remained at Brenton Neck waiting to be loaded aboard the British ships, but poor weather delayed their transfer. Dr. Stiles recalled that

> The Men o' War & Transports drawn up close or near—but it being very rainy & stormy . . . The Men o' War had not took off the Stock tho' they had set Marines to guard it. . . . Resolute, brave [militia] 280 [strong] . . . marched down into the neck & . . . in the sight of the Men o' War . . . boldly bro't off 60 or 70 Head of Cattle, 100 Sheep, besides Hogs, Turkies, &ct. It was expected that there would be Firing from the Ships & Landing Marines— but the Marines ran off—& they fired only two swivels.[36]

The British ships proceeded to Newport where Wallace demanded that the rebel troops in town immediately depart, "otherwise it would become my Duty to destroy them and the Town."[37] This threw the town into a panic as the inhabitants sought to remove their effects and themselves from danger. An account of the chaos appeared in the *Newport Mercury*: "The carts, chaises, riding chairs, and trucks, were so numerous that the streets and roads were almost blocked up with them. . . . Being rainy and muddy, the poor women and children were much exposed in looking out for some place of safety."[38]

Wallace informed Admiral Graves that the rebels withdrew just two miles from town, implying that he would have been justified to fire upon Newport, but he chose not to, concluding that "In this Instance it would have been hard upon the Town to have destroyed it, because it seemed that many of them could not help the [Interruption] of such a Banditti."[39] Wallace instead sailed to Bristol, just north of Rhode Island on the mainland. His fleet of sixteen ships anchored off the town around 6:00 p.m. on October 7.[40] An account of what transpired appeared in the *New York Gazette* two weeks after the incident:

> On Saturday the 7th instant, appeared in sight of this harbour, a very formidable fleet, consisting of 16 sail, viz. three men of war, one bomb ketch, and other armed vessels all of which . . . drew up in line of battle, from one end of the town to the other. Soon after they moored, a barge came from the *Rose*, to the head of a wharf, with a Lieutenant, who asking if there were any gentlemen on the wharf? William Bradford being present, answered yes; whereupon the Lieutenant informed him, Captain Wallace had a demand to make on the town, and desired that two or three of the principal men, or magistrates of the town, would go on board his ship, within an hour, and hear his proposals, otherwise hostilities would be commenced against the town.[41]

Mr. Bradford, who was a magistrate of the town, replied that it would be more proper for Wallace to come ashore in the morning to meet with the town's leaders.[42] Wallace was not amused when this response was conveyed to him and commenced to bombard Bristol.

The inhabitants were shocked by the attack. One observer noted that

> The whole fleet began a most heavy cannonading, and the bomb vessel to bombard and heave shells and carcasses into the town. . . . Such an incessant and hot fire; the streets being full of men, women and children, the whole time; the shrieks of the women, the cries of the children, and the groans of the sick, would have extorted a tear from even the eye of a Nero. . . . Words cannot describe the dreadful scene.[43]

During the bombardment, Colonel Stephen Potter went to the wharf and hailed the *Rose*, upon which he and several other leaders were brought before Captain Wallace. He reported to Admiral Graves that

> I asked them why they did not answer my Summons, that my intention was friendly, that I only came to purchase Stock for the King's forces. Had they given me fair Answers not a Gun would have been fired, however, since it was as it was, I demanded a quantity of Stock for the use of His Majesty, which I would pay for.[44]

Wallace wanted two hundred sheep and thirty cattle but the committee demurred, claiming it was impossible to collect such numbers because most had been driven inland upon the British arrival. They offered fifty sheep, which Wallace accepted and took possession of the next day.[45]

The British bombardment of Bristol, which lasted nearly two hours, caused great fear, but little actual damage and few casualties. Reverend John Burt was found dead in a field near his house the day after the attack, his death believed to be the result of poor health and fear rather than a flying projectile of any kind.[46]

The outcome for the other target of the British navy in October 1775 was far worse.

Burning of Falmouth

The day before Captain Wallace bombarded Bristol, Admiral Graves sent Lieutenant Henry Mowat of the HMS *Canceaux* with a small squadron of ships from Boston to:

Chastize Marblehead, Salem, Newbury Port, Cape Anne Harbour, Portsmouth, Ipswich, Saco, Falmouth in Casco Bay, and particularly Mechias where the *Margaretta* was taken, the Officer commanding her killed, and the [crew] made Prisoners, and where the *Diligent* Schooner was seized and the Officers and Crew carried up the Country, and where preparations I am informed are now making to invade the Province of Nova Scotia. You are to go to all or as many of the above names Places as you can, and make the most vigorous Efforts to burn the Towns, and destroy the Shipping in the Harbours.[47]

These orders were materially different than those sent to Captain Wallace three weeks earlier. Graves sought to destroy nine specific towns in Massachusetts and New Hampshire to both punish the inhabitants for past offenses against the British navy and preempt a possible rebel attack upon Nova Scotia that was rumored to be planned. Lieutenant Mowat had five warships under his command and the latitude to strike at any or all the towns. The only one to suffer his wrath, however, was Falmouth, in mid-October.

Mowat's squadron arrived at Falmouth on October 16, and immediately provoked the ire of the townsfolk by firing on a small schooner in the harbor that refused to heave to. The Reverend Jacob Bailey witnessed the incident and recalled that

Notwithstanding the discharge of several muskets and two cannon [from the British, the schooner] escaped in safety to the town. The populace, which were gazing by hundreds, were immediately thrown into furious agitation by this incident, and vowed revenge with the utmost menace and caution. The Committee, composed of tradesmen and persons of no property, prompted only for a flaming zeal for the liberty of their country, were not less enraged at this hostile appearance and . . . ordered the company of guards to . . . secure the cattle, intimidate the tories and observe the motions of the enemy.[48]

The townsfolk endured an anxious evening and grew more troubled the next day when they observed that the squadron had positioned itself as if to bombard the town. Reverend Bailey recalled, "The whole fleet stood directly up the river, and formed in line of battle before the town. We now plainly discovered one ship of twenty guns, one of sixteen, a large schooner of fourteen, a bomb sloop and two other armed vessels."[49]

Many of Falmouth's residents were confused by the hostile movement of the flotilla because they believed that Mowat held Falmouth in high regard for its assistance in foiling Samuel Thompson's efforts to capture the *Canceaux* in May.[50] They soon learned otherwise when Mowat sent an officer ashore with a warning to the town. Reverend Baily recalled that

[The officer] landed at the lower end of King street, amid a prodigious assembly of people, which curiosity and expectation had drawn together from every quarter. Some of the multitude appeared in arms, who united with the rest to convey the officer with uncommon parade and ceremony along the street to the Town House. His entrance was immediately followed by a confused mixture, which filled the apartment with noise and tumult.[51]

The British officer stunned the gathering with a proclamation from Lieutenant Mowat:

After so many premeditated Attacks on the legal Prerogatives of the best of Sovereigns; After the repeated Instances [of] Britain's long forbearance of the Rod of Correction; and the Merciful and Paternal extension of her Hands to embrace you, again and again, have been regarded as vain and nugatory. And in place of a dutiful and grateful return to your King and Parent state; you have been guilty of the most unpardonable Rebellion. . . . Having it in orders to execute a just Punishment on the Town of Falmouth . . . I warn you to remove without delay the Human Species out of the said town; for which purpose I give you the time of two hours.[52]

Mowat gave the residents of Falmouth just two hours to evacuate the town and avoid the imminent bombardment. Reverend Baily described the reaction of the townsfolk:

It is impossible to describe the amazement which prevailed upon reading this alarming declaration; a frightful consternation ran through the assembly, every heart was seized with terror, every countenance changed colour, and a profound silence ensued for several moments. During the astonishment which had seized the multitude, I quitted the apartment of justice and became a spectator on what passed in the street, where nothing occurred but scenes of tumult, confusion, and bustle.[53]

A committee was hastily formed to appeal to Mowat directly, and he agreed to delay the bombardment until the next morning if the townspeople delivered up their arms. A handful of weapons were delivered in the evening as a gesture of goodwill. This prompted Mowat to proclaim, "If the town would surrender their cannon and musketry, and give hostages for their future good behaviour, he would delay the execution of his orders till he could represent their situation to the Admiral, and intercede for their final deliverance."[54]

Panic swept through Falmouth as residents scrambled to take advantage of the reprieve and save what possessions they could from destruction. Militia from surrounding communities arrived and added to the confusion. It appears that in all the chaos, little consideration was given to Mowat's demand that the town's cannons and muskets, along with a few hostages, be delivered to him by 9 a.m. the next morning. The Falmouth committee informed Lieutenant Mowat the next morning that, "To their . . . astonishment . . . no part of the Inhabitants [had] assembled in the morning [to hand over their muskets] and that the whole town was then in the greatest confusion, with many women and children still remaining in it."[55]

Mowat allowed the 9 a.m. deadline to pass but commenced a bombardment at 9:40 a.m. Reverend Bailey described the result:

The cannon began to roar with incessant and tremendous fury. [Mowat], perceiving the streets replete with people, oxen and horses, directed his men to fire over the tops of the houses, but this solemn exhibition struck the multitude into instant alarm and amazement. The oxen, terrified at the smoak and report of the guns ran with precipitation over the rocks, dashing everything to pieces, and scattering large quantities of goods about the streets. In a few minutes the whole town was involved in smoak and combustion. About a thousand men in arms attended this scene of devastation, besides a prodigious number of both sexes, without attempting any repulsion. The bombardment continued from half after nine till sunset, during which all the lower and middle of the town was reduced to a heap of rubbish. Several houses in the back street and in the upper part, together with the church shared the same fate. The front of the Meeting house was torn to pieces by the bursting of a bomb, and the buildings which were left standing had their glass windows broken, and both walls and apartments terribly shattered. In a word, about three quarters of the town was consumed and between two and three hundred families who twenty four hours before enjoyed in tranquility their commodious habitations, were now in many instances destitute of a hut for themselves and families, and as a tedious winter was approaching they had before them a most gloomy and distressing prospect.[56]

The bombardment lasted until nightfall, after which the British squadron, low on ammunition, sailed out of Falmouth Harbor with two captured vessels. Eleven other boats were destroyed in the harbor.[57]

The once proud community of Falmouth, with nearly four thousand inhabitants, was left a smoldering ruin.[58] British landing parties had added to the destruction by coming ashore with torches to set fires where the shells failed to do so. Despite the presence of hundreds of militiamen, no effective opposition was offered against Mowat. This became a point of criticism for those who believed that Falmouth got what it deserved for its timid response to Mowat. One resident, Daniel Tucker, defended the inhabitants' response: "Many people have blamed the inhabitants of Falmouth for not defending the town against so small a force; but the truth is it was not in their power, for there was not a cannon mounted in town at that time, and there was a great scarcity of powder."[59]

A scarcity of gunpowder was something that George Washington knew all too much about. He had been concerned about the shortage of gunpowder in Cambridge for weeks and, despite the obvious need for gunpowder in Falmouth, was forced to decline a request from the Falmouth Committee of Safety for a supply of it on October 24:

> The Desolation and Misery which . . . has been so lately brought on the Town of Falmouth, I know not, how Sufficiently to detest. Nor can my Compassion for the general Suffering, be Conceived beyond the true Measure of my Feelings. But my Readiness to relieve you, by complying with your Request [for assistance] is Circumscribed by my Inability. The immediate necessities of the Army under my Command, require all the Powder & Ball, that can be collected with the utmost Industry & Trouble.[60]

The Falmouth Committee of Safety expressed its disappointment with Washington's decision in a letter announcing the arrival of yet another British ship, the *Cerberus* (twenty guns), on November 2:

> It gives us inexpressible Concern to find that it is out of your Power to afford us any Aid. And we are the more concerned, on the Arrival yesterday of the ship *Cerberus* [with four hundred men]. . . . How soon they will penetrate the Country, God only knows, for what can a People do without Arms & Ammunition to defend themselves. The Poor distress'd People drove from their Habitations by the late cruel destruction of the Town, can scarcely find sufficient Places for their accommodation, & the Country is so engaged for making provision for them, that we find it difficult to raise the Militia for our present defense. But we have only two half barrels of Powder in Stock, & we almost fear to make an Opposition. . . . We are in great want of some Person of a martial Spirit to conduct the few Forces we already have.[61]

The arrival of the *Cerberus* threw Falmouth into a new frenzy. Its commander, Captain John Symons, threatened to unleash "the most vigorous efforts" against Falmouth if troops were raised or military works erected in response to his arrival.[62] Reverend Samuel Deane described the response of the inhabitants:

The Militia is call'd in, and they with part of the soldiery, are gone to throw up some breast works this night, so that we expect a cannonade at least to-morrow morng. We have cannon that would be able to annoy the ship much if we had ammunition: But we have not half enough for our small arms. Symons has asked for a few cattle and offer'd pay for them and has been refused.[63]

The unexpected resolve of the militia surprised Captain Symons. Jonathan Mitchell, Chairman of the Cumberland County Convention, explained what happened:

A number of the Militia and soldiers repaired to Falmouth . . . but, the weather being very stormy, nothing could be done till [November 4], when the ground was viewed, the men put under some regulation, and tools prepared to begin an intrenchment that night, (while Captain Symons, not thinking it proper to stay and see his orders put in execution, came to sail in the evening, and went out of the harbour).[64]

The destruction of Falmouth and constant harassment of the British navy prompted Massachusetts' leaders to issue letters of marque and reprisal to anyone in the colony who "shall at his or their own Expense fit out & equip for the defence of America any vessel. . . . And that all such Persons . . . shall have full Power . . . to Sail on the Seas, Attack, take and bring into any Port in this Colony all Vessells, offending or Employed by the Enemy."[65] This action helped trigger an escalation of the war into yet another region: the sea.

New Hampshire
The situation in New Hampshire was relatively stable at the start of autumn. Although Governor Wentworth had fled to Boston in August, he tried to maintain an appearance of authority by returning to New Hampshire in late September aboard an armed schooner. He sent a proclamation ashore in Portsmouth that prorogued the General Assembly, which he had dissolved the previous year, until late April and explained his actions to Lord Dartmouth in London:

While the province continues in the state and temper the people are in at present, the meeting of the General Assembly can be of no service, but whenever they are disposed or compelled to return to their duty I shall not fail to meet them and propose to return again as soon as the Admiral will accommodate me with a vessel of such force as may enable me to remain or near the harbour.[66]

Resuming his residence onshore in Fort William and Mary was out of the question because his quarters had been ransacked within half an hour of his departure in August.[67] Strong artillery batteries with cannons as large as 24-pounders, crewed by a hundred men, were erected on two islands in the Piscataqua River to keep at bay British warships.[68]

Good fortune struck New Hampshire in early October when a British merchant ship, the *Prince George*, loaded with nearly 1,900 barrels of flour destined for the British troops in Boston, mistakenly sailed into Portsmouth Harbor. Captain Titus Salter, the commander of the artillery batteries protecting the town, seized the vessel and the Portsmouth Committee made plans to sell some of the flour to the public, who were in great need of it. They reconsidered, however, before acting and wrote to Washington and the New Hampshire Committee of Safety to seek their permission.[69]

When he first learned of the flour, Washington asked that all of it be sent to the army: "I cannot but consider this as a most providential event, the state of this army being defective in that article [flour]."[70] Appeals from both the Portsmouth and New Hampshire Committees of Safety altered Washington's instructions. He informed the New Hampshire Committee that "Had I known their Situation [in Portsmouth] I should have made the Application unnecessary. . . . They have my cheerful Consent to take what is necessary, but perhaps somewhat less than 600 Barrels."[71]

The situation in Portsmouth that he referred to was described to him in the Committee's earlier appeal:

This Colony have upward of a hundred Soldiers stationed at the Batteries erecting in our Port . . . and there is not, nor has there been for some Weeks past a single Barrel of Flour to be purchased within this Colony. We therefore . . . have ordered a hundred Barrels of the Flour to be taken for the use of the said Soldiers. . . . And as the Town of Portsmouth is in great want of Bread, we should be exceeding glad if the Circumstance of the Army will admit . . . that about Five hundred Barrels of the Flour might be sold to the Inhabitants of said Portsmouth.[72]

News of the destruction of Falmouth in mid-October prompted Washington to send John Sullivan and a detachment of Pennsylvania riflemen to Portsmouth under the expectation that it would be the next town attacked by Mowat's force.[73] In addition to the artillery batteries protecting Portsmouth, numerous fire rafts had been built and construction of a boom across the river channel had commenced. General Sullivan was not impressed at what he found, however, and shared his disappointment with Washington:

I was Surprized to find that the Boom So much Talked of was not prepared, that the Bridge Intended for Crossing from the main to the Island whereon Stands the Principal Fort (Called Fort Washington) had nothing more done than one Pier Sunk [and] That there was not a foot of the Parapet over which a man might fire or Even See his Enemy. . . . In Short not a moments Defence Could be made or annoyance given to the Enemy Either with Cannon or Small Arms.[74]

Sullivan moved quickly to address his concerns. He moored boats head to stern and used planks between them to form a rudimentary pontoon bridge that connected Fort Washington to the mainland. "I then Turned my attention to the Boom," he reported, "& in two Days got it across but found it could not Stand the Rapidity of the Tide [and] it Soon Broke & we have again Fixed it So that I hope it may hold."[75] Construction of earthworks for the artillery batteries was also sped up.

Sullivan's efforts proved unnecessary. Captain Mowat had returned to Boston; Falmouth was the only town to suffer his wrath.

The Fourth New Hampshire Provincial Congress reconvened in Exeter on October 31 and addressed the issue of governing the colony. The General Assembly had not met in over a year and with Governor Wentworth's departure in August and his refusal to call it into session, it was unlikely to ever meet again. The Provincial Congresses that met in their place mainly addressed the military crisis with Britain, not routine governmental business. New Hampshire's leaders believed a more permanent solution to the political vacuum that existed in their colony was needed.

The colony's delegates to the Continental Congress in Philadelphia presented a request from New Hampshire's leaders for guidance on a possible new system of government in mid-October, and although the Continental Congress supported the idea, it offered few specific suggestions:

> Resolved, That it be recommended to the provincial Convention of New Hampshire, to call a full and free representation of the people, and that the representatives, if they think it necessary, establish such a form of government, as, in their judgement, will best produce the happiness of the people, and most effectually secure peace and good order in the province, during the continuance of the present dispute between Great Britain and the colonies.[76]

New Hampshire's delegates conveyed Congress's support but noted that "You'll see that the government is limited to the present contest; to ease the minds of some few persons who were fearful of Independence."[77] In other words, whatever New Hampshire's leaders decided to do regarding the governance of their colony should be considered a temporary solution to the crisis with Great Britain. Once this crisis was resolved, it was expected that the former governmental arrangement with Great Britain would be restored. The New Hampshire Provincial Congress moved forward and agreed on November 4 that, "The . . . Representatives [of] this Colony in future shall be chosen by the voices or Votes of the Electors and not by the value of the Estates."[78]

This did not mean, however, that every free man in New Hampshire could vote. The Provincial Congress proposed that voters possess property with a value of at least £20 and representatives £300. Communities could send one representative to the legislature for every one hundred freeholders. Small communities could band together to elect a representative.[79]

Ten days into their consideration, the Provincial Congress formally began to replace its old government by authorizing the right to vote for "Every Legal Inhabitant paying taxes."[80] The property requirement was discarded. The Congress agreed that representatives of future Provincial Congresses would serve one-year terms and be required to own real estate valued at £200 or more. The number of representatives from New Hampshire's largest community, Portsmouth, was capped at three while several other large towns were granted two representatives. The total number of representatives came to eighty-nine.[81] Although this was a step in the process of forming a new, stable government for New Hampshire, most of the work was left to the next Provincial Congress, scheduled to meet in late December.

While the Provincial Congress worked to restore functioning government to New Hampshire, they received a request from Washington to take action against any royal official in the colony who was unfriendly to the patriot cause. Washington's request was prompted by a series of recent proclamations from William Howe, the new British commander in Boston. In response to a renewed crackdown on the inhabitants of Boston, Washington sent duplicate instructions to Governor Cooke in Rhode Island, Governor Trumbull in Connecticut, and General Sullivan in New Hampshire to seize all royal officials still in their respective colonies for further inspection:

> At a time when some of our Sea port Towns are cruelly and Wantonly laid in Ashes; and ruin & Devastation denounced against others—When the Arms are demanded of the Inhabitants, and Hostages required (in effect) to Surrender their Liberties . . . 'tis evident that the most Tyrannical, & cruel system is adopted for the destruction of the rights and liberties of this Continent, that ever disgraced the most despotick Ministry; and ought to be opposed by every means in our power.
>
> I therefore desire, that you will delay no time in causing the Seizure of every Officer of [royal] Government at Portsmouth who have given pregnant proofs of their unfriendly disposition to the

cause we are Ingaged In; and when you have secured them, take the opinion of the Provincial Congress . . . in what manner to dispose of them in that Government. I do not mean that they should be kept in close confinement. If [the Congress] should incline to send them to any of the Interior Towns, upon their Parole not to leave them till released, it will meet with my concurrence.

For the present, I shall avoid giving you the like order in respect to the Tories in Portsmouth; but the day is not far off when they will meet with this, or a worse fate if there is not considerable reformation in their Conduct, of this they may be assured.[82]

Although Washington's motivation for these instructions was aimed more to retaliate for Howe's harsh treatment of Bostonians than to prevent any sort of Tory uprising in New England, there were some, including Governor Wentworth, who believed that such an uprising, at least in New Hampshire, was possible.

Convinced that a few powerful British warships and three thousand redcoats stationed in New Hampshire "would be likely to answer very important purposes," Wentworth repeatedly appealed to British commanders in Boston over the fall to send ships and troops to Portsmouth.[83] He naively claimed that should British troops be sent to New Hampshire:

I . . . would still hope to get a greater number to join in their assistance if means were provided for their support, which the House of Assembly would not in the present state of things supply. I am persuaded that at least such a measure would meet with more success in New Hampshire than in any other part of New England.[84]

Informed by Admiral Graves that he had no ships to spare, Wentworth remained in Boston, frustrated and powerless.

The Fourth New Hampshire Provincial Congress was not powerless, however, and ordered several royal officials still in New Hampshire to leave Portsmouth and reside in the interior of the colony until granted permission to leave.[85] The Congress then adjourned until late December.

RHODE ISLAND

Destruction of coastal towns was very much on the mind of Rhode Island's leaders in the fall of 1775. Captain Wallace and the British naval squadron in Rhode Island bombarded Bristol for nearly two hours in early October, and while damage was surprisingly light, the potential for widespread destruction remained. Panic ensued in Newport at the expected return of Wallace and residents scrambled to escape with their possessions. Reverend Ezra Stiles noted in his diary that

> I removed one Load of my Books & Furniture. The Carting of Goods & Removing of the people continued all day yesterday & yet continues. . . . It is judged that Two Thirds of the Inhabitants are removed up the Island.[86]

While the majority of Newport's inhabitants fled, hundreds of militia under General Esek Hopkins arrived on the island and gathered in Newport to challenge the British should they attempt to land troops upon their return. When Captain Wallace returned with his squadron on October 11, a delegation of town leaders, no doubt concerned that Newport was about to share Bristol's fate, met with Wallace aboard the *Rose*. The British commander reported to Admiral Graves in Boston that they asked

> If I would spare the Town, and suffer the Ferry Boats and Market [boats] to come to Town, they would engage to get the Rebels off the Island and Supply His Majesty's Ships with what they wanted. I answered it would be impossible to be at Peace while such a Body of Rebels hung over the Town if they would remove them off the Island and Supply the Kings Ships I would consent to what they proposed 'till further Orders.[87]

Newport's leaders were open to Wallace's terms and sent a delegation to Providence to meet with Governor Cooke. A committee of the Continental Congress from Philadelphia were passing through Providence and invited to weigh in on the request. They agreed that given Newport's precarious situation, the inhabitants should provide

Wallace with fresh provisions and beer. They also agreed that whatever troops were in Newport should be removed per Wallace's demand, provided the British commander honor the terms he offered. The Committee added, however, that troops should remain on the island. Governor Cooke thus ordered Hopkins to "remove the Troops at a greater Distance from the Town if he shall think the service will not suffer by it."[88]

The Rhode Island General Assembly endorsed Governor Cooke's decision in late October when it convened in Providence.[89] Two weeks later, Wallace formally pledged not to attack Newport, provided his ships continued to be adequately provisioned. He dropped his demand for the rebel troops to leave the island but expected them to remain out of Newport. "Let it remain neuter," he wrote to the town on November 14. "If the rebels enter the town, and break the neutrality, I hold myself disengaged, and at liberty to do my utmost for the King's service."[90]

Although the Rhode Island General Assembly displayed sympathy for Newport's exposed situation, it promised to deal harshly with anyone else, other than the residents of Newport, who aided British forces:

> [Anyone found] holding a traitorous correspondence with the Ministry of Great Britain, or any of their officers or agents; or of supplying the ministerial army or navy that now is . . . employed in America, against the United Colonies . . . shall suffer the pains of death . . . and shall forfeit his lands, goods, and chattels to the colony.[91]

Other actions the assembly took were to authorize the printing of £20,000 of paper currency in a variety of shilling denominations to help pay for the mounting expenses of resistance and authorize the formation of a new five hundred-man regiment for the defense of the colony to serve for a full year.[92]

CONNECTICUT
Like New Hampshire and Rhode Island, Connecticut's focus in the fall of 1775 was largely upon the British navy, particularly Captain

Wallace and the HMS *Rose*. His attack on Stonington at the end of August shook the colony and Governor Trumbull and the Council of Safety scrambled to defend against future attacks. Complicating their effort was a demand from Washington to send the last remnants of Connecticut's Provincial troops still in the colony to Massachusetts. They reluctantly did so and moved to replace them with two hundred newly recruited troops to be posted at several places including Stonington (fifty), New London (seventy), Lyme (twenty), and New Haven (fifty).[93] The new troops were to continue work on the fortifications in these four locations and man them until October 20.[94] When the General Assembly met in October, it authorized a continuation of these troops until the start of December, reducing the number assigned to Stonington (forty), Lyme (fifteen), and New Haven (thirty), but keeping the force at New London at seventy.[95]

Fortunately for the residents of Connecticut the only British force capable of harassing them was under Captain Wallace, and he was preoccupied with Rhode Island, so Connecticut was spared further attacks in 1775. This did not mean, however, that Connecticut men were out of harm's way. Connecticut troops served with Montgomery in Canada, Arnold in Maine and Quebec, Schuyler in New York, and of course, Washington in Massachusetts.

Four

Winter

December 1775–February 1776

T HE BRITISH NAVY, ALTHOUGH STRETCHED THIN ALONG THE
American coast, met little opposition on the seas during the
first six months of the war. A few incidents such as what happened
to the *Margaretta* and *Diligent* off Machias in the summer and the
Prince George off Portsmouth in the fall, annoyed the British, but
none represented a significant threat to the British navy.

General Washington and the New England colonies strove to
change this in the latter half of 1775. Determined to offer more resistance to the British navy and strike at the British supply line, Washington armed the sloop *Hannah* with four 4-pound cannon and a
number of swivel guns in September. A detachment of Massachusetts
soldiers chosen for their seamanship and experience were transferred
to the vessel, which was commanded by Captain Nicholson
Broughton, an officer in Colonel John Glover's Massachusetts regiment. Broughton's mission was to cruise off the Massachusetts coast
and seize supply vessels bound for Boston and the British Army.[1]

The *Hannah*'s first capture was actually a recapture. Captain
Broughton and his crew regained the American merchant ship *Unity*,

which had been seized by a British warship. Its British prize crew sailing to Boston surrendered to the *Hannah* without a shot and the *Unity* was taken to Gloucester, north of Boston. When *Hannah*'s crew learned they would not receive any prize money because the vessel was a recaptured American ship, they mutinied and were arrested. The mutineers were court-martialed, convicted, and then whipped and fined with fourteen crewmen drummed out of the service.[2]

Although troubled by the conduct of *Hannah*'s crew, Washington resolved in October to arm more ships. With the approval of the Continental Congress, he armed several more vessels, christened *Washington, Franklin, Harrison,* and *Lee.* None was a match for a British man-of-war, but they were all adequately armed with several cannons (3- and 4-pounders) and swivel guns in order to attack and seize lightly armed supply and transport ships sailing from Canada or Great Britain. Washington boasted about their success in a letter in early December:

> Finding we had no great prospect of coming to close Quarters with the Ministerial Troops in Boston, I fitted out at the Continental Expence, several Privateers; chiefly with design to Intercept their Fresh Provision Vessels from Nova Scotia & Canada, in which we have succeeded. In this few days, [one has] taken a Store ship from London with a fine brass Mortar, 2000 stand of Arms, Shot, Shells, &ct. to the amount . . . of £16,000, but no Powder—also a Ship of Dry Goods from . . . Scotland . . . worth £3600.[3]

The store ship that Washington referred to was the *Nancy,* loaded with two thousand much needed muskets, bayonets, and cartridge boxes as well as over one hundred thousand musket flints and a large assortment of other military supplies.[4]

A letter written from a British officer in Boston in mid-December confirmed the impact Washington's ships had on the British:

> We are now almost as much blocked up by the sea as we have been for these eight months by land. By this opportunity you will receive a confirmation of the rebels having taken the Ordnance brig. This is a great loss to us and a great acquisition to them. The

rebels have also just taken another vessel from Britain, valued at £10,000 loaded with necessaries for the army.[5]

The author of this letter blamed Admiral Graves for the losses, declaring that "though there are near twenty [warships] in this harbour, I cannot find that there is one vessel cruising in the bay. . . . Our navy never made so disgraceful a figure."[6]

Howe expressed his dissatisfaction with Graves to British officials in London as well as to the admiral himself, who replied,

I wish it was in my power to give your Excellency more Satisfaction on the Subject of your Letter, but altho' fully sensible of the Distress this Garrison will be subjected to by the Rebels taking its Supplies; Yet it is impossible entirely to prevent it with the Men of War alone at this Season. All that I can do is to place the Kings Ships in the most likely Situations to fall in with Vessels expected to arrive.[7]

In other words, the navy simply did not have enough ships to protect all the vessels sailing for Boston. Fortunately for the British, New England's winter and the departure of most of the American sailors when their enlistments ended at the end of the year curtailed the activities of Washington's fledgling navy until the spring.

Although Graves was correct in his insistence that he did not have enough ships to protect every supply vessel sailing to New England, he did have enough to harass the coastline, and Captain Wallace in Rhode Island aboard the HMS *Rose* was ready and willing to do so.

CONANICUT ISLAND RAID
Captain Wallace and his small squadron of British warships had loomed off Newport, Rhode Island, all year, an ever-present threat to the town's inhabitants. An accommodation and agreement to keep Wallace from attacking the town had held, but in his view, it did not apply to other targets in Rhode Island or in the colony. So, in the predawn hours of December 10, approximately two hundred British marines and sailors landed on Conanicut Island, across from Newport. Reverend Ezra Stiles described the raid in his diary:

This Morng we were awaked with the Conflagration of Jamestown on Conanicott. An awful Sight! The Bomb Brig & several Tenders full of Marines went over last Night, & about 5 o'clock or a little before day landed and set fire to the Houses. The men continued ravaging & firing till about Noon & returned.[8]

Henry Babcock witnessed the raid from the mainland west of Conanicut Island and rushed to intervene:

On Sunday morning, at break of day, we were alarmed with the cry of Fire, upon which we found that five houses were in flames upon the Island of Conanicutt. The country was alarmed as soon as possible. Fifty Provincials were upon the Island. I immediately repaired to Narragansett Ferry, where I found a number of people collected. Out of a hundred, thirty-six volunteered who put themselves under my command, [and we] embarked on board of a Sloop. We imagined [Captain Wallace] designed to burn every house on the Island.

We were told that the enemy had landed a number of field pieces. I observed to the people at the Ferry, that even if they had, they were not so terrible as some people imagined; that it was a shame to afford no relief to the distressed inhabitants, and that the party on the Island might be entirely cut to pieces, for the want of our assistance; and that it would be a noble prize to take Capt. Wallace prisoner. The Col. of the Militia and several other officers I urged hard to step on board the Sloop, but they tho't the attempt too hazardous, and chose to keep themselves out of danger. We arrived time enough to save one house.

Capt. Wallace landed with 75 marines, 125 seamen and 20 women. They plundered and burnt 15 houses; took off 50 head of cattle, 30 sheep and 40 hogs. A number of barns full of hay, and several cribs full of corn were likewise committed to the flames. He landed at three o'clock in the morning, with five tenders; surprized the guard; took two of them prisoners, and several women and children and sundry of the inhabitants.[9]

Wallace's raid upon Conanicut Island in mid-December reignited debate in Rhode Island about whether the inhabitants of Newport should continue to supply Wallace with provision. Reverend Stiles reported on December 13 that "The Town [is] generally for supplying him notwithstanding his Barbarity in Burning Conanicott [Island]."[10]

The following day they voted to continue to provide provision and sent a committee to Wallace to inform him. That same evening an express from Rhode Island's Committee of Safety in Providence arrived that ordered all communication and trade with Wallace and the British navy to stop. Another town meeting was held where a vote took place to send a committee to Providence to once again plead Newport's case in favor of supplying the British with provision. Wallace agreed to await the Committee's decision before taking further action, expressing his desire to "save the town."[11]

Although Wallace took no action against Newport, he had hungry livestock to feed aboard his ships and needed forage, so he sent a landing party ashore south of Newport to gather hay. Reverend Stiles recorded in his diary that

> The infamous Capt. Wallace at 10 a.m. sent one Brig & 2 Tenders & landed Marines on Brentons Point to take off hay as they have 13 head of Cattle starving. Two companies marched from Head Quarters down the Neck & joined Capt. Bartons Company there—in all about 120 men to oppose the Landing. The Brig fired—the Marines & sailors had got to the Stacks—our soldiers fired on them, & they instantly quitted, left the Hay & fled on board ship.[12]

Preparations for a New Continental Army

The inhabitants of Newport were not the only ones who found themselves in a precarious situation in December of 1775. With the enlistments of most of the army due to expire at the end of the year, Washington scrambled to raise a new force to replace them.

The Continental Congress had authorized twenty-seven new Continental regiments in November to replace Washington's existing army for the upcoming year. Each regiment consisted of 728 officers and men, exclusive of the artillery units and riflemen. Massachusetts was to provide sixteen regiments, Connecticut five, New Hampshire three, and Rhode Island two.[13] With the addition of the riflemen, who formed their own regiment, and artillerists, Washington's new army for 1776 should have surpassed twenty thousand men. Recruitment for the new army was slow, however, and the unexpected departure of most of the Connecticut troops in early December greatly troubled Washington.

Washington and others appealed to the Connecticut troops to remain until January but with little success. He described his efforts and disappointment to Governor Trumbull in early December:

> The reason of my giving you the trouble of this, is the late extraordinary and reprehensible conduct of some of the Connecticut Troops. Some time ago . . . I applied to the Officers of the several Regiments, to know whether it would be agreeable to the men to continue till the first of January, or till a sufficient number of other forces could be raised to supply their place, who informed me, that they believed the whole of them would readily stay till [replacements] could be effected. To my great surprise, last week I discovered their great uneasiness at the Service, and determination to leave it.[14]

The impending loss of thousands of troops had to be addressed immediately, so Washington appealed to Massachusetts and New Hampshire for five thousand militia to fill the void until the new Continental Army could be fully raised. He then appealed again to the Connecticut troops to remain until the militia arrived to take their place, but to his chagrin most ignored him, and some departed early with their weapons. He expressed his displeasure to the entire army in his orders of December 3:

> It is with surprise and Astonishment the General learns, that notwithstanding the Information that was communicated to the Connecticut Troops, of the [militia] being ordered to supply their places, by the 10th of this month; that many of them have taken their Arms with them, and gone off, not only without leave, but contrary to express Orders.[15]

Two days later, a discouraged Washington wrote to all the New England governments:

> By sad experience It is found, that the Connecticut Regiments have deserted and are about to desert the noble cause we are engaged in; nor have I any reason to believe, that the forces of New Hampshire, this Government or Rhode Island will give stronger proofs of their Attachment to it, when the period of their dismission . . . arrives. For after every stimulus which I have been able to throw in their way, and near a months close endeavour, we have Inlisted but five thousand men, 1500 of which, are to be absent at a Time on Furlough.[16]

To address the looming shortage of troops, Washington called again upon Massachusetts and New Hampshire to send five thousand militia as soon as possible for several weeks of service with the army. To his surprise and satisfaction, both colonies did so. Washington praised them in a letter to Congress in mid-December: "The Militia are coming fast, I am much pleased, with the Alacrity which the good people of this Province, as well as those of New Hampshire, have Shewn upon this occasion."[17]

General Sullivan conveyed Washington's praise for New Hampshire, who raised two thousand of the militia, to the Committee of Safety: "General Washington, and all the other officers, are extremely pleased, and bestow the highest encomiums on you and your troops, freely acknowledging that New-Hampshire forces, for bravery and resolution, far surpass the other Colonies; and that no Province discovers so much zeal in the common cause."[18]

While New Hampshire and Massachusetts received Washington's esteem, Nathanael Greene struggled to reenlist his Rhode Island troops for the Continental Army of 1776. He acknowledged to a friend that it was a challenge to do so:

> In my last I mentioned to you that the troops inlisted very slowly in general; I was in hopes then that ours would not have deserted the cause of their country, but they seem to be so sick of this way of life, and so home-sick, that I fear the greater part, and the best

of the troops from our Colony, will go home. . . . The [new Provincial] regiment raised in the Colony of Rhode-Island has hurt our recruiting amazingly; they are fond of serving in the army at home, and each feels a desire to protect his own family.

I harangued the troops yesterday; I hope it had some effect; they appear of a better disposition to-day; some have inlisted, and others discover a complying temper. I leave nothing undone or unsaid that will promote the recruiting service. But I fear the Colony of Rhode-Island is upon the decline.[19]

A week later, Greene sounded more optimistic about raising the new army: "The army is filling up slowly: I think the prospect is better than it has been. Recruits come in out of the country plentifully, and the soldiers in the army begin to show a better disposition, and to recruit cheerfully."[20] It is likely that the cause for much of Greene's optimism was the arrival of the militia troops from New Hampshire and Massachusetts.

While Washington and his officers struggled to raise a new army from the ashes of the old one, significant events to the north unfolded at Quebec.

CANADA: ATTACK ON QUEBEC

The American thrust into Canada in the fall of 1775 had achieved much by the start of winter. Richard Montgomery had captured the bulk of British forces in Canada at St. Johns as well as the city of Montreal and was on the march to Quebec to join Benedict Arnold and his force. Arnold and his men had successfully completed an epic march through the Maine wilderness and reached Quebec in November, but then withdrew to await Montgomery.

The two forces united on December 2, at Point-aux-Tremble, twenty miles southwest of Quebec. Montgomery had less than four hundred troops and together with Arnold's six hundred men, he led the united American force back to Quebec. Comprised of troops from all four New England colonies as well as New York, he faced a much smaller British force under Governor Guy Carleton that relied on the walls of Quebec and the Canadian militia within to repel the Americans.

Montgomery's demand to surrender the town was rejected by Governor Carleton, so the Americans commenced a siege of Quebec. Lacking adequate cannons, men, or supplies, the siege was more of a pause to await an opportunity to storm the city than it was an actual siege.

The opportunity came on December 31 when a blizzard provided cover for the Americans to advance upon Quebec. Montgomery's plan called for a small detachment to feign an attack upon the western approach to Quebec, while two columns of troops converged from opposite directions upon Lower Town, which sat just below the city's walls on the eastern side of the city along the St. Lawrence River. Montgomery led three hundred New York troops along the river to reach the lower town from the south while Arnold, with six hundred men, circled around the city and attacked Lower Town from the north. Once Lower Town was secured, the united American force would storm Upper Town.

With snow beating in their faces, the Americans kicked off their attack in the predawn hours of December 31. The diversionary force engaged British sentinels on the west side of the city while Montgomery and Arnold led the main American force in a pincer movement around the city. Montgomery's advance along the St. Lawrence River shore ended abruptly when a blast of grapeshot from a guardhouse smashed into his column, killing the general and several officers instantly. Rattled by the loss of their commander, the surviving officers ended the attack and withdrew.

Arnold's column moved through the northern suburbs of Quebec along the Saint Charles River toward Lower Town. Abner Stocking of Connecticut provided a detailed description of the attack:

> The division . . . moved in files . . . along the street of St. Roques, towards the Sault des Matelots. In imitation of Montgomery, [Arnold] too led the [advance guard] in person, and was followed by Captain Lamb with his company of artillery, and a field piece mounted on a sled. Close in rear of the artillery was the main body, in front of which was Morgan's company of riflemen. . . . At the Sault des Matelots, the enemy had constructed their first barrier, and had erected a battery of two twelve pounders, which

it was necessary to force. . . . Arnold advanced with the utmost intrepidity along the St. Charles, against the battery. The alarm was immediately given, and the fire on his flank commenced, which, however, did not prove very destructive. As he approached the barrier, [Arnold] received a musket ball in the leg which shattered the bone, and he was carried off the field to the hospital. Morgan rushed forward to the battery at the head of his company, and received from one of the [cannons] a discharge of grape shot which killed only one man. A few rifles were immediately fired into the embrazures . . . and the barricade being instantly mounted with the aid of the ladders, brought by the men on their shoulders, the battery was deserted without discharging the other gun. The captain of the guard, with the greater number of his men, fell into the hands of the Americans, and the others made their escape.[21]

Daniel Morgan confirmed Stocking's account with his own years later:

I had to attack a two-gun battery, supported by Captain M'Leod and 50 regular troops. The first gun that was fired missed us, the second flashed, when I ordered the ladder, which was on two men's shoulders, to be placed; (every two men carried a ladder.) This order was immediately obeyed, and, for fear the business might not be executed with spirit, I mounted myself, and was the first man who leaped into the town, among M'Leod's guard, who were panic struck, and, after a faint resistance, ran into a house that joined the battery and platform. I [landed] on the end of a heavy piece of artillery, which hurt me exceedingly and perhaps saved my life, as I fell from the gun upon the platform, where the bayonets were not directed. Charles Porterfield, who was then a Cadet in my company, was the first man who followed me; the rest lost not a moment, but sprang in as fast as they could find room; all this was performed in a few seconds. I ordered the men to fire into the house, and follow up their fire with their pikes (for besides our rifles we were furnished with long espontoons) this was done, and the guard was driven into the street. I went through a sally-port at the end of the platform; met them in the street; and ordered them to lay down their arms, if they expected quarter; they took me at my word and every man threw down his gun.[22]

With Arnold wounded in the leg and evacuated to the rear and the bulk of Arnold's force scattered amid Lower Town in the blinding storm, the Americans at the first barricade paused their advance for nearly an hour. Morgan finally led them forward, about two hundred in all.[23] Private Stocking recalled,

> We . . . were proceeding to the second barrier, when on turning an angle in the street, we were hailed by a Captain Anderson who had just issued from the gate with a body of troops to attack us. Captain Morgan who led our little band in this forlorn hope, answered the British Captain by a ball through his head, his soldiers drew him within the barricade and closed the gate; a tremendous fire from the windows of the buildings and port holes of the wall was directed against [us].[24]

An account of the attack printed in the *New York Gazette* in mid-January praised Morgan's conduct in the fight: "The dispute remained obstinate for some time, (in which an attempt to scale [the barricade] twice was made by the intrepid Captain Morgan, whose uncommon presence of mind, and gallant behaviour in this critical situation, were truly conspicuous)."[25]

Private George Morrison of Pennsylvania also commented on Morgan's gallant behavior at the second barricade in his journal:

> We are now attacked by thrice our number, the battle becomes hot, and is much scattered; but we distinguish each other by hemlock springs previously placed in our hats. All our officers act most gallantly. Betwixt every peal the awful voice of Morgan is heard, whose gigantic stature and terrible appearance carries dismay among the foe wherever he comes.[26]

Despite Morgan's bold leadership, the American situation at the second barricade was critical. "We are now attacked in our rear,"

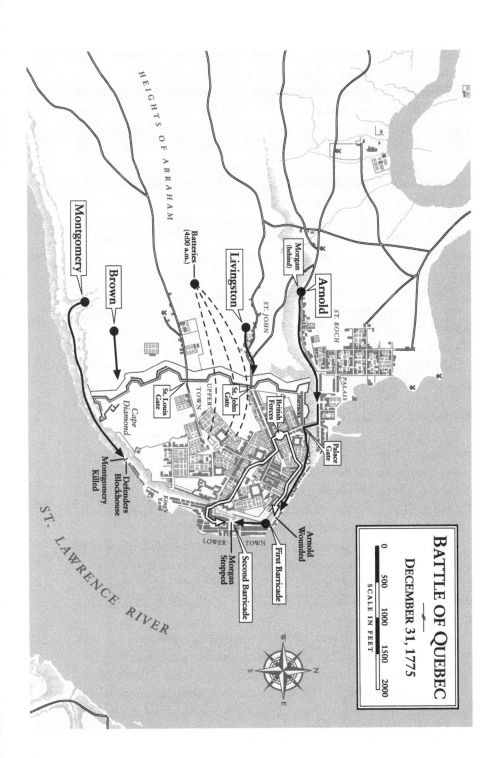

BATTLE OF QUEBEC
DECEMBER 31, 1775

SCALE IN FEET
0 500 1000 1500 2000

Montgomery

Brown

Batteries
(4:00 a.m.)

Livingston

Morgan
(behind)

Arnold

HEIGHTS OF ABRAHAM

ST. JOHN

ST. ROCH

PALAIS

St. Louis
Gate

St. John
Gate

UPPER TOWN

British
Forces

Barracks

Palace
Gate

Cape
Diamond

Defenders
Blockhouse

Montgomery
Killed

King's
Yard

LOWER TOWN

Morgan
Stopped

Second Barricade

First Barricade

Arnold
Wounded

ST. LAWRENCE RIVER

wrote Morrison, "the enemy increase momentarily—they call out to us to surrender but we surrender them our bullets."[27]

While the fight raged on at the second barricade, approximately two hundred British and Canadian troops moved to retake the first barricade and seal the Americans within Lower Town.[28] Trapped between two strong forces, the Americans fought on, hoping that Montgomery's arrival would turn the tide. By midmorning it was obvious that help was not coming and with the promise of good treatment from their enemy, Arnold's men surrendered.

Over half of Arnold's force was lost in the attack on Quebec. Most (three hundred) were captured but at least sixty were killed or wounded.[29] Despite all the fighting, the British lost just a handful of men.

Command of the approximately five hundred remaining Americans and two hundred Canadians who joined them fell to Arnold, who continued the weak siege. Governor Carleton in Quebec, with a small contingent of British troops and many more French militia whose loyalty was uncertain, was content to remain in the fortified city, protected from the Americans and the brutal Canadian winter.

GRIM START TO THE NEW YEAR

News of the American loss at Quebec shocked the rebellious colonists. Oliver Wolcott, a delegate to the Continental Congress from Connecticut, described the impact of the news to Philip Schuyler, the commanding American officer in New York and Canada: "The unfortunate Death of General Montgomery and the Disaster of his Troops pierced every Heart."[30]

Thomas Lynch of South Carolina was also in Philadelphia with the Continental Congress when the news of Quebec arrived and informed Schuyler, "Never was any City so universally Struck with grief, as tis [this] on hearing of the Loss of Montgomery. Every lady's Eye was filled with Tears."[31]

Both congressmen assured Schuyler that Congress would take measures to offset the loss and secure Canada from the British, but such measures would take time. Washington did not wait for Congress to act. On January 18, he held a war council where it was agreed that although the army outside of Boston was too "feeble" to send reinforcements to Canada, the governments of Massachusetts, Connecticut, and New Hampshire should each be asked to raise a new regiment of 728 Continental officers and men as quickly as possible to do so.[32]

Two days earlier, another war council had recommended that Washington request from the three New England colonies, "exempting Rhode Island . . . on Account of the repeated Insults of the Enemys ships of War, and the Exposed Situation of the Sea Coasts of that Colony," that thirteen regiments of militia be raised to reinforce the army outside of Boston for two months.[33] The war council that met two days later, after learning of Montgomery's defeat at Quebec, recommended that the militia regiments requested for Washington's army be reduced from thirteen to ten, and the remaining three, one from each colony except Rhode Island, become new Continental regiments to serve for a year and reinforce the army in New York and Canada.[34] Washington sent out the requests the next day.[35]

The need for more troops to offset American losses in Canada only added to the difficulty Washington faced in bringing the Continental Army in Massachusetts to full strength. News from across the Atlantic at the start of 1776, however, made it imperative that those troops be raised.

In early January, copies of King George III's speech to Parliament in late October concerning the dispute with the colonies reached Boston. Tories in the city printed copies and gleefully sent them to the American camp. The king aligned himself squarely with Parliament and against the colonists, declaring that

Those who have long too successfully laboured to inflame My People in America, by gross Misrepresentations, and to infuse into their Minds a System of Opinions repugnant to the true Constitution of the Colonies, and to their subordinate Relation to *Great Britain*, now openly avow their Revolt, Hostility, and Rebellion. They have raised Troops, and are collecting a Naval Force; they have seized the publick Revenue, and assumed to themselves Legislative, Executive, and Judicial Powers, which they already exercise in the most arbitrary Manner over the Persons and Properties of their Fellow Subjects. And although many of these unhappy

People may still retain their Loyalty, and may be too wise not to see the fatal Consequence of this Usurpation, and wish to resist it, yet the Torrent of Violence has been strong enough to compel their Acquiescence till a sufficient Force shall appear to support them.[36]

King George claimed that the true goal of the "Authors and Promoters of this desperate Conspiracy, [was to prepare] for a general Revolt," and that he and Parliament had acted in, "a Spirit of Moderation and Forbearance . . . to prevent, if . . . possible, the Effusion of the Blood of My Subjects, and the Calamities which are inseparable from a State of War; still hoping that My People in *America* would have discerned the traiterous Views of their Leaders."[37] The king then declared that

The rebellious War now levied is become more general, and is manifestly carried on for the Purpose of establishing an independent Empire. I need not dwell upon the fatal Effects of the Success of such a Plan. The Object is too important, the Spirit of the *British* Nation too high, the Resources with which God hath blessed her too numerous, to give up so many Colonies which she has planted with great Industry, nursed with great Tenderness, encouraged with many Commercial Advantages, and protected and defended at much Expence of Blood and Treasure.

It is now become the Part of Wisdom and (in its Effects) of Clemency, to put a speedy End to these Disorders by the most decisive Exertions. For this Purpose I have increased my Naval Establishment, and greatly augmented My Land Forces; but in such a Manner as may be the least burthensome to My Kingdoms. . . .

When the unhappy and deluded Multitude, against whom this Force will be directed shall become sensible of their Error, I shall be ready to receive the Misled with Tenderness and Mercy: And in order to prevent the Inconveniencies which may arise from the great Distance of their Situation, and to remove as soon as possible the Calamities which they suffer, I shall give Authority to certain Persons upon the Spot to grant general or particular Pardons . . . to such Persons as they shall think fit; and to receive the Submission of any Province or Colony, which shall be disposed to return to its Allegiance.[38]

Washington received a copy on January 3, sent out from Boston, "by the Boston Gentry."[39] He wrote to Congress the next day and described the speech as "full of rancour & resentment, and explicitly holds forth his Royal will to be, that vigorous measures must be pursued to deprive us of our constitutional rights & liberties."[40] The American commander added that he hoped that whatever measures the king had in store for the colonies would be "opposed by more vigorous ones" by Congress and the united colonies.[41]

The impact of the king's October speech was significant. Many colonists had held out hope that King George might still intervene or influence Parliament on their behalf, but his speech put an end to any thought of that. Nathanael Greene wrote as much to his wife in mid-January:

It is generally agreed that George the Tyrant's last Graceless Speech made to that Stupid, Ignorant, wicked, Pensiond, Perjur'd Parliament shuts the Door of hope for a Reconciliation between us and great Britain. The Calamities of a War are shocking, but the consequences of Slavery are dreadful. May God in Mercy preserve us from so great an Evil.[42]

There appeared to be no hope for a peaceful resolution now and many began to consider independence for the first time.

MASSACHUSETTS

Although Washington and his army were not strong enough to force the British from Boston, their siege of the city, combined with the harassment of Washington's armed ships and the logistical challenge of supplying an army from across the ocean, made life for the British Army and the civilians still in the city difficult. A British officer bleakly noted in late December that

But four of the thirty Sail of provision fuel & Store Ships are as yet arrived from England. One said to be the *Spy* was taken last

Sunday Morning and carried into Salem, her Cargo is Chiefly Coal, an Article we much want. . . . Last Week there were orders for pulling down the useless houses and breaking up the Wharfs to form Magazines of fuel in the different districks of the Regiments; they have been at Work two days. . . . The Torys in this place . . . are really to be pittied, many families with whome you were acquainted last Winter, & had their Seven or Eight fires in their Houses, are now reduced to one, to Cook and sit by it, with their Servants. In short, we are Caught in the Toil, and it will be some time before we shall be able to work our way out of it. The Yankies will have [fun] pelting at us with Shot & Shells this Winter, they have left no place unoccupied round us but Dorchester Neck.[43]

Encouraged by the recent success of Washington's armed ships as well as reports that "several of the united Colonies have of late thought it expedient and necessary to fit out armed Vessels for the Defence of American Liberty," the Massachusetts Council, or upper house of their legislature, formed a committee that included John Adams, to draft a plan to do the same.[44]

When the committee reported its plan two weeks later, it called for the construction of two large warships: "One suitable to carry Thirty-Six Guns, vizt Twenty Guns carrying twelve Pound Shot, & Sixteen Guns for Six Pound Shot; and the other Ship suitable to carry Thirty-two Guns, vizt Twenty Guns for nine Pound Shott, & Twelve for six Pound Shot."[45]

The committee wanted the ships to be built "in a manner best calculated for swift sailing" and of strong timber and other material "suitable for Ships of War."[46]

A month later, a committee proposed to vastly expand the naval force of Massachusetts by authorizing the construction of ten armed sloops of over one hundred tons each. They were to mount from fourteen to sixteen cannons each (6- and 4-pound cannons).[47] The proposal was adopted by the Massachusetts General Court on February 7.[48]

On January 19, Massachusetts acted on Washington's request for six new militia regiments to serve for two months and one new Continental regiment to be sent to Canada.[49] Colonel Elisha Porter of Western Massachusetts commanded the new continental regiment.[50]

New Hampshire

In Exeter, New Hampshire, the Provincial Congress finally acted in early January to establish a more permanent governing body for the colony. The Congress declared that

> The sudden and abrupt departure of his Excellency John Wentworth Esq., our Governour, and several of the Council, leaving us destitute of legislation; and no Executive Courts being open to punish criminal offenders, whereby the lives and property of the honest people of this Colony are liable to the machinations and evil designs of wicked men. Therefore, for the preservation of peace and good order, and for the securities of the lives and property of the inhabitants of this Colony, we consider ourselves reduced to the necessity of establishing a form of Government, to continue during the present unhappy and unnatural contest with Great Britain: protesting and declaring that we never sought to throw off our dependence upon Great Britain, but felt ourselves happy under her protection, while we could enjoy our constitutional rights and privileges; and that we shall rejoice if such a reconciliation between us and our Parent State can be effected as shall be approved by the Continental Congress, in whose prudence and wisdom we confide.[51]

The Provincial Congress then proclaimed itself New Hampshire's new colonial legislature, specifically, the House of Representatives, and formed a twelve-person council to act as an upper house. All legislative and executive authority in New Hampshire was to reside in these two houses for as long as the "present unhappy dispute with Great Britain" should continue.[52]

Responding to requests from the Continental Congress for a new regiment of Continentals and from Washington for a regiment of Continentals to serve for a year in Canada and a regiment of militia to serve with his army for two months, the assembly complied. It voted to raise a regiment of Continentals to serve for a year on January 20.[53] Colonel Timothy Bedel was appointed colonel of the new Continental regiment, which was raised primarily from the western part of New Hampshire. The assembly also supported John Sullivan's efforts to raise a regiment of two-month men from New Hampshire's militia who were still with Washington's army in January. Sullivan reported his success in late January and thanked the assembly when it forwarded pay for the recruits.[54]

One of the last actions the assembly took in late January was to petition the Continental Congress for assistance in defending Portsmouth:

> As you have been pleased to order a Number of Battalions of men to be raised to Guard other Colonies, and as this is by far the Poorest Colony on the Continent, according to the Number of Inhabitants—We most humbly pray your Honours would order such a Number of men to be raised and Stationed at Portsmouth (and in case of any Emergency to assist our Neighbour Colonies) as you in your Wisdom Shall see fit.[55]

The assembly's reference to battalions of men raised to guard other colonies was likely directed at Georgia and North Carolina, who were encouraged in the fall to raise troops for their colonies at the expense of the Continental Congress. It took Congress four months to agree to do so for New Hampshire.[56] Colonel Nicholas Long commanded this new regiment.

Rhode Island

The issue of providing British warships anchored off Newport, Rhode Island, with fresh provision to avoid the destruction of the town weighed heavy on Rhode Island's leaders in December. While the inhabitants of Newport waited for a decision from the Committee of Safety in Providence, a dispatch from Washington arrived announcing the departure of several British transport ships from Boston. Although their destination was unknown, Governor Cooke was alarmed at the news and appealed to Washington for help:

> Should the Force [that] sailed from Boston be destined for Rhode Island I tremble for the Consequences, as the Colony in its present

exhausted State cannot without Assistance defend the Island. . . .
I apply to your Excellency for a Detachment from the Continental
Army of One Regiment to be stationed upon Rhode Island; and
that you would please to appoint a General Officer to take the
Command of the whole Force there. . . . We have at Head Quarters about 250 Men and shall immediately place on there about
400 more, and hold as many more in Readiness as possible.[57]

Washington was not convinced that Rhode Island was the destination of the British squadron and declined to send a regiment. He
did, however, send a general officer to Rhode Island, Charles Lee.[58]
He arrived in Newport on Christmas Day accompanied by a detachment of riflemen from the army and urged the remaining residents
of Newport to leave within ten days because he expected a conflict
with the British navy.[59]

On his own authority he called for suspected Tories to renounce
their Loyalist views and swear an oath of allegiance to the Continental Congress. The handful of Tories who refused to do so, including
Joseph Wanton, the former governor, were sent to Providence under
arrest.[60] Reverend Stiles noted, "General [Lee's] Presence here strikes
Awe through the Tories. They are as obsequious & submissive as
possible. They wait upon him & invite him to dine."[61]

This submission, however, evaporated when Lee departed just two
days after he arrived. Captain Wallace, still offshore on the HMS
Rose, observed, "Upon the departure of Lee, [the town] offered us
every thing we wanted; I accepted 'till the 8th of January."[62]

Washington disapproved of this arrangement and expressed his
concern to Governor Cooke in January:

> I am told that Capt. Wallace's ships have been supplied for some
> time with provisions by the Town of Newport, on certain condi-
> tions stipulated between him and the Committee. When this
> Treaty [was] first Obtained, perhaps it was right, then there might
> have been some hopes of an accommodation taking place; But
> now, when every prospect of it, seems to be cut off by his
> Majesties late Speech; when the Throne from which we had sup-
> plicated redress, breaths forth vengeance & indignation, & a firm

determination, to remain unalterable in its purposes, & to prose-
cute the system & plan of ruin formed by the Ministry against us,
should not an end be put to it, & every possible method be fallen
upon, to prevent their getting necessaries of any kind? We need
not expect to conquer our Enemies by good offices, and I know
not what pernicious consequences may result from a precedent of
this sort; other places circumstanced as Newport is, may follow
the example, and by that means their whole fleet and Army will
be furnished with what, it highly concerns us to keep them from.[63]

Washington left the decision to Cooke, however, and the British
navy continued to receive supplies from Newport.

While Rhode Island's leaders continued to relent to Newport's
pleas for accommodation in its interaction with the British navy, they
also took stronger measures to challenge the navy. The General Assembly authorized the construction of several row galleys with a crew
of fifty men each, as well as two frigates "for the service of the Continent of America."[64]

Wallace and the British navy had been relatively quiet during the
first two weeks of 1776, but that changed on January 12, when he
landed 250 marines and sailors on Prudence Island, about eight miles
northwest of Newport. He explained his action to the new British
naval commander, Vice Admiral Molyneux Shuldham, who replaced
Admiral Graves in late December:

The Rebels having for some time past kept from one to two Hundred Men upon the Islands, to prevent our Supplies—and by a
Law, making it Death for anyone to Supply us, have put us to a
great inconvenience, being much in want of Hay. On Friday
Morning the 12th Instant I stood up the Bay, with His Majesty's
Ships *Glasgow*, *Swan*, and Tenders, in order to procure some. At
about . . . Noon, being abreast of Prudence [Island] we saw a Body
of Armed Men, with a Field Piece, who followed us as we Sailed
along. At the South end of the Island, I saw a Quantity of Hay,
and determined to Land and Seize it, this they perceived, and set
fire to the Stacks, and retired to their Stone Fences to oppose us.
. . . We landed [and] beat them from fence to fence for four Miles

into their Country, firing and wasting the Country as we advanced along; We burnt twelve or Fifteen Farm Houses, took a great deal of Stock, when Night coming on, we gave over the pursuit, and retired back to our Ships, bringing with us the Stock.[65]

Wallace reported that they had killed two rebels and captured two others while only three of his men were slightly wounded. An account of the fight in the *Providence Gazette* described it differently:

Captain Wallace . . . at Four o'Clock in the Afternoon landed about 250 Men on the Island of Prudence, where about 40 or 50 of our Men were stationed, under the Command of Capt. [Job] Pearce. They were soon fired upon by the Enemy, which was returned with much Spirit; but Capt. Pearce finding the Enemy greatly superior in Number, retreated, and with his Men went off the Island; he had one Man wounded and taken prisoner, and it is said several of the Enemy were killed and wounded. The Enemy about Sunset burnt seven Houses on the Island.[66]

Fighting resumed the next day on Prudence Island when a detachment of militia some ninety strong returned in whaleboats. The newspaper account of what occurred reported that

About Nine o'Clock in the Morning the Enemy landed 250 Men, and attacked Lieut. Carr, who was stationed with a Guard of 40 Men to observe their motions; the Remainder of our Men, about 50 in Number, soon coming up, a smart Engagement ensued, which lasted three Hours. The Enemy several Times sent out flanking Parties, where were as often drove back to their main Body. They were at length drove to their Vessels, leaving our People in Possession of the Island, having the Night before got on board about 100 Sheep, but no Cattle are missing.[67]

Wallace's account of the second day's action noted, "Some of the *Swan's* and *Glasgow's* Men, straying too far from the Main Body, fell into an Ambush, and one Man of the *Swan's* was killed, two Mortally wounded, and one Slightly."[68] Wallace blamed the losses, as well as two others from the *Glasgow*, on the spirit of his men, who recklessly charged into the ambush.

Despite this bloodshed, the Rhode Island Assembly continued to allow Newport to supply Wallace with provision, specifically two thousand pounds of beef and beer, to prevent the town's destruction.[69] The fact that Wallace was regularly committing depredations upon the colony's islands was conveniently overlooked by the assembly, apparently for Newport's sake.

Governor Cooke, aware of Washington's displeasure over supplying the British navy, pointed to the Continental Congress for justification. He noted that it "appeared to us that the Members of the Continental Congress were of Opinion that [trade with Captain Wallace] should be continued."[70] It was another convenient interpretation, this time of the sentiment of Congress as expressed by Rhode Island's delegates to the Continental Congress. The result was that despite Washington's displeasure, the inhabitants of Newport continued to supply beef and beer to the British navy anchored off their town.

CONNECTICUT

The Connecticut General Assembly in mid-December called for one-quarter of the colony's militia to be formed into minute companies to "hold themselves in constant readiness to march on the shortest notice for the defence of this or any other of the United Colonies."[71] These minutemen were to be volunteers who drilled half a day every two weeks with their company.[72] The General Assembly also cracked down upon those who assisted the enemy, declaring that should anyone be convicted of such acts, their entire estate would be forfeited and they would face imprisonment for up to three years.[73]

Like the other New England colonies, the Connecticut legislature acted to better resist the British navy. An effort to do so in the fall fizzled when the crew of the *Minerva*, an armed vessel authorized by Connecticut, mutinied and never sailed. The legislature authorized the purchase of a brigantine and four row galleys "to be suitably manned, armed, and equipp'd for the defence of this and the neighbouring Colonies."[74] The cannon and military stores on the *Minerva* were to be transferred to the new brigantine when it was ready.

At the start of the new year, Governor Trumbull reported to Washington that two armed vessels, one of sixteen guns the other of fourteen, plus the schooner *Spy* with four guns and four row galleys were being prepared for action by Connecticut.[75]

Trumbull wrote Washington on January 22 that Connecticut would raise a new Continental regiment for Canada and three militia regiments to serve in Massachusetts for two months.[76] Colonel Charles Burral was selected to command the new Continental regiment.[77] These troops were in addition to the 1,500 militia officers and men that Trumbull informed Washington a week earlier that Connecticut was raising to reinforce New York City.[78] Washington feared the British intended to strike at New York and had ordered Charles Lee to take charge there of the defense of that city.[79]

In early February, David Bushnell approached the Connecticut Council of Safety with a proposal for a radical new weapon against the British navy. It was essentially a one-man submarine, described by Dr. Benjamin Gale, who helped construct it, as resembling "the two upper shells of a Tortoise joined together."[80] Nearly eight feet tall and made of wood, it was designed to approach its target underwater and attach an explosive mine below the waterline.

The Council of Safety listened intently to Bushnell and asked many questions, then approved his plan to use his machine, dubbed the *Turtle*, against the British navy and encouraged him to proceed with the preparations.[81]

The first attempt to sink a British ship with the *Turtle* occurred in September against the HMS *Eagle*, a sixty-four-gun warship anchored in New York Harbor. Although the *Turtle* successfully approached the ship undetected, it failed to attach the explosive mine, which was on a timer, to the hull. When the mine exploded, it did little but make a big splash and startle the crew of the *Eagle* and other nearby ships.[82] Two other attempts against the British were thwarted by difficult conditions before the *Turtle* was lost in early October when the American sloop transporting it was sunk by the British.

WASHINGTON'S CONTINENTAL ARMY OF 1776

Washington reported to Congress on December 31 that only 9,650 men had enlisted into the twenty-six New England regiments of the new Continental Army, well short of the 20,000 authorized.[83] Under the new arrangement, Massachusetts was to field sixteen regiments, Connecticut five, New Hampshire three, and Rhode Island two for the army outside of Boston. The troops were to serve for a year, and although most of the regimental commanders of the past year continued to command regiments, their unit designations were no longer connected to their colony. The regiments were all designated Continental regiments and given a number. The honor of the First Continental Regiment went to Colonel William Thompson's Pennsylvania rifle battalion. Colonel James Reed's New Hampshire regiment was designated the Second Continental Regiment and Colonel Ebenezer Learned's Massachusetts regiment became the Third Continental Regiment.

The addition of the Massachusetts and New Hampshire militia brought Washington's troop strength in January up to 13,500 men, but over 3,000 were sick, on furlough, or on command, so his effective troop strength in early January was just over 10,000 men.[84] He described the challenge he faced to Congress:

> It is not in the pages of History perhaps, to furnish a case like ours; to maintain a post within Musket Shot of the Enemy for Six months together, without [powder] and at the same time to disband one Army and recruit another, within the distance of Twenty odd British regiments, is more probably than ever was attempted; But if we succeed as well in the last, as we have heretofore in the first, I shall think it the most fortunate event of my whole life.[85]

One of the causes for the disappointing recruitment numbers was a chronic shortage of nearly everything an army needed, including blankets. Just before Christmas, Washington appealed to the New England governments to seek out blankets for his troops from among their inhabitants:

> Notwithstanding the great pains taken by the Quarter Master General, to procure Blankets for the Army, he finds it impossible to procure a Number Sufficient. Our Soldiers are in great distress & I know of no way to remedy the evil than applying to you; can-

not some be got from the different Towns? Most Houses could spare One, some of them many.[86]

The shortage of blankets might not have been so dire had there not also been a severe shortage of wood for shelter, warmth, and cooking. Nathanael Greene noted on December 31 that

> We have suffered prodigiously for want of Wood. Many Regiments have been Obligd to Eat their Provisions Raw for want of [firewood] to Cook, and notwithstanding we have burnt up all of the fences and cut down all the Trees for a mile round the Camp, our suffering has been inconceivable. The Barracks has been greatly delayed for want of Stuff. Many of the Troops are yet in their Tents and will be for some time, especially the Officers. The fatigues of the Campaign, the suffering for want of Wood and Cloathing, has made an abundance of the Soldiers heartily sick of service.[87]

More challenges confronted Washington in mid-January. Not only were the recruitment numbers for the new army disappointing, but a shortage of arms arose as many of the troops who left the army took their weapons with them.[88] Washington expressed his regret to Joseph Reed, a former aide-to-camp from Pennsylvania, that he did not attack Boston in October when the army was much stronger. His generals had advised against such an attack and Washington relented, but in mid-January he declared to Reed,

> Could I have foreseen the difficulties which have come upon us— could I have known that such a backwardness would have been discovered in the old Soldiers to the Service, all the Generals upon Earth should not have convinced me of the propriety of delaying an Attack upon Boston till this time. When it can now be attempted I will not undertake to Say, but this much I will answer for, that no opportunity can present itself earlier than my wishes."[89]

Complicating the situation further, the New Hampshire and Massachusetts militia that had turned out in December to reinforce the rapidly shrinking Continental Army, expected to be dismissed in mid-January, and new Continental recruits continued to enlist slowly. A war council with his top officers recommended that Washington request from the New England governments thirteen regiments of militia to reinforce the army during the crucial months of February and March. This was reduced to ten regiments when news of Montgomery's death at Quebec arrived. Washington hoped that this influx of troops, combined with his Continental troops, might allow him to strike at the British in Boston before they were reinforced in the spring.[90]

Some good news finally arrived when Henry Knox appeared in camp from his expedition to Fort Ticonderoga in New York. He rode ahead of a large train of artillery and ordnance taken from the fort and hauled over the Berkshire Mountains. Knox's successful return meant that the American army would soon have much needed cannons and firepower.

Despite the disappointing news of the failed American attack upon Quebec and his continued struggle to recruit troops to complete the undermanned regiments outside of Boston, Washington resolved to use the cannons delivered by Knox against the city. To do so, however, required more men and even more importantly, more gunpowder and muskets.

Shortages continued to plague the American commander in February, despite his pleas to the New England governments to canvas their communities for weapons.[91] Washington expressed his frustration to Joseph Reed on February 10: "So far from my having an Army of 20,000 Men well Armd &ct. I have been here with less than one half of it, including Sick, furloughd, & on Command, and those neither Arm'd or Cloathed, as they should be. In short my Situation has been such that I have been obligd to use art to conceal it from my own Officers."[92]

Despite these many shortfalls, Washington saw an opportunity a week later to strike Boston. Much of the Back Bay had frozen by mid-February and Washington believed his army might cross the ice and successfully drive the British from the city. He sought the input of his officers and was once again disappointed by their response:

It is the Opinion of this Council that the King's forces in the Town of Boston . . . amount to a much larger Number than 5,000—furnished with Artillery, Assisted by a Fleet, and possessed of every advantage the situation of the place affords. . . . Our Army is at present very defective in the Number . . . sufficient for the purpose of Offensive War, and also deficient in Army to the amount of 2,000 Stand [of arms]. The Militia Ordered & expected to be here by the first of the Month are not more than half arrived, so that to Assault the Town of Boston [and] guard [our] Works & Stores, there remain only 12,600 Men, militia, [and officers]—a force not more than sufficient to defend the Lines and maintain the Blockade.[93]

Although the war council rejected Washington's bid for a full attack on Boston, it did support a movement against the unoccupied high ground of Dorchester Heights, which overlooked Boston Neck, in order to draw the British out of Boston (as they did at Bunker Hill) or be in position to either attack the town elsewhere or bombard it once an adequate supply of gunpowder arrived.[94] The council believed that if a large enough British force sallied out of Boston to attack the new American position at Dorchester Heights, it might present an opportunity for the Americans to attack the weakened British force inside Boston. As a result, the war council advised that in conjunction with the occupation of Dorchester Heights, four thousand select troops under the command of Generals Sullivan and Greene be ready to attack Boston by boat from Cambridge.[95]

A disappointed Washington once again vented to Joseph Reed about what he considered a half measure by the war council:

About ten days ago the severe freezing Weather formed some pretty strong Ice from Dorchester to Boston Neck, and from Roxbury to the Common—this I thought (knowing the Ice could not last) a favourable opportunity to make an Assault upon the Troops in Town—I proposed it in Council; but behold! though we had been waiting all the year for this favourable Event, the enterprize was thought too dangerous! Perhaps it was. Perhaps the irksomeness of my Situation led me to undertake more than could be warranted by prudence—I did not think so, and am sure, yet, that the Enterprize if it had been undertaken with resolution must have succeeded . . . but it is now at an end, and I am preparing to take Post on Dorchester to [see] if the Enemy will be so kind as to come out to us.[96]

Washington was determined to confront the British, and occupying Dorchester Heights just south of the city, offered the best chance to do so.

Part II

1776

Five

Spring

WITH THE SUPPORT OF HIS OFFICERS, WASHINGTON PRESSED forward in early March to seize and fortify Dorchester Heights. Reinforced by approximately five thousand militia from Massachusetts and New Hampshire, many unarmed, Washington's troop strength in the beginning of March surpassed 14,500 men, still well short of the 20,000 authorized, but strong enough for Washington to proceed.[1]

As the ground was still frozen, the usual tactic of using gabions (large woven baskets made of saplings) filled with dirt dug from the location of the earthwork, was impractical. Lieutenant Colonel Rufus Putnam, who had overseen the construction of most of the American lines outside Boston, was tasked by Washington to find a solution. Putnam discovered a reference to chandeliers in a book about field fortifications that he had borrowed from General William Heath.[2] These were wooden rectangular frames built of heavy timber and filled with fascines (which were themselves long bundles of brush and branches bound tightly together). Both could be built behind the American lines and then transported to Dorchester Heights and erected under cover of darkness. Although not as strong as typical earthworks, the chandeliers would likely stop small arms fire and obscure the Americans from view, making it harder for the British to inflict casualties. Pressed hay, wooden barrels filled with gravel and sand, and twisted branches to create abatis, which served as eighteenth-century barbed wire and was placed in advance of fortifications to slow an enemy's assault, were also gathered in camp.

The operation against Dorchester Heights began on the evening of March 2, with a steady American bombardment of Boston from cannons and mortars posted in Roxbury, Cobble Hill, and Lechmere Point.[3] This was repeated the following night and an even heavier bombardment occurred on March 4, to cover the American movement upon Dorchester Heights. Washington described the movement to Congress:

> As soon as our firing commenced [on the evening of March 4] a considerable detachment of our men under the command of Brigadier General Thomas crossed the Neck and took possession of the Two Hills without the least interruption or annoyance from the Enemy, and by their great activity and Industry, before morning advanced the Works so far, as to be secure against their Shot.[4]

Captain Samuel Richards of Connecticut participated in the advance upon the heights and recalled,

> On the 4th night of March, a detachment from our army moved to the heights of Dorchester point—this is also a peninsula joined to the main by a narrow neck; on this was placed—on the side looking toward the enemy—a line of bundles of pressed hay to defend our troops from the enemies fire while passing it.[5]

Another Connecticut officer recalled that about 2,400 men with three hundred wagons marched onto Dorchester Neck early in the evening of March 4:

> The division to which I was assigned, commanded by Colonel Whitcomb, was ordered on, to the northerly hill where in one hour's time we had a fort enclosed, with fascines placed in chan-

delears; and we immediately employed as many men at intrenching as could be advantageously used for that purpose. A larger party was assigned the high hill, where they erected a larger fort, built much in the same manner as ours.[6]

William Heath recalled another clever adaptation employed by the Americans at Dorchester Heights:

The Americans took possession of Dorchester heights, and nearly completed their works on both the hills by morning. Perhaps there never was so much work done in so short a space of time. The adjoining orchards were cut down to make the abbattis; and a very curious and novel mode of defence was added to these works. The hills on which they were erected were steep, and clear of trees and bushes. Rows of barrels, filled with earth, were placed round the works. They presented only the appearance of strengthening the works; but the real design was, in case the enemy made an attack, to have rolled them down the hill. They would have descended with such increasing velocity, as must have thrown the assailants into the utmost confusion, and have killed and wounded great numbers.[7]

The British posted at Boston Neck, distracted by the American bombardment of the city, initially failed to notice the American movement onto Dorchester Heights. The British were thus shocked to discover the American works on Dorchester Heights in the morning. A British officer noted the significance of the American action in a letter home:

This is, I believe, likely to prove as important a day to the British Empire as any in our annals. We underwent last night a very severe cannonade, which damaged a number of houses, and killed some men. This morning, at daybreak, we discovered two redoubts on the hills on Dorchester-Point, and two smaller works on their flanks. They were all raised-during the night, with an expedition equal to that of the Genii belonging to Aladin's wonderful lamp. From these hills they command the whole town, so we must drive them from their post, or desert the place. The former is determined upon, and five regiments are already embarked. . . . I think it is likely to be . . . a general affair . . . Adieu balls, masquerades, &ct., for this may be looked upon as the opening of the campaign.[8]

General Howe initially planned to carry out the attack foretold by the British officer in his letter. British cannon fire from the town and ships in Boston Harbor proved ineffectual, so storming the position was Howe's only choice. Several thousand British troops were embarked aboard transports and then offloaded upon Castle Island, which was the staging area for an assault by boat.

A violent storm delayed these plans and during the disruption, Howe reconsidered his attack and opted instead to evacuate Boston. He had been in the process of preparing an evacuation to Halifax before Washington took Dorchester Heights and despite the uncomfortable appearance that they were fleeing from the Americans, Howe cancelled his attack and continued with preparations to abandon the city.

Washington, confident that his troops on Dorchester Heights would repulse a British attack and eager to attempt his own attack upon Boston with the troops waiting in Cambridge, expressed disappointment in Howe's decision: "It is much to be wished, that [Howe's attack] had been made—The event I think must have been fortunate, and nothing less than success and victory on our side, as our Officers and men appeared Impatient for the appeal, and to have possessed the most animated sentiments and determined resolution."[9]

What occurred instead was an awkward pause, while Washington waited for Howe to act. Washington learned on March 8, in a letter from several of Boston's selectmen that Howe had decided to abandon the town. Eager to spare their town from destruction at the hands of the departing British, the selectmen informed Washington that Howe had assured them that "He has no intention of destroying the Town Unless the Troops under his Command are molested during their Embarkation, or at their departure."[10] In other words, if the American army held its fire while the British loaded their ships with men and equipment, the British would spare Boston and simply sail away.

Washington was noncommittal to this proposal and continued to improve his fortifications on Dorchester Heights. He also held his fire, however, and began preparations for the army to march. Concerned that Howe's destination was New York, Washington ordered the riflemen from Pennsylvania, Virginia, and Maryland to prepare to march.[11] They started for New York on March 14 and were soon followed by five regiments under William Heath.[12]

By March 17, the last of the British troops, along with approximately one thousand Tories, boarded transport ships crammed with gear, supplies, and people, and made their way out of Boston Harbor. Washington shared the news with Congress:

> It is with the greatest pleasure I inform you that on Sunday last, the 17th Instant, about 9 O'Clock in the forenoon, The Ministerial Army evacuated the Town of Boston, and that the Forces of the United Colonies are now in actual possession thereof. I beg leave to congratulate you Sir, & the honorable Congress—on this happy Event, and particularly as it was effected without endangering the lives & property of the remaining unhappy Inhabitants.[13]

Washington added, "The Town, although it suffer'd greatly is not in so bad a state as I expected to find it."[14] The American commander was particularly pleased to inform Mr. Hancock that his residence and personal belongs remained largely unscathed.

Washington observed to Joseph Reed that the British retreat had been hasty, caused undoubtedly by the American seizure of Dorchester Heights.[15] He was surprised by the amount of gear and supplies left behind (there was no room on the ships) and the condition of the British works, which were largely left standing.

Although the British fleet puzzled Washington by remaining anchored off Boston for over a week (to refit and stock up on fresh water) he remained concerned that their next destination was New York and ordered another portion of his army to march there under John Sullivan.[16]

When the British fleet finally sailed out to sea on March 27, Washington ordered the rest of the army to New York, leaving five regiments (approximately two thousand officers and men) in Boston under Artemas Ward "to protect the Continental Stores and to assist in fortifying the Town and Harbour."[17] Washington marched to New York with the remainder of the army in early April. He left behind a city scarred by a two-year British occupation and an eleven-month American siege.

In the weeks following the departure of the British from Boston, the inhabitants of coastal New England remained on edge, concerned that Howe might return at any moment.

REACTION TO THE BRITISH DEPARTURE IN NEW ENGLAND
The New Hampshire House of Representatives was in session in March when Washington took Dorchester Heights and Howe announced that he was leaving Boston. Concerned that Howe's movement could bring British troops to New Hampshire, the assembly voted to raise a new Provincial regiment of 725 officers and men to serve for the rest of the year. A forty-two-man company of artillery and three companies of one hundred men each were also to be raised, all to defend the colony in case the British suddenly arrived.[18]

House Speaker Meshech Weare wrote to Washington following the votes to ask for a return of gunpowder that New Hampshire had provided the army the previous summer:

> Our Assembly have very readily determind upon the most effectual Measures in our power, for the Defence of the Sea Coast, & in particular Piscataqua Harbour—but We must beg Leave to remind your Excellency of a Matter of the utmost Consequence to Us, Our Magazine of powder being very low not exceeding twelve Barrels, We are under the Necessity of asking The Return of the Supply of Powder made by this Colony last summer for the Continental Service.[19]

Washington replied two days later, explaining, "I am exceedingly sorry that It is not in my power at this time to comply with your requisition for powder and to make a return of what was generously lent for the Continental use, the low state of stock of that article will not allow me to spare the smallest quantity."[20] Fortunately for New Hampshire, Howe had no intention of paying the colony a visit.

Although the initial urgency of manning defenses in Portsmouth subsided as each day of British inactivity passed, concern lingered among New Hampshire's leaders that their proximity to Halifax could result in a sudden appearance of the British. To their good fortune, no such appearance occurred.

Rhode Island placed its militia on alert at the news of the British departure from Boston, concerned that Howe and his troops were heading their way. Governor Nicholas Cooke provided a bleak assessment of Rhode Island's military preparedness to Washington on March 19: "We must inform your Excellency that the great Number of Troops sent out of this Colony [to join the Continental Army] have considerably thinned our Numbers." Rhode Island's militia suffered from a severe deficiency of firearms, prompting Cooke to solicit "all the Assistance your Excellency can afford us consistent with the general Good." [21] Washington, however, had no troops to spare and even fewer arms.

Washington informed Governor Trumbull of Connecticut on March 14 about the departure of the British from Boston and speculated that New York was their next destination. He asked the governor to "throw two thousand men into that City, from the Frontiers of Connecticut, to maintain the place until I can arrive there with the Army."[22] The Connecticut Council of Safety voted on March 18 to organize and form two regiments of militia raised from among seven established militia regiments. Each was to have nine hundred officers and men and were to march to New York City as soon as possible, where they were to remain until Washington arrived with the army.[23] Colonel Gold Selleck Silliman was selected to command the first regiment of militia and Colonel Matthew Talcott, the second.

In early April, the Council of Safety called upon each militia regiment to draft between one-quarter and one-third of their men and ensure that they were properly equipped and ready to march on a moment's notice.[24] They were to be minutemen, similar to those raised in New England prior to the war.

By April, it was apparent that the evacuated British Army had not sailed to New York or elsewhere in New England. They had sailed to Halifax, Nova Scotia, to reorganize, refit, and await British reinforcements. The coast of New England, however, was still patrolled by powerful British warships that seized colonial shipping and threatened to destroy colonial ports.

CLASHES WITH THE BRITISH NAVY

HMS *Rose* had been stationed off Newport, Rhode Island, since 1775 and remained there after the British withdrawal from Boston. HMS *Glasgow* (20 guns, 160 crew), HMS *Swan* (14 guns, 125 crew), HMS *Nautilus* (16 guns, 125 crew), and HMS *Bolton* (eight guns, 30 crew) were with the *Rose* in early April 1776 when Commodore Esek Hopkins's Continental fleet out of Philadelphia approached.

Hopkins, who had commanded Rhode Island militia in the fall of 1775, had been appointed by the Continental Congress in late 1775 to command the fledgling Continental Navy that was assembled in the mid-Atlantic. His fleet included the frigates *Alfred* (30 guns, 280 crew) and *Columbus* (28 guns, 280 crew), the brigs *Andrew Doria* (16 guns, 160 crew) and *Cabott* (14 guns, 150 crew), the sloops *Providence* (12 guns, 118 crew) and *Hornet* (eight guns, 60 crew), the schooner *Wasp* (eight guns and 60 crew), and the sloop-tender *Fly* (four guns, 29 crew).[25] Commodore Hopkins had successfully raided the Bahamas a month earlier and sought to offload captured stores and prisoners, including the governor of the Bahamas, Montfort Browne.

When the American fleet approached Block Island off Rhode Island on April 5, most of the British squadron was anchored at Newport, preparing to disperse and sail to several different locations. Captain Wallace of the HMS *Rose* had just received orders to send the *Glasgow* southward to Virginia and the *Bolton* and *Swan* to cruise along St. Georges Bank, off Nova Scotia.[26] HMS *Bolton*, several tenders, and HMS *Glasgow*, were not in Newport Harbor, but out to sea off Block Island when the Americans approached. They were not within sight of each other however, so when the American ship *Alfred* bore down and seized the *Bolton* in the afternoon of April 5, the *Glasgow* was unaware of it.

Early in the morning of April 6, the *Glasgow* discovered the American fleet and prepared for battle. Captain Tryingham Howe of the *Glasgow* recalled that

At half past two [in the morning] a Brig much like the *Bolton*, but larger, came within hail, and seemed to hesitate about giving any answers, but still kept standing towards us, And on being asked what other Ships were in Company with her, they answered, "the *Columbus* and *Alfred*, a two and twenty Gun frigate." And almost immediately, a hand Grenadoe was thrown out of her top. We exchanged our Broadsides, she then shot ahead, and lay on our bow, to make room for a large Ship, with a top light, to come on our Broadside, and another Ship ran under our Stern, Raked us as she passed.[27]

Captain Samuel Nicholas, in command of the marines onboard the *Alfred*, shared similar details of the fight. Awakened by the call of "all hands to quarters" at 1:30 a.m., Nicholas recalled that

We soon discovered a large ship standing directly for us. The *Cabot* was foremost of the fleet, our ship close after, not more than one hundred yards behind, but to windward withal. When the [*Cabot*] came up close, she was hailed by the ship, which we then learned was the *Glasgow* man-of-war: The [*Cabot*] immediately fired a broadside, and instantly received a return of twofold, which, owing to the weight of metal, damaged her so much in her hull and rigging, as obliged her to retire for a while to refit. Our ship then came up, not having it in our power to fire a shot before without hurting the [*Cabot*], and engaged her side by side for three glasses [ninety minutes], as hot as possibly could be on both sides. The first broadside she fired, my Second Lieutenant fell dead close by my side; he was shot by a musket-ball through the head.[28]

Concerned at one point that his ship would fall to the rebels, Captain Howe had a packet of dispatches he was charged to deliver thrown overboard, weighed down by a cannonball.[29]

Sailing for Newport to gain the protection of the rest of the British squadron, Howe was relieved to see the Americans suddenly break off their chase. Hopkins aboard the *Alfred* explained his decision to end the three-hour engagement:

We lost six men killed and as many Wounded. The *Cabot* four men killed and Seven Wounded. The Captain among the latter— the *Columbus* had one Man lost his Arm. We receiv'd considerable damage in our Ship but the greatest was in having our Wheel Rope & blocks shot away which gave the *Glascow* time to make Sail. I did not think proper to follow as it would have brought on an Action with the whole of their Fleet and as I had upwards of thirty of our best Seamen on board the Prizes [several ships captured earlier in his voyage], and some that were onboard had got too much Liquor out of the Prizes to be fit for Duty, thought it most prudent to give over Chase and secure our Prizes.[30]

The American fleet sailed into New London, Connecticut, the next day.

In Newport, Wallace aboard the *Rose* heard the cannon fire out to sea but remained unaware of its cause. Anchored between Gould Island and Coddington's Point, just north of Newport, he was greeted at sunrise with rebel cannon fire from two 18-pound cannons that had been moved to the point during the evening. The cannon fire reportedly "hulled the *Rose* 2 or 3 times, the *Nautilus* once or twice, and sent one shot through and through one of the armed tenders."[31] It also forced the British squadron to slip their cables and sail out of range of the cannons. The battered *Glasgow* rejoined the British squadron at 11:00 a.m., her arrival and condition described in the *Newport Mercury*: "Away came the poor *Glasgow*, under all the sail she could set, yelping from the mouths of her cannon (like a broken leg'd dog) in token of her being badly wounded. . . . It was plainly perceived by the holes in [her sails] and by the hanging of her yards, that she had been treated in a very rough manner."[32]

The *Rose*, *Nautilus*, and *Swan* put out to sea in search of the rebel fleet, leaving the battered *Glasgow* and three small vessels at anchor off Brenton's Point. In the evening, militia hauled four cannons to the point, an 18-pounder, a 9-pounder, and two 4-pounders, and early the next morning

[they] saluted the *Glasgow* with such warmth that she slipped her cable and pushed up the river without firing a gun, under all the

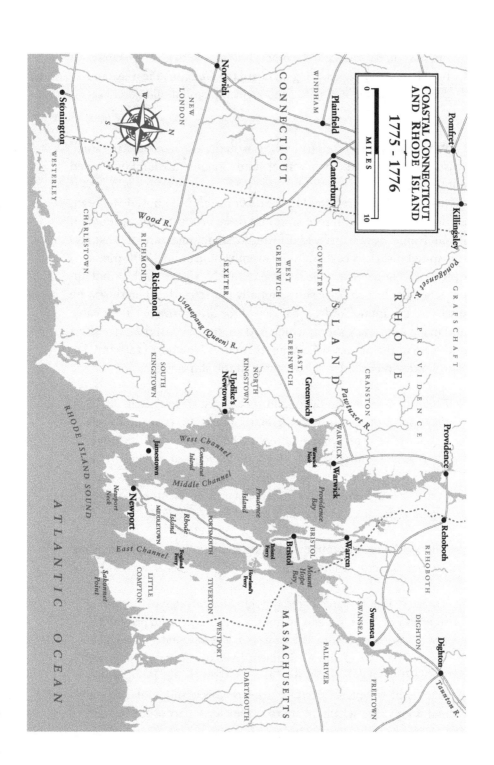

COASTAL CONNECTICUT
AND RHODE ISLAND
1775 - 1776

sail she could make, and the others followed with great precipitation. By the terrible cracking on board the *Glasgow*, the noise and confusion among her men, tis thought the cannon did good execution.[33]

When the wind shifted from the north, the *Glasgow* and the small vessels with her made their way around Conanicut Island and sailed out to sea.[34]

Just four days later, the HMS *Scarborough* (20 guns, 130 crew), escorting a sixteen-gun transport and three prizes it had captured on its sail from Georgia, arrived off Rhode Island, unaware of what had transpired just days earlier. In the evening at around 10:00 p.m. two of Rhode Island's row galleys came out of Newport Harbor and approached the British prize ships, initially undetected. When they were discovered, Captain Andrew Barkley of the *Scarborough* cut his cable and made after the galleys, which had secured two of the prize ships and were in the process of towing them into Newport Harbor. Captain Barkley recorded what occurred in the ship's log:

> Begun to Cannonade them, and they us, & struck often. At 11 they towed the prizes into the Harbour. At 1/2 past the Rebels began to fire at us, from a Battery at the North end of the Town. . . . A great number of shot struck us, & did great damage to the Lower Shrouds & Running Rigging, one shot struck the main mast. . . . At 5 the Rebells got three Guns on Brintons point & begun to fire at us, several shot came Close to us.[35]

A more detailed account of the engagement appeared in the *Constitutional Gazette* in late April:

> Thursday last, towards night, the ship *Scarborough* of 20 guns, a transport of 200 tons, and 16 guns, a brig loaded with provisions, and a sloop loaded with salt, came into this bay, and anchored between Goat-Island and Connanicut [Island]. In the evening two row galleys, commanded by Captains Grimes and Hyer, with a number of volunteers from the army on this island, took the brig and sloop; after which a battery at the North part of the town, a

battery at Brenton's Point, and the gallies play'd so briskly upon the ships, that they were soon obliged to move out of the reach of the batteries, and went under Conanicut [Island]. Capt. Hyer, in one of the gallies, lay within musket shot of the *Scarborough*, firing upon her, while Grimes boarded and sent off the brig and sloop. The *Scarborough* did the galley some damage in her hull and rigging, and the musketry from her tops wounded one of Capt. Hyer's people, which was all the injury received on the American side. This bold action, of taking two vessels close under the stern of a 20 gun ship, may possibly convince our enemies that the Yankees are not such dastards, as the Tories in this country have represented them.[36]

The *Scarborough* moved further up the bay, just past Newport, close to Conanicut Island and the crew commenced to repair the damage done to it. Captain Barkley observed militia construct a new cannon battery at the entrance of Newport Harbor but did nothing to prevent it.[37] In the evening, cannons on Conanicut Island fired upon the *Scarborough* for two hours, but apparently did little damage.[38] The cannon fire resumed at daylight and when a shot hit the mainmast, Barkley moved the *Scarborough* away from Conanicut Island.[39] This just put the ship closer to Rhode Island and the rebel batteries there, which commenced to fire upon the *Scarborough* at 9:00 a.m. Barkley noted in his journal that

> The Rebels firing so brisk at us, & the Tide of Ebb setting so strong, to avoid the Tide sitting us Close to their Battery's, Cutt the Cable, 2/3 from the Anchor, made sail, & Run Close under the South Shore, the [transport] and Sloop in Company. The Rebells kept a continual fire at us from their 2 Battery's which we return'd all the way going out, one shot struck the Middle of the fore Mast & several struck the Hull & Lower Rigging. At 1/2 past 11 got out of Gun shott.[40]

Barkley had had enough of Rhode Island and sailed out to sea. For the first time in over a year, the colony was free of the looming presence of the British navy.

Washington was enroute to New York when the naval clash off Block Island occurred. He met with Commodore Hopkins on April 9 in New London, no doubt congratulating him on his recent successful voyage.[41] Washington reached New York a few days later.

In Boston, General Ward and the civilian leaders of Massachusetts were slow to construct new defensive works to protect the harbor and town, but by May some progress was achieved.[42] British warships hovered in Massachusetts Bay, seizing a handful of colonial vessels that unwisely sailed within sight of the British warships.

The British were not the only ones, however, who seized ships. An assortment of New England privateers, armed merchant ships commissioned by both the Continental Congress and colonial authorities to engage the enemy or those who supported the enemy, also patrolled the waters off New England. Usually outgunned by the British navy, these daring New England mariners were, in most cases, careful about whom they challenged and attacked.

Captain James Mugford of Marblehead, aboard the armed schooner *Franklin*, one of the ships Washington authorized the previous fall, threw caution to the wind on May 17 when he encountered the British transport *Hope*, loaded with one thousand stand of carbines (short muskets), numerous entrenching tools, and most importantly, 1,500 barrels of gunpowder estimated to weigh seventy-five tons.[43] The *Hope* had sailed from Ireland in March and was unaware of the British evacuation of Boston. The transport sailed unnoticed in the early morning hours past several British warships stationed in Massachusetts Bay (that were there in part to redirect such transport ships to Halifax) and continued toward Boston Harbor. By the time the British warships noticed the transport, it was too late. Captain Mugford had spotted the ship as well and was bearing down from Boston to seize it. An account of what happened appeared in the local paper:

> Notwithstanding she appeared to be an armed ship, and was in sight of the enemy's men of war laying in Nantasket, Capt. Mugford resolutely bore down upon her, and took her without opposition. [The transport] mounted 6 carriage guns, a number of swivels, and had on board 18 men. The *Franklin* at that time, had only 21 men.[44]

Eager to secure what was the richest prize seized by the Americans to date, Mugford quickly brought the transport into Boston Harbor. When it grounded before reaching the dock, boats were used to unload its valuable cargo and deposit it in Boston.[45]

News of the capture spread quickly, and Massachusetts leaders jockeyed to retain as much of the captured cargo as they could. Thomas Cushing wrote to John Hancock and the Continental Congress on the day the *Hope* was captured, requesting that the seized weapons and entrenching tools remain in Boston for the use of the troops posted there. He also requested that ten tons of the captured gunpowder be used to compensate Massachusetts for gunpowder it had provided the Continental Army during the siege of Boston.[46] The Continental Congress left the decision on what to do with the captured items to Washington, who instructed Ward at the end of May to send eight hundred of the carbines and four hundred barrels of gunpowder to New York. The remaining weapons and gunpowder were to remain in Massachusetts, the weapons to be used as needed by the Continental troops there and the gunpowder to be stored in a secure location outside of Boston.[47]

Captain Mugford and the crew of the *Franklin* did not concern themselves with what became of the captured military stores. Joined by the small schooner *Lady Washington* with a crew of just six, the *Franklin* set out on another cruise two days after its stunning seizure and immediately ran into trouble when it became grounded before it reached the open sea.[48] Spotted by two British warships, which sent sailors and marines in tenders and longboats to seize the *Franklin*, Mugford managed to free his vessel just before the British reached his ship.[49] An account of what happened next appeared in the *New England Chronicle*:

> Capt. Mugford . . . between 9 and 10 o'clock [at night] discovered a number of boats, which he hailed, and received for answer, that they were from Boston. He ordered them to keep off, or he would fire upon them. They begged him, for God's sake, not to fire, for they were going on board him. Capt. Mugford instantly fired, and was followed by all his men; and cutting his cable, brought his broadside to bear, when he discharged his cannon [likely just two

light cannon], loaded with musquet ball, directly in upon them. Before the cannon could be charged a second time, two or three boats were along side, each of them supposed to have as many men on board as the *Franklin*, which were only 21, including officers.[50]

A desperate fight ensued as the crew of the *Franklin* and *Lady Washington* (which had remained near the *Franklin* to assist) struggled to keep the British from boarding their ships. Accounts of the engagement vary in detail, but it is clear that a pitched fight occurred in the dark. A barge from the HMS *Renown* (50 guns, 350 crew) was sunk, costing the lives of an officer, two sailors, and two marines.[51] The HMS *Experiment* (50 guns, 350 crew) reported two marines killed and several others wounded.[52] The Americans were convinced that British losses were much higher. General Ward estimated that the British lost between sixty to seventy men in their attempt to capture the *Franklin*. He informed Washington that

> The intrepid Captain Mugford fell a little before the Enemy left his Schooner, he was run through with a lance while he was cutting off the hands of the Pirates as they were attempting to board him; and it is said that with his own hands he cut off five pair of theirs; no other Man was either killed or wounded onboard the *Franklin*.[53]

Another account of the fight noted that the "Decks of the Privateers were cover'd with the hands and fingers of the Enemy," who had tried to climb aboard the ships.[54]

Yet another account, published in the *New England Chronicle*, agreed that British losses were heavy, but maintained that "while the heroic Mugford, with out-stretched arms, was righteously dealing death and destruction to our base and unnatural enemies, he received a fatal ball in his body, which in a few minutes put a period to his life."[55] In other words, claimed this account, Mugford had been shot during the struggle. His loss was noted by many, including Washington, who commented that "The two schooners . . . behaved extremely well in repelling the Attack . . . and It is only to be lamented that the affair was attended with the death of Captn Mugford—he seemed to deserve a better fate."[56]

A month after the loss of Captain Mugford, New England privateers scored another decisive seizure when they captured several British troop transports that had sailed from Scotland. Like the captured British transport *Hope*, the troop transports *George* and *Annabella*, with approximately two hundred men of the 71st Regiment of Highlanders including their commander Lieutenant Colonel Archibald Campbell, were unaware that Howe had abandoned Boston.[57] Campbell, who was aboard the *George*, informed Howe what happened:

> On [June] 17, at day light, we found ourselves opposite to the harbour's mouth of Boston. . . . Four schooners, which we took to be pilots, or armed vessels in the service of his Majesty (but which were afterwards found to be four American privateers of eight carriage guns, twelve swivels, and forty men each) were bearing down upon us at four o'clock in the morning, at half an hour thereafter two of them engaged us, and about eleven o'clock the other two were close along side.[58]

Campbell noted that the two transport ships were lightly armed, the *George* with just six light cannons and the *Annabella* with only two swivel guns. They still managed to keep the privateers at bay all day with the loss of only a handful of men.[59]

Still unaware that Boston was held by the rebels, the transports pushed on into Boston Harbor. Suddenly, rebel cannons posted on a nearby island fired upon the transports, finally revealing to Campbell that Boston was no longer in British hands. With the tide and wind against them, the transports were forced to anchor out of range of the rebel cannons.[60]

Captain Seth Harding, in command of the brig *Defence* out of Connecticut with sixteen cannons and over one hundred crew, arrived on the scene and anchored his ship between the two transports at around 11:00 p.m. Captain Harding recalled that he hailed the larger ship and

Ordered her to strike her Colours to America. They answered by asking What Brigg is that? I told them the *Defence*. I then haild them again and told them I did not want to kill their Men but have the Ship I would.[61]

He was answered with gunfire, which Harding immediately returned. Joined by the four smaller privateer schooners, a ninety-minute battle raged, ending only when the British transports ran out of ordnance for their cannon.[62] Campbell reported that

Under such circumstances, hemmed in as we were with six privateers, in the middle of an enemy's harbour, beset with a dead calm, without the power of escaping, or even the most distant hope of relief, I thought it became my duty not to sacrifice the lives of our gallant men wantonly in the arduous attempt of an evident impossibility.[63]

Harding reported that none of his men were killed in the fight, but nine were wounded.[64] He claimed that eighteen of the enemy were killed, but Campbell reported eight deaths (seven privates and a major) and twelve other soldiers wounded.[65]

More important than the losses in battle, however, were the number of captured 71st Highlanders. When Campbell arrived in Boston, he discovered that two other transports carrying more of his regiment were also captured, bringing the total number of captured Scottish Highlanders to over four hundred.[66]

THE NEED FOR MORE CANNONS

While New England's leaders welcomed the naval successes that occurred offshore in the spring and worked to build, equip, and man even more armed vessels to challenge the British navy, they also sought to defend their coastline from shore. Large commercial ports like Portsmouth, Boston, Newport, and New London were particularly important to defend.

The latter two towns found themselves locked in a dispute over possession of a number of heavy cannons brought by Commodore Hopkins in April from his raid upon New Providence in the Bahamas. Before the Continental Congress had decided what to do with the cannons, Hopkins had delivered twenty-four to Newport and left the remaining thirty-four cannons at New London.[67] Both communities happily accepted the weapons and went to work building defensive positions upon which to mount the guns.

The Continental Congress, however, had other plans for most of the cannons delivered to Newport. On May 7, Congress ordered that twenty of the heaviest cannons sent to Newport be retrieved and sent to Philadelphia instead.[68] Two commissioners were sent from Philadelphia to take possession of the cannons, but before they arrived, Hopkins learned about the decision and attempted to retrieve the cannons from Newport himself.

The Rhode Island General Assembly, acting in place of the governor, who was unavailable at the time Hopkins made his request, refused to deliver the cannons and instead, sent an appeal to Congress to reconsider its decision to take them.

Noting that prior to the arrival of the cannons, Newport was "entirely defenceless, surrounded by a powerful Naval Armament, and daily threatened with, and in Danger of, immediate Destruction," it was thus no surprise, the assembly declared, that nearly one-third of the population had fled and those that remained sought to appease the British to avoid an attack.[69]

The assembly claimed that the arrival of Hopkins with the cannons in April elated many of Newport's inhabitants, who readily agreed to build fortifications on which to place them. "This decisive Resolution gave every Friend to the United Colonies a new Spring," declared the assembly, who asserted that Newport's newfound ability to defend itself strengthened support for the colonial cause.[70]

The Rhode Island Assembly asked of the consequences should the cannons be removed: "All the disaffected, all the lukewarm, and all the timid cry out that this Colony hath been totally neglected by Congress, while every other Colony that is exposed is defended by Continental Troops." The removal of the cannons would only reinforce this view and then, predicted the assembly, "the Town of Newport and the island of Rhode Island are lost." The assembly stressed that without the cannon "It will be impossible for the Inhabitants to defend themselves. They will not even attempt it. Leave us the Cannon," urged the assembly, "we can save Newport."[71]

The assembly's appeal produced a compromise. On May 30, Congress ordered that six of the heaviest cannons at Newport and fourteen of the heaviest cannons at New London be transported to Philadelphia as soon as possible.[72]

Although the New England colonies did not retain all of the troops and cannons they desired, they had enough to offer some resistance to the British, should General Howe or the British navy decide to pay them a visit. The British, however, had other plans. Their attention was focused on Canada and New York.

The day after Washington arrived in New York in mid-April, he ordered three regiments of Massachusetts Continentals and one from New Hampshire to Canada to reinforce the American army there.[73] Colonels John Patterson, John Greaton, and William Bond commanded the Massachusetts regiments, which totaled over 1,300 officers and men on paper but less than 1,000 fit for duty.[74] Colonel Enoch Poor commanded the New Hampshire regiment detached to Canada. He had nearly 500 officers and men fit for duty when he arrived in May.[75]

Two weeks after he ordered these four regiments to Canada, Washington complied with a request from the Continental Congress and sent six more regiments north, two from New Hampshire, two from Pennsylvania, and two from New Jersey, all under the command of John Sullivan.[76] The New Hampshire regiments were commanded by Colonels James Reed and John Stark and totaled over nine hundred officers and men.[77] Colonel Timothy Bedel joined them in Canada with five companies of his newly raised New Hampshire regiment (under two hundred men), so by mid-May all of New Hampshire's Continental regiments were attached to the American northern army in Canada.[78] They would all be needed very shortly.

Six

Summer

THE CANADIAN CAMPAIGN THAT HAD COMMENCED THE PREVIOUS fall had seen mixed success for the Americans. Although Richard Montgomery had managed to capture St. Jeans and Montreal in 1775, his attack on Quebec at the end of the year ended in failure and cost him his life. Governor Guy Carleton managed to defend the walled city with a handful of British redcoats and French militia, many of the latter who were ambivalent about the conflict. Benedict Arnold, who was wounded in the leg in the assault on Quebec, remained outside the city with less than one thousand American troops, several hundred from New England, waiting for reinforcements and better weather.

General David Wooster of Connecticut had arrived in Montreal during the winter to assume command of all the American troops in Canada. He spent most of the winter in Montreal and joined Arnold outside Quebec with reinforcements in March. This brought the American force to approximately 2,500 troops, but over one-quarter of them were sick, many with smallpox or under inoculation.[1] Equally troubling was that the enlistments of hundreds of men were due to expire in mid-April. Wooster offered a bounty to those who agreed to reenlist for a year, but after a harsh winter during which they had been poorly supplied, most declined the offer.[2]

General John Thomas of Massachusetts, who had been appointed by Congress in early March to take command of the American army in Canada, arrived outside Quebec on May 1. He found nearly half of the two thousand American troops that remained outside Quebec unfit for service, due mostly to illness (smallpox). Additionally, the supply of gunpowder and provisions were critically low. Thomas and his officers agreed that it was time to retreat to Trois-Rivieres (Three Rivers), eighty miles up the St. Lawrence River.[3]

The arrival of British warships and transports with thousands of British troops under General John Burgoyne the day following the decision to retreat turned the American movement to Trois-Rivieres into a disorderly flight. Several hundred of the American sick fell into British hands as did most of their cannons and gunpowder at Quebec. Thomas and the remainder of his dispirited force retreated all the way to Sorel, 120 miles from Quebec, leaving a small rear guard at Trois-Rivieres.[4]

Knowing that the sudden turn of events would come as a shock to a recently arrived delegation from Congress, Thomas explained to them that

> The Army here have now for two days been entirely destitute of meat; that no contractor is provided, nor have I any money to purchase provisions, were they to be procured in this country. . . . In order to judge truly my situation, you will be pleased to figure to yourselves a retreating Army, disheartened by unavoidable misfortunes, destitute of almost every necessity to render their lives comfortable, or even tolerable, sick, and (as they think) wholly neglected, and no probable prospect of a speedy relief. . . . In short, such are our present circumstances that, unless some effectual spirited steps are immediately undertaken for our relief, it will not be possible to keep the Army together, but we must unavoidably be obliged to abandon a country of infinite importance to the safety of the Colonies, and to leave our friends here a prey to those whose mercies are cruelties.[5]

Fortunately for the Americans, Carleton and Burgoyne did not aggressively pursue the fleeing Americans. Time was now on their side, and they were in no rush.

BATTLE OF THE CEDARS

Newly promoted General Benedict Arnold was not with the American troops who fled to Trois-Rivieres in May. He had gone to Montreal weeks earlier to assume command of the American troops posted there. Reports that a regiment of British troops and "a number of Savages" were approaching from the west prompted Arnold to post four hundred men in early May at a narrow pass about forty-five miles west of Montreal known as the Cedars.[6] He reported to Washington that this detachment had "two pieces [of] Cannon & [are] well entrenched by which the Enemy must pass."[7] The men posted at the Cedars were mostly from New Hampshire, raised and commanded by Colonel Bedel over the winter.

There are conflicting accounts of what happened when the garrison at the Cedars learned of the approach of the enemy. An inquiry by the Continental Congress found that Colonel Bedel received intelligence of their approach on May 15 and that he set out himself to Montreal to "procure reinforcements," leaving Major Isaac Butterfield in command.[8] If this is indeed what occurred, it certainly places Bedel in a cowardly light.

Another account however, brought up at Bedel's court-martial, claims that he had left the Cedars before word of the enemy's approach arrived in order to meet with a delegation of Caughnawaga Indians just a few miles outside of Montreal and "cultivate friendly relations."[9] When he learned of the enemy's approach at the Cedars, Bedel rode to Montreal, which was much closer than the Cedars, in order to obtain reinforcements. Sick with smallpox, he was unable to return.[10]

Whichever account is true, it was left to Butterfield to command the garrison at the Cedars, some 390 men strong. Approximately forty British Regulars, one hundred Canadians, and five hundred Indians, all commanded by Captain George Forester, surrounded the fort on May 17.[11] Butterfield and his men, protected by the fort, suffered no casualties over two days of sporadic fighting, yet the American commander seemed determined to surrender. A congressional inquiry into the affair reported that "Major Butterfield proposed, from the very first, to surrender the post, and refused repeated [requests] from his officers and men to permit them to sally out on the enemy."[12] The inquiry reported that not only did the garrison suffer no casualties during the two days of scattered fighting, but they also remained well armed and provisioned and could have easily held out much longer. Furthermore, Butterfield knew that reinforcements were on the way.[13]

Yet when Captain Forster summoned the garrison to surrender on May 19 or face the wrath of the Indians once the fort was taken by force, Butterfield, against the wishes of his fellow officers, surrendered.[14]

The surrender of Butterfield's force at the Cedars enabled Forester to turn his attention to the 150-man American relief party under Major Henry Sherbourne. They were ambushed by Forester and his Indian allies a few miles from the fort the next day.[15] An American officer recalled that

They were attacked by a large body of savages and Canadians, who under cover of a wood fired upon them. Our people, though entirely exposed, without shelter, maintained an obstinate engagement for one hour and forty minutes; when the savages, having surrounded, rushed upon and disarmed them. Then a scene of savage barbarity ensued, and many of our people were sacrificed to their fury—butchered with tomahawks and other instruments of murder.[16]

In two days, Captain Forster had managed to capture nearly five hundred Americans at the loss of just a handful of men. Forster handed Sherborne's men over to the Indians who "stripped [them] of their baggage and wearing apparel" and put several to death.[17] The congressional inquiry claimed that one poor soul was "first shot, and while retaining life and sensation, was roasted" by the Indians.[18]

Forster, burdened with as many prisoners as he had men and unable to prevent their abuse by the Indians, proposed a cartel with Sherbourne and Butterfield to free the captured Americans in exchange for a like number of British prisoners held by the Americans. The freed Americans would also have to pledge to never "again bear arms against the British government," a stipulation not applied to the prisoners held by the Americans.[19] Although they had no authority to agree to such an arrangement, the captured American commanders, "being under the absolute power of the enemy," reluctantly signed the proposal.[20]

When Arnold arrived with 350 troops, Forster informed him of the cartel and declared that if Arnold "rejected the cartel, and attacked him, every man of the prisoners would be put to instant death."[21] Forester stressed that the Indians were determined to kill the prisoners if attacked and he was powerless to stop them, so for humanity's sake he urged Arnold to accept the stipulations of the cartel.[22]

Arnold initially rejected Forster's proposal, but eventually relented to save the prisoners "from cruel and inhuman death, threatened in such terms as left no doubt it was to be perpetrated."[23] A few prisoners were retained as hostages by Forster to ensure implementation of the agreement.

Congress refused to accept the terms, however, and declared the released American captives prisoners of war to be considered on parole (and thus not able to fight until exchanged).[24] British prisoners would only be released through an official exchange that would then release the paroled Americans and allow each to return to the war.

Back at Sorel, the first of Washington's reinforcements, including three regiments from New Hampshire and three more from Massachusetts, began to arrive. These troops swelled the American presence in Canada to over six thousand officers and men, nearly half of which were from New England.[25] General Thomas had little opportunity to use the reinforcements, however. Struck down by smallpox, he resigned his command and went to Chambly, forty-five miles south of Sorel along the Richelieu River in an effort to recover. He suffered terribly and died on June 1. Command of the American troops at Sorel passed briefly to General William Thompson, who sent two regiments, one from Pennsylvania and the other from New Jersey, totaling approximately seven hundred men, to attack, if possible, a detachment of British and Canadian troops reportedly posted at Trois-Rivieres.[26]

When General Sullivan arrived in Sorel on June 3, he assumed command of the American army.[27] Confident that he could hold Sorel and eager to strike a blow against the enemy, whom he was informed numbered just three hundred men at Trois-Rivieres, Sullivan sent Thompson with two more regiments from Pennsylvania and New Jersey to reinforce the two already sent to Trois-Rivieres earlier.[28]

BATTLE OF THREE RIVERS

Thompson and his men arrived at the village of Nicolet early in the morning of June 7. He determined that there was not enough time to complete a crossing of the St. Lawrence River and then attack Trois-Rivieres before dawn, so he let his tired men rest. They waited until evening to cross several miles upriver from the British ships at Trois-Rivieres. The plan was to attack the British at dawn of June 8.[29] Thompson informed Sullivan of his decision and added that the latest reports on British troop strength at Trois-Rivieres ranged from 500 to 1,500 strong. The actual number of British troops Trois-Rivieres approached 2,000, many who had recently arrived aboard transport ships.[30]

At nightfall on June 7, the Americans, over 1,500 strong, crossed the river nine miles from Trois-Rivieres.[31] They struggled in the darkness to advance, directed by guides who either purposefully misled or incompetently led them. As they approached Trois-Rivieres, they were fired upon by British warships in the river.

The Americans pressed on and engaged British troops, briefly pushing them back. Initially successful, heavy British cannon and musket fire from the ships and entrenchments at Trois-Rivieres halted the American advance.[32] An unidentified American officer involved with the battle noted that

> The great body of the enemy, which we knew nothing of, consisting of two or three thousand men, covered with intrenchments, and assisted with the cannon of the shipping and several field pieces, began a furious fire, and continued it upon our troops in the front; it was so heavy that [Colonel Anthony Wayne's] division gave way. . . . Colonel [Arthur] St. Clair's division advanced, but the fire was too heavy. Part of Colonel [William] Irvine's division

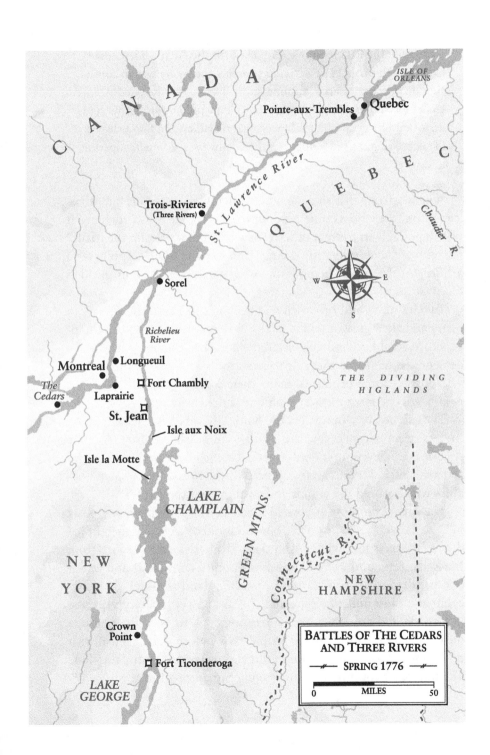

ISLE OF
ORLEANS

CANADA

Pointe-aux-Trembles ● ● **Quebec**

QUEBEC

St. Lawrence River

Trois-Rivieres ●
(Three Rivers)

Chaudier R.

N
W   E
S

● Sorel

*Richelieu
River*

THE   DIVIDING
HIGLANDS

Montreal ● Longueuil

*The
Cedars* ●

□ Fort Chambly

Laprairie ●

St. Jean □

Isle aux Noix

Isle la Motte

*LAKE
CHAMPLAIN*

GREEN MTNS.

Connecticut R.

NEW
YORK

NEW
HAMPSHIRE

Crown
Point ●

□ Fort Ticonderoga

*LAKE
GEORGE*

**BATTLES OF THE CEDARS
AND THREE RIVERS**

— SPRING 1776 —

0   MILES   50

(especially the Riflemen) went up towards the enemy. Lieutenant-Colonel [Thomas] Hartley, understanding the Army was in confusion, led up the reserve within a short distance of the enemy. . . . Under all of these disadvantages, our men would fight, but we had no ground for it. We had no covering, no artillery, and no prospect of succeeding, as the number of the enemy was so much superior to ours.[33]

When a strong British detachment attempted to cut off the Americans from their boats nine miles upriver, a retreat was ordered. "It was impossible to [retreat orderly] as we could not regain the road," remembered the unidentified American officer. "The shipping and artillery of the enemy being in the way; small parties went through the swamp."[34]

Two hundred and fifty men had been left to guard the American boats and they grew anxious at the first reports of what had happened. Several hundred exhausted men reached the boats before the detachment guarding them fled across the river, leaving the bulk of Thompson's force behind to make their escape by foot.[35] Over the next few days, most of these men found their way back to Sorel.[36]

Those killed or wounded in the Battle of Trois-Rivieres amounted to less than twenty for the British and around fifty for the Americans.[37] Several hundred Americans, including General Thompson and Colonel Irvine, were captured by the British and French Loyalists who scoured the woods and swamp after the battle.[38]

The American army at Sorel, Montreal, and several smaller posts in Canada numbered just over four thousand officers and men fit for duty in the days following the Battle at Trois-Rivieres.[39] Troops from Massachusetts and New Hampshire, both Continental and about two hundred state troops from Connecticut and Massachusetts, accounted for just under half the total.[40] Most had only recently arrived in Canada and now they were retreating back to Fort Ticonderoga on Lake Champlain. Months would pass before the feared British push down Lake Champlain commenced and the troops at Fort Ticonderoga kept busy over the summer preparing for it.

DEFENDING NEW YORK

In New York City, Washington was also preparing for the arrival of the British. He had confidently informed his brother in late April, "We have already gone to great lengths in fortifying this City & the Hudsons River—a fortnight more will put us in a very respectable posture of Defence."[41]

Of the 8,411 officers and men fit for duty with Washington in mid-May, over 7,000 were from New England.[42] Eight of the eighteen continental regiments at New York were from Massachusetts, commanded by Colonels Ebenezer Learned, John Nixon, William Prescott, Moses Little, Joseph Read, Jonathan Ward, John Bailey, and Loammi Baldwin. They accounted for over 3,500 men or approximately 44 percent of Washington's effective infantry.[43] Connecticut contributed five regiments to Washington's army. They were commanded by Colonels Samuel Holden Parsons, Jedediah Huntington, Charles Webb, Samuel Wyllys, and Lieutenant Colonel John Durkee in place of Benedict Arnold. They accounted for 2,500 men or 30 percent of Washington's force.[44] Rhode Island's two regiments, commanded by Colonels James Varnum and Daniel Hitchcock, totaled nearly 800 men fit for duty or 10 percent of Washington's army at New York.[45]

The Continental Congress authorized the recruitment of four more Continental regiments from New England in May, two from Massachusetts and one each from New Hampshire and Connecticut.[46] In early June, Congress requested that the New England colonies send even more troops outside their borders, calling 13,500 New England militia into the field to serve until December. Massachusetts was requested to send 3,000 militia to Canada and 2,000 militia to New York; Connecticut, 1,500 militia to Canada and 5,500 to New York. New Hampshire and Rhode Island, as smaller colonies, were asked to send just 750 militia each to Canada.[47]

None of the militia ordered to Canada arrived in time to fight, but they did strengthen General Schuyler's battered army at Fort Ticonderoga. Nearly 2,000 militia from Massachusetts, over 1,100 from New Hampshire, and 800 from Connecticut arrived at Fort Ticonderoga over the summer to increase the garrison there to over 6,000 men.[48] Rhode Island failed to send its requested troops.

Informed by Joseph Hawley, a member of the Massachusetts General Court in early July that, "This colony I imagine will raise the Men required by Congress before Snow falls—But in No season for the relief of either New York or Canada," Hawley recommended that Washington transfer some or all the continental regiments still posted in Boston in place of the militia.[49]

Washington wrote to Congress about the proposal on July 4, and that body authorized him to transfer the troops to either Canada or New York.[50] He ordered three regiments to Fort Ticonderoga on July 9 and the two remaining Continental regiments in Boston to New York two days later.[51] Like the other New England colonies, Massachusetts would now have to rely on its own resources to defend against a return of the British. It became obvious, however, by the end of June, that New York City was the objective of the British. The arrival of over one hundred British ships crowded with thousands of troops made that clear. They arrived too late to prevent the Americans from declaring independence but were determined to crush Washington's army and strangle American independence in its infancy.

INDEPENDENCE

Sentiment in favor of American independence from Great Britain was non-existent prior to April 1775, even in New England. Colonel George Washington acknowledged this in October 1774 while attending the First Continental Congress. Writing to Robert McKenzie, a British officer whom he had served with in the French and Indian War, Washington declared, "I think I can announce it as a fact, that it is not the wish or interest of [Massachusetts] or any other [colony] upon this Continent, separately, or collectively, to set up for Independency."[52]

Despite bloodshed at Lexington and Concord, few colonists initially considered independence from Great Britain as a serious option. Silas Deane of Connecticut expressed the sentiment of most colonists when he shared with his wife a congressional committee resolution in late May:

In the most Explicit terms that the foundation of the present unhappy dispute between the British Ministry & Parliament &

America, is a Right claimed by the former to tax the Subjects of the latter without their consent—and not an inclination on Our part to set up for independence, which we utterly disavow.[53]

Time and again, accusations from Great Britain that independence was the true goal of the rebellious colonists were denied by colonial leaders. Yet, as the bloodshed continued in 1775, support for independence grew. Nathanael Greene noted in late October that his troops began "heartily to wish [for] a Declaration of Independence," and he agreed with it for a practical reason. "The French never will agree to furnish us with Powder," believed Greene, "as long as there is the least probability of an Accommodation between us and Great Britain."[54]

The king's speech to Parliament in October, which did not reach the colonies until the start of 1776, dashed hopes for reconciliation for many colonists and increased support for independence. Washington, acknowledging to Joseph Reed that he had supported independence ever since Bunker Hill, wrote, "The Kings Speech has confirmed the Sentiments [in favor of independence] I entertained upon the News of [Bunker Hill]."[55] Washington candidly noted that

The Ministers of G.B. should know, in a few Words, upon what Issue the cause should be put. I would . . . in open, undisguised, and Manly terms, proclaim our Wrongs & our Resolutions to be redressed. I would tell them, that we had born much—that we had long, & ardently sought for reconciliation upon honourable terms—that it had been denied us—that all our attempts at Peace had provd abortive and had been grossly misrepresented—that we had done everything that could be expected from the best of Subjects—that the Spirit of Freedom beat too high in us, to Submit to Slavery; & that, if nothing else would satisfie a Tyrant & his diabolical Ministry, we were determined to shake off all Connexions with a State So unjust, & unnatural.[56]

A growing number of colonists likely agreed with Washington by the start of 1776, especially after news of Parliament's Prohibitory Act, which targeted all American shipping on the seas, arrived in December and Thomas Paine's pamphlet *Common Sense*, which argued strongly for independence, was published in January.

Leaders in all the colonies began to seriously consider independence, and by spring many acted. The Rhode Island Assembly moved to the brink of independence on May 6, 1776, by renouncing the colony's allegiance to King George:

> Whereas George III, King of Great Britain . . . entirely departing from the duties and character of a good King, instead of protecting, is endeavouring to destroy the good people of this Colony, and of all the United Colonies, by sending Fleets and Armies to America, to confiscate our property, and spread fire, sword, and desolation, throughout our country, in order to compel us to submit to the most debasing and detestable tyranny; whereby we are obliged by necessity, and it becomes our highest duty; to use every means with which God and nature has furnished us, in support of our invaluable rights and privileges, to oppose that power which is exerted only for our Destruction.[57]

While not a direct declaration of independence, it drew the colony to the edge of such an act.

The issue of independence was certainly on the minds of many delegates to the Continental Congress in May. Stephen Hopkins, informed of the Rhode Island Assembly's action, wrote to Governor Cooke seeking more explicit instructions on the issue of independence:

> I observe that you have avoided giving me a direct answer to my queries concerning dependence or independence. However, a copy of the act of Assembly which you have sent me, together with our instructions, leave me little room to doubt what is the opinion of the Colony I came from. I suppose that it will not be long before Congress will throw off all connection, as well, in name as in substance, with Great Britain, as one thing after another seems gradually to lead them to such a step.[58]

Leaders in Massachusetts called upon the colony's inhabitants to meet and discuss the issue of independence in town meetings. By

June, it was clear that sentiment in favor was overwhelming.[59] One observer wrote to Elbridge Gerry, a Massachusetts delegate in Philadelphia, in mid-June to inform him that the colony was ready for independence:

> You cannot declare Independence too soon. . . . When the present House here called, last week, for the instructions of the several towns touching Independency . . . it appeared that about two-thirds of the towns in the Colony had met, and all instructed in the affirmative, and generally returned to be unanimously. As to the other towns, the accounts of their Members were, either that they were about to meet, or that they had not received the notice, as it was given only in the newspapers. . . . In a short time undoubtedly we shall have returns from all, and it is almost certain that the returns will be universally to support the Congress, with their lives and fortunes, in case of a declaration of Independence.[60]

Both the New Hampshire and Connecticut assemblies specifically instructed their delegates in Philadelphia to vote for independence in mid-June. New Hampshire's assembly, citing self-defense as its justification, instructed its delegates on June 15 to join the other colonies in support of independence should it be proposed in Congress:

> Whereas it now appears an undoubted fact that, notwithstanding all the dutiful petitions . . . from the American Colonies . . . the British Ministry, arbitrary and vindictive, are yet determined to reduce by fire and sword our bleeding country to their absolute obedience; and for this purpose, in addition to their own forces, have engaged great numbers of foreign mercenaries, who may now be on their passage here, accompanied by a formidable fleet, to ravage and plunder the sea-coast from all which we may expect the most dismal scenes of distress the ensuing year, unless we exert ourselves by every means and precaution possible. . . . We do hereby declare, that it is the opinion of this Assembly, our Delegates at the Continental Congress . . . are hereby instructed to join with the other Colonies in declaring the thirteen United Colonies a free and independent State.[61]

The Connecticut Assembly took an even stronger stand. Apparently unaware that Richard Henry Lee of Virginia had already done so on June 7, the Connecticut Assembly directed its delegates in Philadelphia on June 14 to propose independence to the Continental Congress:

> Resolved unanimously by this Assembly, that the Delegates of this Colony in General Congress . . . are hereby, instructed to propose to that respectable body to declare the United American Colonies free and independent States, absolved from all allegiance to the King of Great Britain, and to give the assent of this Colony to such Declaration.[62]

Weeks of deliberation and debate in Congress resulted in a unanimous vote (with New York abstaining) in favor of independence on July 2. Two days later, Congress adopted Thomas Jefferson's Declaration of Independence and announced its decision to the public.

News of the historic vote by Congress reached Connecticut within a week. The *Connecticut Journal*, printed in New Haven, squeezed in one sentence in its July 10 edition announcing, "The CONGRESS unanimously Resolved to declare the United Colonies FREE and INDEPENDENT STATES."[63] Two days later, a full copy of the text appeared in the *Connecticut Gazette*, printed in New London.[64]

The *Providence Gazette* in Rhode Island printed a copy of the Declaration of Independence in its July 13 edition, announcing that it was received from Philadelphia the previous day.[65] When Rhode Island's General Assembly met soon after the news, it formally approved the Continental Congress's Declaration of Independence and then changed the name of the colony to The State of Rhode Island and Providence Plantations.[66] The assembly had the Declaration of Independence read at the head of a brigade of militia in Newport on July 20 where "It was received with joy and applause by all ranks."[67]

The *New-England Chronicle*, printed in Boston, broke the news, not of the Declaration of Independence but of Congress's July 2 vote for independence. Likely informed in a letter by one of Massachusetts's delegates, the printer had time for just a one sentence announcement in its July 11 edition.[68] A week later, the Declaration was formally read from the balcony of the Massachusetts State House before two regiments of troops and a large gathering of people. They reportedly listened to the Declaration "with great joy, expressed by three huzzas from a great concourse of people assembled."[69] It was read that same day in Portsmouth, New Hampshire, before two companies of troops and "a numerous and respectable audience. The pleasing countenances of the many patriots present spoke a hearty concurrence in the interesting measure, which was confirmed by three huzzas, and all was conducted in peace and good order," remembered one observer."[70]

TWELVE YEARS OF POLITICAL CONFLICT AND FIFTEEN MONTHS of bloodshed and war culminated with the Declaration of Independence on July 4. Massachusetts, which from the start was at the center of the long dispute with Great Britain, together with its New England neighbors, who stood alongside Massachusetts the entire time, were truly the spark of American Independence. It remained to be seen in the fall of 1776 whether the British could extinguish that spark and return their former colonies to the British Empire, or whether the American states would persevere and keep their newly declared independence.

NOTES

INTRODUCTION

1. U.S. Census Bureau, "Estimated Population of American Colonies: 1610 to 1780," in *Historical Statistics of the United States: Colonial Times to 1970*, Part 2. (Washington, DC: U.S. Census Bureau, 1975), 1169–70.

2. Peter Force, ed., "Proceedings of the Massachusetts House of Representatives, June 17, 1774," in *American Archives, Fourth Series*, Vol. 1 (Washington, DC: M. St. Clair Clarke and Peter Force, 1837), 421.

3. Worthington Chauncey Ford, ed., "Proceedings of the Continental Congress, May 18, 1775," in *Journals of the Continental Congress, 1774–1789*, Vol. 1 (Washington, DC: Government Printing Office, 1905), 32–36.

4. Paul H. Smith, ed., "John Adams to Abigail Adams, September 18, 1774," in *Letters of the Delegates to Congress*, Vol. 1 (Washington, DC: Library of Congress, 1976), 79.

5. Smith, "John Adams Proposed Resolutions, October 1, 1774 and Richard Henry Lee's Proposed Resolutions, October 3, 1774," in *Letters of the Delegates to Congress*, Vol. 1, 1976), 131–32, 140.

6. Force, ed., "Massachusetts Provincial Congress, October 5, 1774," in *American Archives, Fourth Series*, Vol. 1, 829.

7. Force, ed., "Proceedings of the Massachusetts Provincial Congress, October 25–26, 1774," in *American Archives, Fourth Series*, Vol. 1, 842–43.

8. Ibid., 843–44.

9. Ibid., 844.

10. Force, ed., "Proceedings of the Massachusetts Provincial Congress, December 3, 1774," in *American Archives, Fourth Series*, Vol. 1, 998.

11. Force, ed., "Extract of a Letter from a Gentleman in Massachusetts to his Friend in London, dated January 21, 1775," in *American Archives, Fourth Series*, Vol. 1, 1167–68.

12. William B. Clark, ed., "Petition from a Number of Inhabitants of Scituate and Marshfield, January 20, 1775," in *Naval Documents of the American Revolution*, Vol. 1, (Washington, DC: Department of the Navy, 1964), 65–66.

13. Clark, "Narrative of Vice Admiral Graves, March 7, 1775," in *Naval Documents of the American Revolution*, Vol. 1, 130.

14. Clark, "Thomas Gilbert to Captain James Wallace, March 23, 1775," in *Naval Documents of the American Revolution*, Vol. 1, 159.

15. Ibid.

16. Clark, "Thomas Gilbert to Captain James Wallace, March 23, 1775," in *Naval Documents of the American Revolution*, Vol. 1, 159; Franklin B. Dexter, ed., "April 11, 1775," in *The Literary Diary of Ezra Stiles, President of Yale College*, Vol. 1 (New York: Charles Scribner's Sons, 1901), 533.

17. Force, ed., "Proceedings of the Massachusetts Provincial Congress, February 15, 1775," in *American Archives, Fourth Series*, Vol. 1, 1340.

18. Force, ed., "Proceedings of the Massachusetts Provincial Congress, February 9, 1775," in *American Archives, Fourth Series*, Vol. 1, 1332.

19. Henry S. Nourse, "A Forgotten Patriot," *American Antiquarian Society*, October, 1890, 101.

20. Force, ed., "Instructions of General Gage to Captain Brown and Ensign D'Bernicre, February 22, 1775" and "Narrative of Ensign D'Bernicre," in *American Archives, Fourth Series*, Vol. 1, 1263.

21. Force, ed., "Instructions of General Gage to Captain Brown and Ensign D'Bernicre, February 22, 1775" and "Narrative of Ensign D' Bernicre," in *American Archives, Fourth Series*, Vol. 1, 1263–68.

22. Samuel and Ebenezer Hall, "Salem, February 28, 1775," *The Essex Gazette*, 3.

23. Ibid.

24. Ibid.

25. Clark, "Major John Pitcairn to Lord Sandwich, March 4, 1775," in *Naval Documents of the American Revolution*, Vol. 1, 124–26.

26. Ibid.

27. Force, ed., "Proceedings of the Massachusetts Provincial Congress, March 25, 1775 and April 1, 1775," in *American Archives, Fourth Series*, Vol. 1, 1344, 1347.

28. Force, ed., "Proceedings of the Massachusetts Provincial Congress, April 5, 1775," in *American Archives, Fourth Series*, Vol. 1, 1351.

29. U.S. Census Bureau, "Estimated Population of American Colonies: 1610 to 1780," in *Historical Statistics of the United States: Colonial Times to 1970*, Part 2, 1170.

30. Force, ed., "Extract of a Letter from Governor Wentworth to the Earl of Dartmouth, August 29, 1774," in *American Archives, Fourth Series*, Vol. 1, 745–46.

31. Force, ed., "Extract of a Letter from Governor Wentworth to the Earl of Dartmouth, September 13, 1774," in *American Archives, Fourth Series*, Vol. 1, 786–87.

32. Force, ed., "Extract of a Letter from Governor Wentworth to the Earl of Dartmouth, December 14, 1774," in *American Archives, Fourth Series*, Vol. 1, 1041–42.

33. Ibid.

34. Force, ed., "Captain Cochran to Governor Wentworth to the Earl of Dartmouth, December, 1774," in *American Archives, Fourth Series*, Vol. 1, 1042.

35. Force, ed., "Extract of a Letter from Governor Wentworth to the Earl of Dartmouth, December 16, 1774," in *American Archives, Fourth Series*, Vol. 1, 1042.

36. Clark, "John Wentworth to Vice Admiral Samuel Graves, December 20, 1774," in *Naval Documents of the American Revolution*, Vol. 1, 37.

37. Force, ed., "To the Inhabitants of the Province of New Hampshire, January 25, 1775," in *American Archives, Fourth Series*, Vol. 1, 1182.

38. K. G. Davies, ed., "Governor John Wentworth to Earl of Dartmouth, March 10, 1775, in *Documents of the American Revolution*, Vol. 9 (Shannon, Ireland: Irish University Press, 1975), 70.

39. Ibid.

40. Force, ed., "To Governor Wentworth, March 17, 1775" and "Portsmouth (New Hampshire) Volunteers, April 6, 1775," in *American Archives*, Fourth Series, Vol. 2, 159, 298–99.

41. U.S. Census Bureau, "Estimated Population of American Colonies: 1610 to 1780," in *Historical Statistics of the United States: Colonial Times to 1970*, Part 2, 1171.

42. Ibid.

43. John Russell Bartlett, ed., Proceedings of the Rhode Island General Assembly, June 13, 1774, in *Records of the Colony of Rhode Island and Providence Plantations in New England*, Vol. 7 (Providence, RI: A. Crawford Greene, State Printer, 1862), 246.

44. Bartlett, Proceedings of the Rhode Island General Assembly, October 26, 1774, in *Records of the Colony of Rhode Island and Providence Plantations in New England*, Vol. 7, 257–58.

45. Bartlett, Proceedings of the Rhode Island General Assembly, December 5, 1774, in *Records of the Colony of Rhode Island and Providence Plantations in New England*, Vol. 7, 262.

46. Bartlett, ed., Proceedings of the Rhode Island General Assembly, December 5, 1774, in *Records of the Colony of Rhode Island and Providence Plantations in New* England, Vol. 7, 263, 267.

47. Dexter, "December 9, 1774," in *Literary Diary of Ezra Stiles*, Vol. 1, 499–500.

48. Force, ed., "Extract of a Letter to a Gentleman in New York, dated Newport, Rhode Island, December 14, 1774," in *American Archives, Fourth Series*, Vol. 1, 1041.

49. Clark, "Captain James Wallace to Vice Admiral Samuel Graves, December 12, 1774," in *Naval Documents of the American Revolution*, Vol. 1, 15.

50. Ibid.

51. Dexter, "March 14, 1775," in *Literary Diary of Ezra Stiles*, Vol. 1, 525.

52. U.S. Census Bureau, "Estimated Population of American Colonies: 1610 to 1780," in *Historical Statistics of the United States: Colonial Times to 1970*, Part 2, 1169.

53. Charles Hoadly, ed., "In the House of Representatives of the Colony of Connecticut, June 3, 1774," in *The Public Records of the Colony of Connecticut: From October 1772 to April 1775* (Hartford, CT: Lockwood & Brainard Co., 1887), 324.

54. Force, ed., "Meetings of the Committee of Correspondence, July 13 and August 3, 1774," in *American Archives, Fourth Series*, Vol. 1, 895.

55. Worthington C. Ford, ed., "Silas Deane to Charles Thomson, July 14, 1774," in *Correspondence and Journals of Samuel Blachley Webb* (New York: Arno Press, 1969), 36.
56. Ford, "Samuel Blachley Webb to Silas Deane, October 10, 1774," in *Correspondence and Journals of Samuel Blachley Webb*, 41.
57. Force, ed., "Danbury (Connecticut) Town Meeting, December 12, 1774," and "Fairfield (Connecticut) Committee, December 29, 1774," in *American Archives, Fourth Series*, Vol. 1, 1038–39, 1075–76.
58. Force, ed., Danbury (Connecticut) Town Meeting, December 12, 1774," in *American Archives, Fourth Series*, Vol. 1, 1038–39.
59. Force, ed., "Joseph Trumbull to Governor Trumbull, December 30, 1774," in *American Archives, Fourth Series*, Vol. 1, 1077.
60. Force, ed., "Letter from Connecticut to a Gentleman in New York, dated January 21, 1775," in *American Archives, Fourth Series*, Vol. 1, 1173.
61. Force, ed., "Ridgefield (Connecticut) Resolutions, January 30, 1775," in *American Archives, Fourth Series*, Vol. 1, 1202.
62. Force, ed., "Newtown, Connecticut, February 6, 1775," in *American Archives, Fourth Series*, Vol. 1, 1215.
63. Force, ed., "Fairfield County (Connecticut) Resolutions, February 14, 1775," in *American Archives, Fourth Series*, Vol. 1, 1238.
64. Ibid.
65. Force, ed., "Reading (Connecticut) Association, February 23, 1775," in *American Archives, Fourth Series*, Vol. 1, 1258–59.
66. Ibid.
67. Force, ed., "Reading (Connecticut) Committee, February, 1775," in *American Archives, Fourth Series*, Vol. 1, 1259–60.
68. Hoadly, "At a General Assembly . . . of the English Colony of Connecticut, March 2–10, 1775," in *The Public Records of the Colony of Connecticut*, 392–93.
69. Ibid., 409, 393–40.

CHAPTER ONE: SPRING 1775

1. Davies, "General Gage to Lord Dartmouth, February 20, 1775," in *Documents of the American Revolution*, Vol. 9, 52.
2. Davies, "Lord Dartmouth to General Gage, January 27, 1775," in *Documents of the American Revolution*, Vol. 9, 37–38.
3. Ibid., 38–39.
4. Ibid., 39.
5. Ibid.
6. Frederick Mackenzie, "April 18, 1775," in *The Diary of Frederick Mackenzie*, Vol. 1 (Cambridge, MA: Harvard University Press, 1930), 18.
7. David Hackett Fischer, *Paul Revere's Ride* (New York: Oxford University Press, 1994), 114.
8. Ibid., 180.
9. Ibid., 189.
10. Ibid., 190.

11. Ibid., 197.

12. Fischer, Appendix Q, British Casualties, April 19, 1775, *Paul Revere's Ride,* 321.

13. Fischer, Appendix P, American Casualties, April 19, 1775, *Paul Revere's Ride,* 320–21.

14. Force, ed., "To All Friends of American Liberty . . . Watertown, New York ten o' clock, April 19, 1775," in *American Archives, Fourth Series,* Vol. 2, 363.

15. Daniel Fowle, "Bloody News, April 21, 1775," *New Hampshire Gazette,* 1; Force, ed., "Committee of Newburyport to the Massachusetts Committee of Safety, April 21, 1775," in *American Archives, Fourth Series,* Vol. 2, 373.

16. Force, ed., "Proceedings of the Massachusetts Committee of Safety, April 21, 1775," in *American Archives, Fourth Series,* Vol. 2, 744.

17. Force, ed., "Proceedings of the Massachusetts Committee of Safety, April 21, 1775," in *American Archives, Fourth Series,* Vol. 2, 745.

18. Force, ed., "Dr. Joseph Warren to General Gage, April 20, 1775, in *American Archives, Fourth Series,* Vol. 2, 370.

19. Force, ed., "Agreement Between General Gage and the Town of Boston, April 23, 1775," in *American Archives, Fourth Series,* Vol. 2, 376.

20. Fischer, Appendix F: The British Army in Boston: Returns of Strength, 1775, *Paul Revere's Ride,* 309; Richard Frothingham, *History of the Siege of Boston and of the Battles of Lexington, Concord, and Bunker Hill* (Boston, MA: Little, Brown, 1896), 93.

21. Force, ed., "Agreement Between General Gage and the Town of Boston, April 23, 1775," in *American Archives, Fourth Series,* Vol. 2, 376–77.

22. Richard Frothingham, *History of the Siege of Boston and of the Battles of Lexington, Concord, and Bunker Hill* (Boston, MA: Little, Brown & Co., 1896), 95.

23. Clark, "General Gage to Vice Admiral Graves, April 20, 1775," in *Naval Documents of the American Revolution,* Vol. 1, 201.

24. Force, ed., "Proceedings of the Massachusetts Provincial Congress, April 23, 1775," in *American Archives, Fourth Series,* Vol. 2, 765.

25. Ibid.

26. William Lincoln, ed., "Massachusetts Provincial Congress to the Continental Congress, May 3, 1775," in *Journals of each Provincial Congress of Massachusetts in 1774 and 1775, and of the Committee of Safety* . . . (Boston, MA: Dutton and Wentworth, Printers to the State, 1838), 188.

27. Charles Martyn, *The Life of Artemas Ward, the First Commander in Chief of the American Revolution* (New York: A. Ward, 1921), 89.

28. Ibid., 90.

29. William Henshaw, "General Orders, April 22, 1775," in *The Orderly Book of Colonel William Henshaw, of the American Army, April 20—Sept. 26, 1775* (Boston: A. Williams and Co., 1881), 15.

30. William Abbott, ed., *Memoirs of Major-General Heath* . . . , (New York: Wm. Abbott, 1901), 11–12.

31. Clark, "Minutes of the Committee of Inspection of Falmouth, Maine Province, April 10, 1775," in *Naval Documents of the American Revolution,* Vol. 1, 174–75.

32. Clark, "Enoch Freeman, Chairman of the Committee of Falmouth, to Samuel Freeman, a Delegate to the Massachusetts Provincial Congress, April 12, 1775," in *Naval Documents of the American Revolution*, Vol. 1, 179–80.

33. Clark, "Journal of His Majesty's Ship, *Canceaux*, May 9, 1775," in *Naval Documents of the American Revolution*, Vol. 1, 297.

34. Clark, "Enoch Freeman to the Massachusetts Committee of Safety, May 10, 1775," in *Naval Documents of the American Revolution*, Vol. 1, 301; William Williamson, *The History of the State of Maine*, Vol. 2, (Hallowell, ME: Glazer, Masters & Smith, 1839), 423.

35. Williamson, *The History of the State of Maine*, 423.

36. Ibid., 424.

37. Derek W. Beck, "The First Naval Skirmish of the Revolution," *Journal of the American Revolution* (October 7, 2013) (online at *allthingsliberty.com*).

38. Ibid.

39. Isaiah Thomas, "May 24, 1775," *Massachusetts Spy*, 3.

40. Ibid.

41. Fowle, "Bloody News, April 21, 1775," *New Hampshire Gazette*, 1.

42. Fowle, "Extract of a Letter from New Hampshire, dated April 26, 1775, printed May 5, 1775," *New Hampshire Gazette*, 1.

43. Force, ed., "Andrew McClary to the New Hampshire Congress, April 23, 1775," in *American Archives, Fourth Series*, Vol. 2, 378.

44. Force, ed., "Benjamin Greenleaf to the Committee of Correspondence in Hampton, April 22, 1775," in *American Archives, Fourth Series*, Vol. 2, 378.

45. Force, ed., "To the Provincial Congress of Massachusetts, April 26, 1775," in *American Archives, Fourth Series*, Vol. 2, 401.

46. Ibid.

47. Force, ed., "Andrew McClary to the New Hampshire Congress, April 23, 1775," in *American Archives, Fourth Series*, Vol. 2, 378.

48. Frothingham, *History of the Siege of Boston and of the Battles of Lexington, Concord, and Bunker Hill*, 99.

49. Force, ed., "Proceedings of the New Hampshire Provincial Congress, May 20-22, 1775," in *American Archives, Fourth Series*, Vol. 2, 652–53.

50. Force, ed., "Proceedings of the New Hampshire Provincial Congress, May 23, 1775," in *American Archives, Fourth Series*, Vol. 2, 654.

51. Force, ed., "Proceedings of the New Hampshire Provincial Congress, June 3, 1775," in *American Archives, Fourth Series*, Vol. 2, 657.

52. Force, ed., "Proceedings of the New Hampshire Provincial Congress, May 24, and June 1, 1775," in *American Archives, Fourth Series*, Vol. 2, 654, 656.

53. Davies, "Governor John Wentworth to Earl of Dartmouth, May 17, 1775," in *Documents of the American Revolution*, Vol. 9, 135–36.

54. Davies, "Governor John Wentworth to Earl of Dartmouth, June 14, 1775," in *Documents of the American Revolution*, Vol. 9, 171.

55. Clark, "Governor Wentworth to General Gage, June 15, 1775," in *Naval Documents of the American Revolution*, Vol. 1, 684.

56. Davies, "Governor John Wentworth to Earl of Dartmouth, June 14, 1775," in *Documents of the American Revolution*, Vol. 9, 171.

57. Nathaniel Bouton, ed., "Address of the New Hampshire Provincial Congress to Governor Wentworth, June 8, 1775," in *Provincial Papers, Documents and Records Relating to the Province of New Hampshire*, Vol. 7 (Nashua, NH: Orren C. Moore, State Printer, 1873), 509–10.

58. Ibid.

59. Clark, "Captain Andrew Barkley to Vice Admiral Samuel Grave, May 30, 1775," in *Naval Documents of the American Revolution*, Vol. 2, 567–68.

60. Ibid., 568.

61. Ibid.

62. Solomon Southwick, "Providence, April 22," *Newport Mercury*, April 24, 1775, 3.

63. Ibid.

64. Bartlett, "Proceedings of the General Assembly of Rhode Island, April 22, 1775," in *Records of Rhode Island*, Vol. 7, 310–11.

65. Force, ed., "James Angell to the Massachusetts Congress, April 28, 1775," in *American Archives, Fourth Series*, Vol. 2, 431.

66. Ibid.

67. Force, ed., "Proceedings of the Rhode Island General Assembly, May 3, 1775," in *American Archives, Fourth Series*, Vol. 2, 1146.

68. Force, ed., "Metcalf Bowler to the Massachusetts Committee of Safety, May 6, 1775," in *American Archives, Fourth Series*, Vol. 2, 520.

69. Force, ed., "General Assembly of Rhode Island, May 20, 1775," in *American Archives, Fourth Series*, Vol. 2, 662.

70. Richard K. Showman, ed., "Introduction," xviii; "Nathanael Greene to Colonel James Varnum, October 31, 1774," in *The Papers of General Nathanael Greene*, Vol. 1 (Chapel Hill: University of North Carolina Press, 1976), 75.

71. Showman, "Appointment as Brigadier-General of the Rhode Island Army, May 8, 1775," in *The Papers of General Nathanael Greene*, Vol. 1, 78–79.

72. Showman, "General Greene to General John Thomas, May 23, 1775," in *The Papers of General Nathanael Greene*, Vol. 1, 80.

73. Force, ed., "General Assembly of Rhode Island, May 17, 1775," in *American Archives, Fourth Series*, Vol. 2, 1148.

74. Clark, "Some of the Principal Inhabitants of Newport to Captain James Wallace, May 1, 1775," in *Naval Documents of the American Revolution*, Vol. 2, 255–56.

75. Clark, "Vice Admiral Graves to Philip Stephens, Secretary of the British Admiralty, May 13, 1775," in *Naval Documents of the American Revolution*, Vol. 2, 324–25.

76. Dexter, "Diary Entry, May 23, 1775," in *The Literary Diary of Ezra Stiles*, Vol. 1, 561.

77. Ibid.

78. Dexter, "Diary Entry, June 3, 1775," in *The Literary Diary of Ezra Stiles*, Vol. 1, 566.

79. Clark, "Captain Wallace to Vice Admiral Graves, June 5, 1775," in *Naval Documents of the American Revolution*, Vol. 1, 615.

80. Force, ed., "Connecticut Committee of Correspondence to John Hancock, April 21, 1775," in *American Archives, Fourth Series*, Vol. 2, 372–73.

81. Force, ed., "Extract of a Letter from Weathersfield, Connecticut, April 23, 1775," in *American Archives, Fourth Series*, Vol. 2, 362.

82. Eben Watson, "News of the battle reported," *Connecticut Courant*, April 24, 1775, 3.

83. Force, ed., "Proceedings of the Connecticut Assembly, April 26, 1775," in *American Archives, Fourth Series*, Vol. 2, 411.

84. Ibid., 411–14.

85. Ibid., 414.

86. William Cutter, *The Life of Israel Putnam, Major-General of the Army of the American Revolution*, Third Edition (New York: George F. Cooledge & Brother, 1848), 151.

87. Henshaw, *The Orderly Book of Colonel William Henshaw of the American Army, April 20–Sept. 26*, 1775, 15.

88. Force, ed., "Jedediah Huntington to Jonathan Trumbull, April 27, 1775," in *American Archives, Fourth Series*, Vol. 2, 423.

89. Force, ed., "Proceedings of the Connecticut Assembly, April 26, 1775," in *American Archives, Fourth Series*, Vol. 2, 416–17.

90. Ibid., 420.

91. Force, ed., "Proceedings of the Committee of New York City, May 3, 1775," in *American Archives, Fourth Series*, Vol. 2, 480.

92. Lincoln, "Governor Trumbull to General Gages, April 28, 1775," in *Journals of each Provincial Congress of Massachusetts in 1774 and 1775, and of the Committee of Safety . . .*, 180–81.

93. Ibid.

94. Lincoln, "Massachusetts Provincial Congress to Connecticut General Assembly, May 2, 1775," in *Journals of each Provincial Congress of Massachusetts in 1774 and 1775, and of the Committee of Safety . . .* , 179–80.

95. Ibid.

96. Force, ed., "Agreement Subscribed by Captain Arnold and his Company of fifty persons. . . . ," April 24, 1775," in *American Archives, Fourth Series*, Vol. 2, 383–84.

97. Force, ed., "Benedict Arnold to the Massachusetts Committee of Safety, April 30, 1775," in *American Archives, Fourth Series*, Vol. 2, 450.

98. Ibid.

99. Force, ed., "Extract of a Letter from a Gentleman in Pittsfield, to an Officer in Cambridge, dated May 4, 1775," in *American Archives, Fourth Series*, Vol. 2, 507.

100. Force, ed., "Committee at Ticonderoga to the Massachusetts Congress, May 10, 1775" and "Edward Mott to the Massachusetts Congress, May 11, 1775," in *American Archives, Fourth Series*, Vol. 2, 556, 557–58.

101. Force, ed., "Orders to Benedict Arnold, May 3, 1775," in *American Archives, Fourth Series*, Vol. 2, 485.

102. Force, ed., "Edward Mott to the Massachusetts Congress, May 11, 1775," in *American Archives, Fourth Series*, Vol. 2, 557–58.

103. Force, ed., "Veritas, June 25, 1775," in *American Archives, Fourth Series*, Vol. 2, 1086–87.

104. Force, ed., "Benedict Arnold to the Massachusetts Committee of Safety, May 19, 1775," in *American Archives, Fourth Series*, Vol. 2, 646.

105. Lincoln, "Circular Letter to Several Towns from the Committee of Safety, April 29, 1775," in *Journals of each Provincial Congress of Massachusetts in 1774 and 1775, and of the Committee of Safety . . .*, 526.

106. Henshaw, "General Orders, April 27, 1775," in *The Orderly Book of Colonel William Henshaw, of the American Army, April 20—Sept. 26, 1775*, 19.

107. Henshaw, "General Orders, May 8, 1775," in *The Orderly Book of Colonel William Henshaw, of the American Army, April 20—Sept. 26, 1775*, 23.

108. Bouton, ed., "Colonel Stark to the New Hampshire Congress, May 18, 1775," in *Provincial Papers, Documents and Records relating to the Province of New Hampshire*, Vol. 7, 474.

109. Force, ed., "General Ward to the Massachusetts Congress, May 19, 1775," in *American Archives, Fourth Series*, Vol. 2, 647.

110. Force, ed., "Proceedings of the Massachusetts Congress, May 19, 1775," in *American Archives, Fourth Series*, Vol. 2, 813.

111. Frothingham, *History of the Siege of Boston*, 101.

112. Showman, "General Greene to Jacob Greene, June 6–10, 1775," in *The Papers of General Nathanael Greene*, Vol. 1, 85.

113. Ibid.

114. Force, ed., "Colonel Stark to the New Hampshire Congress, May 29, 1775," in *American Archives, Fourth Series*, Vol. 2, 739.

115. Clark, "*New England Chronicle*, May 25, 1775," in *Naval Documents of the American Revolution*, Vol. 1, 522.

116. Force, ed., "Circumstantial Account of the Battle of Chelsea, Hog Island, Etc., in Massachusetts," in *American Archives, Fourth Series*, Vol. 2, 719.

117. Ibid.; Amos Farnsworth, *Amos Farnsworth Journal* (Massachusetts Historical Society, January, 1898), 80.

118. Farnsworth, *Amos Farnsworth Journal*, 80.

119. Clark, "Journal of His Majesty's Ship *Preston* . . . May 27, 1775," in *Naval Documents of the American Revolution*, Vol. 1, 546.

120. Farnsworth, *Amos Farnsworth Journal*, 81.

121. Force, ed., "Circumstantial Account of the Battle of Chelsea, Hog Island, Etc., in Massachusetts," in *American Archives, Fourth Series*, Vol. 2, 719.

122. Clark, "Report to the Massachusetts Committee of Safety of the Battle of Noodle's Island," in *Naval Documents of the American Revolution*, Vol. 1, 545–46.

123. Force, ed., "Circumstantial Account of the Battle of Chelsea, Hog Island, Etc., in Massachusetts," in *American Archives, Fourth Series*, Vol. 2, 720.

124. Clark, "Vice Admiral Samuel Graves to Philip Stevens, June 7, 1775," in *Naval Documents of the American Revolution*, Vol. 1, 622–23.

125. Force, ed., "Circumstantial Account of the Battle of Chelsea, Hog Island, Etc., in Massachusetts," in *American Archives, Fourth Series*, Vol. 2, 720.

CHAPTER TWO: SUMMER 1775

1. John Howard Ahlin, "Petition from the Residents of Machias to the Massachusetts Provincial Congress, May 25, 1775," in *Maine Rubicon: Downeast Settlers during the American Revolution* (Camden, ME: Picton Press, 1966), 15–16.
2. Ahlin, 15–16; Clark, "Committee of Penobscot to the Massachusetts Provincial Congress, June 7, 1775," in *Naval Documents of the American Revolution*, Vol. 1, 620.
3. Ibid.
4. Clark, "James Lyons, Chairman of the Machias Committee, to the Massachusetts Provincial Congress, June 14, 1775," in *Naval Documents of the American Revolution*, Vol. 1, 676–77.
5. Clark, "Pilot Nathaniel Godfrey's Report on the Action Between the Schooner *Margaretta* and the Rebels at Machias, June 11, 1775," in *Naval Documents of the American Revolution*, Vol. 1, 655.
6. Ibid.
7. Clark, "James Lyons, Chairman of the Machias Committee, to the Massachusetts Provincial Congress, June 14, 1775," in *Naval Documents of the American Revolution*, Vol. 1, 676–77.
8. Clark, "Pilot Nathaniel Godfrey's Report on the Action Between the Schooner Margaretta and the Rebels at Machias, June 11, 1775," in *Naval Documents of the American Revolution*, Vol. 1, 655.
9. Ibid.
10. Clark, "James Lyons, Chairman of the Machias Committee, to the Massachusetts Provincial Congress, June 14, 1775," in *Naval Documents of the American Revolution*, Vol. 1, 676–77.
11. Clark, "Pilot Nathaniel Godfrey's Report . . . June 11, 1775," in *Naval Documents of the American Revolution*, Vol. 1, 655–56.
12. Williamson, 431.
13. Ahlin, 22.
14. Ibid.
15. Rick Atkinson, *The British Are Coming: The War for America, Lexington to Princeton, 1775–1777* (New York: Henry Holt & Co., 2019), 92.
16. Ibid.
17. Letter from Peter Brown to his Mother, June 25, 1775, Massachusetts Historical Society.
18. Ibid.
19. Atkinson, 99–100.
20. Ibid., 100.
21. Richard Ketchum, *Decisive Day: The Battle for Bunker Hill* (New York: Henry Holt & Co., 1962), 160, 245.
22. Atkinson, 101.
23. Ketchum, 160.

24. Letter from William Prescott to John Adams, August 25, 1775, Massachusetts Historical Society.
25. Ibid.
26. Ibid.
27. Letter from Lt. J. Waller to a Friend, June 21, 1775, Massachusetts Historical Society.
28. Mark M. Boatner, *Encyclopedia of the American Revolution* (Essex, CT: Stackpole Books, 1966), 129.
29. Davies, "General Gage to Lord Dartmouth, June 25, 1775," in *Documents of the American Revolution*, Vol. 9, 199.
30. Force, ed., "Colonel John Stark to the New Hampshire Congress, June 19, 1775," in *American Archives, Fourth Series*, Vol. 2, 1029.
31. Ibid.
32. Force, ed., "General Nathaniel Folsom to the New Hampshire Committee of Safety, June 27, 1775," in *American Archives, Fourth Series*, Vol. 2, 1121.
33. Clark, "Minutes of the New Hampshire Committee of Safety, June 15, 1775," in *Naval Documents of the American Revolution*, Vol. 1, 683.
34. Clark, "Captain Barkley to Vice Admiral Graves, June 16, 1775," in *Naval Documents of the American Revolution*, Vol. 1, 689.
35. Ibid.
36. Clark, "Vice Admiral Graves to Philip Stephens, June 22, 1775," in *Naval Documents of the American Revolution*, Vol. 1, 739.
37. Ibid.
38. Davies, "Governor Wentworth to Lord Dartmouth, August 18, 1775," in *Documents of the American Revolution*, Vol., 11, 76–77.
39. Ibid., 77.
40. Ibid.
41. Ibid., 78.
42. Fowle, "Portsmouth, August 15, 1775," *New Hampshire Gazette*, 1.
43. Clark, "Journal of the General Assembly of Rhode Island, June 12, 1775," in *Naval Documents of the American Revolution*, Vol. 1, 664.
44. Bartlett, "Deputy-Governor Cooke to Captain James Wallace, June 14, 1775," in *Records of Rhode Island*, Vol. 7, 338.
45. Clark, "Mr. Savage Gardner's Report to Captain James Wallace, June 19, 1775," in *Naval Documents of the American Revolution*, Vol. 1, 721.
46. Ibid.
47. Clark, "Captain Wallace to Vice Admiral Graves, June 19, 1775," in *Naval Documents of the American Revolution*, Vol. 1, 720–21.
48. Ibid.
49. Ibid., 720.
50. Southwick, "Newport, July 10, 1775," *Newport Mercury*, 3.
51. Clark, "Nicholas Cooke to Samuel Ward and Stephen Hopkins, July 18, 1775," in *Naval Documents of the American Revolution*, Vol. 1, 914–15.
52. Ibid.
53. Ibid.
54. Southwick, "Newport, July 24, 1776," *Newport Mercury*, 3.

55. Ibid.

56. Clark, "*New York Journal* August 17, 1775," in *Naval Documents of the American Revolution*, Vol. 1, 1167.

57. Clark, "Jonathan Trumbull to Nicholas Cooke, August 24, 1775," and "Journal of the Rhode Island General Assembly, August 25, 1775," in *Naval Documents of the American Revolution*, Vol. 1, 1220, 1230.

58. Clark, "Journal of HMS *Glasgow*, August 13, 1775," in *Naval Documents of the American Revolution*, Vol. 1, 1134.

59. Clark, "Journal of the Rhode Island General Assembly, August 26, 1775," in *Naval Documents of the American Revolution*, Vol. 1, 1236.

60. Ibid.

61. David Price, "Thomas Knowlton's Revolution," *Journal of the American Revolution* (September 2, 2021, online).

62. Hoadly, "Meeting of the Connecticut Council of Safety, June 20, 1775," in *The Public Records of the Colony of Connecticut: From May 1775 to June 1776*, 89.

63. Hoadly, "An Act of the Connecticut General Assembly, July 1, 1775," in *The Public Records of the Colony of Connecticut: From May 1775 to June 1776*, 92–93.

64. Ibid., 93, 95.

65. Ibid., 99–100.

66. Hoadly, "At a Meeting of the Governor & Council of Safety, July 24, 1775," in *The Public Records of the Colony of Connecticut: From May 1775 to June 1776*, 109.

67. Hoadly, "At a Meeting of the Governor & Council of Safety, August 7, 1775," in *The Public Records of the Colony of Connecticut: From May 1775 to June 1776*, 114–15.

68. Clark, "General David Wooster to Governor Jonathan Trumbull, August 9, 1775," in *Naval Documents of the American Revolution*, Vol. 1, 1105.

69. Clark, "Joseph Stanton Jr., to Deputy-Governor Nicholas Cooke, September 1, 1775," in *Naval Documents of the American Revolution*, Vol. 1, 1285.

70. Green, "September 1, 1775," *Connecticut Gazette and Universal Intelligencer*, 3.

71. Clark, "Joseph Stanton Jr., to Deputy-Governor Nicholas Cooke, September 1, 1775," in *Naval Documents of the American Revolution*, Vol. 1, 1285.

72. Clark, "Extract of a Letter from New-London, August 31, 1775," in *Naval Documents of the American Revolution*, Vol. 1, 1275.

73. Philander, D. Chase, ed., "General Orders, July 3–4, 1775," in *The Papers of George Washington, Revolutionary War Series*, Vol. 1 (Charlottesville: University Press of Virginia, 1985), 49, 54.

74. Charles H. Lesser, ed., "General Return of the Army of the United Colonies . . . July 29, 1775," in *Sinews of Independence: Monthly Strength Reports of the Continental Army* (Chicago and London: University of Chicago Press, 1976), 2–3.

75. Ibid.

76. Chase, "General Washington to the Continental Congress, July 10, 1775," in *The Papers of George Washington, Revolutionary War Series*, Vol. 1, 85–90.

77. Ibid., 91.

78. Chase, "General Washington to the Continental Congress, August 4–5, 1775," in *The Papers of George Washington, Revolutionary War Series*, Vol. 1, 223–24.

79. Ibid., 224.

80. Ibid., 225.

81. Chase, "General Washington to Lund Washington, August 20, 1775," in *The Papers of George Washington, Revolutionary War Series*, Vol. 1, 335–36.

82. Chase, "General Washington to Richard Henry Lee, August 29, 1775," in *The Papers of George Washington, Revolutionary War Series*, Vol. 1, 372.

83. Ibid.

84. Ibid.

85. Chase, "General Washington to John Hancock, July 9, 1775," in *The Papers of George Washington: Revolutionary War Series*, Vol. 1, 85–86.

86. Bouton, "Journal of the New Hampshire Provincial Congress, August 24, 1775," in *Provincial Papers, Documents and Records Relating to the Province of New Hampshire*, Vol. 7, 577.

87. Chase, "General Washington to John Hancock, July 9, 1775," in *The Papers of George Washington: Revolutionary War Series*, Vol. 1, 85–86.

88. Lesser, "General Return of the Army . . . Commanded by General Washington, July 29, 1775," in *Sinews of Independence: Monthly Strength Reports of the Continental Army*, 2.

89. Chase, "General Orders, July 22, 1775," in *The Papers of George Washington: Revolutionary War Series*, Vol. 1, 153–54; Lesser, "General Return of the Army . . . Commanded by General Washington, July 29, 1775," in *Sinews of Independence: Monthly Strength Reports of the Continental Army*, 2.

90. Chase, "General Orders, July 22, 1775," in *The Papers of George Washington: Revolutionary War Series*, Vol. 1, 153–54.

91. Ibid.

92. Lesser, "General Return of the Army . . . Commanded by General Washington, July 29, 1775," in *Sinews of Independence: Monthly Strength Reports of the Continental Army*, 2.

93. B. Floyd Flickinger, "Captain Morgan and His Riflemen," *Winchester-Frederick County Historical Society Journal*, 14 (2002): 58–59.

94. Chase, "General Orders, August 4, 1775," in *The Papers of George Washington: Revolutionary War Series*, Vol. 1, 218–19.

95. Henry S. Commager and Richard B. Morris, "Jesse Lukens to Mr. Shaw, September 13, 1775," in *The Spirit of Seventy-Six: The Story of the American Revolution as Told by its Participants* (New York: Harper Collins Publishers, Inc., 1967), 156–57.

96. Ibid.

97. Chase, "General Washington to John Augustine Washington, September 10, 1775," in *The Papers of George Washington: Revolutionary War Series*, Vol. 1, 447–48.

98. Chase, "General Orders, September 11, 1775," in *The Papers of George Washington: Revolutionary War Series*, Vol. 1, 450–51.

CHAPTER THREE: FALL 1775

1. Chase, "General Washington to General Schuyler, August 21, 1775," in *The Papers of George Washington, Revolutionary War Series*, Vol. 1, 332.
2. Chase, "General Washington to Reuben Colburn, September 3, 1775" and General Washington to Nathaniel Tracy, September 2, 1775," in *The Papers of George Washington, Revolutionary War Series*, Vol. 1, 409, 404–5.
3. Chase, "General Orders, September 5, 1775," in *The Papers of George Washington, Revolutionary War Series*, Vol. 1, 414–15.
4. Kenneth Roberts, ed., "Journal of Caleb Haskell, September 24, 1775," in *March to Quebec: Journals of the Members of Arnold's Expedition* (Garden City, NY: Doubleday & Co., 1938), 474.
5. Roberts, "Journal of Joseph Henry, September 23, 1775," in *March to Quebec: Journals of the Members of Arnold's Expedition*, 303.
6. Roberts, "Journal of Caleb Haskell, September 28, 1775," in *March to Quebec: Journals of the Members of Arnold's Expedition*, 474.
7. Roberts, "Journal of Abner Stocking, September 28–29, 1775," in *March to Quebec: Journals of the Members of Arnold's Expedition*, 548.
8. Roberts, "Journal of Simon Thayer, September 30, 1775," in *March to Quebec: Journals of the Members of Arnold's Expedition*, 250.
9. Roberts, "Journal of Dr. Isaac Senter, October 5, 1775," in *March to Quebec: Journals of the Members of Arnold's Expedition*, 202–3.
10. Frothingham, *History of the Siege of Boston*, 274.
11. Ibid., 254.
12. Chase, "General Washington to John Hancock, September 21, 1775," in *The Papers of George Washington, Revolutionary War Series*, Vol. 2, 24–25.
13. Ibid., 29.
14. Worthington C. Ford, ed., Proceedings of the Continental Congress, November 4, 1775," in *Journals of the Continental Congress*, Vol. 3 (Washington, DC: Government Printing Office, 1905), 320–24.
15. Ford, Proceedings of the Continental Congress, November 4, 1775," in *Journals of the Continental Congress*, Vol. 3, 325.
16. Ford, "Proceedings of the Continental Congress, October 9 and 12, 1775," in *Journals of the Continental Congress, 1774–1789*, Vol. 3, 285, 291.
17. Commager and Morris, "Observations by Benjamin Thompson, November 4, 1775," in *The Spirit of Seventy-Six*, 153–54.
18. Ibid.
19. Chase, "General Washington to Lieutenant Colonel Joseph Reed, November 28, 1775," in *The Papers of George Washington, Revolutionary War Series*, Vol. 2, 449.
20. Roberts, "George Morison, October 9, 1775," in *March to Quebec: Journals of the Members of Arnold's Expedition*, 513–14.
21. Roberts, "Journal of Dr. Isaac Senter, October 14, 1775," in *March to Quebec: Journals of the Members of Arnold's Expedition*, 205.

22. Roberts, "Journal of Dr. Isaac Senter, October 21, 1775," in *March to Quebec: Journals of the Members of Arnold's Expedition*, 208.

23. Roberts, "Journal of Dr. Isaac Senter, October 22, 1775," in *March to Quebec: Journals of the Members of Arnold's Expedition*, 208.

24. Roberts, "Journal of Dr. Isaac Senter, October 25, 1775," in *March to Quebec: Journals of the Members of Arnold's Expedition*, 210.

25. Roberts, "Journal of Captain Henry Dearborn, October 27, 1775," in *March to Quebec: Journals of the Members of Arnold's Expedition*, 137.

26. Roberts, "Journal of Dr. Isaac Senter, November 1, 1775," in *March to Quebec: Journals of the Members of Arnold's Expedition*, 218–19.

27. Roberts, "Journal of Caleb Haskell, November 2, 1775," in *March to Quebec: Journals of the Members of Arnold's Expedition*, 478.

28. Roberts, "Journal of Caleb Haskell, October 31, 1775," in *March to Quebec: Journals of the Members of Arnold's Expedition*, 478.

29. Roberts, "Journal of Joseph Henry, October 30, 1775," in *March to Quebec: Journals of the Members of Arnold's Expedition*, 336.

30. Clark, "Vice Admiral Graves to Captain James Wallace, September 17, 1775, and to Philip Stephens, September 26, 1775," in *Naval Documents of the American Revolution*, Vol. 2, 129, 210.

31. Clark, "Vice Admiral Graves Orders to Captain James Wallace, September 17, 1775," in *Naval Documents of the American Revolution*, Vol. 2, 129–30.

32. Clark, "Vice Admiral Graves to Captain James Wallace, September 17, 1775," in *Naval Documents of the American Revolution*, Vol. 2, 129.

33. Clark, "Rhode Island Recess Committee to Esek Hopkins and William West, October 4, 1775," in *Naval Documents of the American Revolution*, Vol. 2, 295.

34. Ibid., 295–96.

35. Clark, "Captain James Wallace to Vice-Admiral Samuel Graves, October 14, 1775," in *Naval Documents of the American Revolution*, Vol. 2, 451.

36. Dexter, "October 4, 1775," in *The Literary Diary of Ezra Stiles, President of Yale College*, Vol.1, 621.

37. Clark, "Captain James Wallace to Vice-Admiral Samuel Graves, October 14, 1775," in *Naval Documents of the American Revolution*, Vol. 2, 451.

38. Southwick, "Newport, October 9, 1775," *Newport Mercury*, 3.

39. Clark, "Captain James Wallace to Vice-Admiral Samuel Graves, October 14, 1775," in *Naval Documents of the American Revolution*, Vol. 2, 451.

40. Clark, "Letter from Bristol, Rhode Island to a New York Correspondent, October 12, 1775," in *Naval Documents of the American Revolution*, Vol. 2, 420.

41. Ibid.

42. Ibid.

43. Ibid.

44. Clark, "Captain James Wallace to Vice-Admiral Samuel Graves, October 14, 1775," in *Naval Documents of the American Revolution*, Vol. 2, 451.

45. Clark, "Letter from Bristol, Rhode Island to a New York Correspondent, October 12, 1775"and "Captain James Wallace to Vice-Admiral Samuel Graves,

October 14, 1775," in *Naval Documents of the American Revolution*, Vol. 2, 421, 451–52.

46. Clark, "Letter from Bristol, Rhode Island to a New York Correspondent, October 12, 1775," in *Naval Documents of the American Revolution*, Vol. 2, 421.

47. Clark, "Vice Admiral Graves to Lieutenant Henry Mowat, H.M. Armed Vessel *Canceaux*, October 6, 1775," in *Naval Documents of the American Revolution*, Vol. 2, 324.

48. Clark, "Letter from Rev. Jacob Bailey, October 16, 1775," in *Naval Documents of the American Revolution*, Vol. 2, 471.

49. Clark, "Letter from Rev. Jacob Bailey, October 17, 1775," in *Naval Documents of the American Revolution*, Vol. 2, 487.

50. Clark, "Narrative of Daniel Tucker of Falmouth, October 17, 1775," in *Naval Documents of the American Revolution*, Vol. 2, 488.

51. Clark, "Letter from Rev. Jacob Bailey, October 17, 1775," in *Naval Documents of the American Revolution*, Vol. 2, 487.

52. Clark, "Lieutenant Henry Mowat to the People of Falmouth, October 16, 1775," in *Naval Documents of the American Revolution*, Vol. 2, 471.

53. Clark, "Letter from Rev. Jacob Bailey, October 17, 1775," in *Naval Documents of the American Revolution*, Vol. 2, 487.

54. Ibid., 488.

55. Clark, "Lieutenant Henry Mowat to Vice Admiral Samuel Graves, October 19, 1775," in *Naval Documents of the American Revolution*, Vol. 2, 515.

56. Clark, "Letter from Rev. Jacob Bailey, October 18, 1775," in *Naval Documents of the American Revolution*, Vol. 2, 500.

57. Donald A. Yerxa, "The Burning of Falmouth, 1775: A Case Study in British Imperial Pacification," *Maine Historical Society Quarterly*, 14, no. 3 (1975): 142.

58. James S. Leamon, *Revolution Downeast: The War for American Independence in Maine* (Amherst: University of Massachusetts Press, 1993), 9.

59. Clark, "Narrative of Daniel Tucker of Falmouth, October 18, 1775," in *Naval Documents of the American Revolution*, Vol. 2, 500–1.

60. Chase, "General Washington to the Falmouth Committee of Safety, October 24, 1775," in *The Papers of George Washington, Revolutionary War Series*, Vol. 2, 225–26.

61. Chase, "The Falmouth Committee of Safety to General Washington, November 2, 1775," in *The Papers of George Washington, Revolutionary War Series*, Vol. 2, 286–87.

62. Clark, "Captain John Symons to the People of Falmouth, November 1, 1775," in *Naval Documents of the American Revolution*, Vol. 2, 831–32.

63. Clark, "Rev. Samuel Deane to Benjamin Greenleaf, November 4, 1775," in *Naval Documents of the American Revolution*, Vol. 2, 877.

64. Clark, "Cumberland County Convention to the Massachusetts General Court, November 8, 1775," in *Naval Documents of the American Revolution*, Vol. 2, 926–27.

65. Clark, "Massachusetts Act Authorizing Privateers and Creating Courts of Admiralty, November 1, 1775," in *Naval Documents of the American Revolution*, Vol. 2, 835.

66. Davies, "Governor John Wentworth to the Earl of Dartmouth, September 29, 1775," in *Documents of the American Revolution*, Vol. 11, 134.

67. Ibid.

68. Bouton, "Report of Portsmouth Committee on Fortifications, August 23, 1775," in *Documents and Records Relating to the Province of New Hampshire . . . 1623–1776*, Vol. 7, 580; Chase, "New Hampshire Committee of Safety to General Washington, October 11, 1775," in *The Papers of George Washington, Revolutionary War Series*, Vol. 2, 141.

69. Bouton, "Portsmouth Committee to Committee of Safety, October 7, 1775," in *Documents and Records Relating to the Province of New Hampshire . . . 1623–1776*, Vol. 7, 618.

70. Chase, "General Washington to the Portsmouth Committee of Safety, October 5, 1775," in *The Papers of George Washington, Revolutionary War Series*, Vol. 2, 113.

71. Chase, "General Washington to the Portsmouth Committee of Safety, October 15, 1775," in *The Papers of George Washington, Revolutionary War Series*, Vol. 2, 170.

72. Chase, "New Hampshire Committee of Safety, October 11, 1775," in *The Papers of George Washington, Revolutionary War Series*, Vol. 2, 141.

73. Chase, "General Washington to John Hancock, October 24, 1775," in *The Papers of George Washington, Revolutionary War Series*, Vol. 2, 227.

74. Chase, "General Sullivan to General Washington, October 29, 1775," in *The Papers of George Washington, Revolutionary War Series*, Vol. 2, 252.

75. Ibid.

76. Ford, "Proceeding of Congress, November 3, 1775," in *Journals of the Continental Congress: 1774–1789*, Vol. 3, 319.

77. Bouton, "Letter from our Delegates in the Continental Congress, November 3, 1775," in *Documents and Records Relating to the Province of New Hampshire . . . 1623–1776*, Vol. 7, 641–42.

78. Bouton, "Provincial Congress Proceedings, November 4, 1775," in *Documents and Records Relating to the Province of New Hampshire . . . 1623–1776*, Vol. 7, 644–45.

79. Ibid.

80. Bouton, "Provincial Congress Proceedings, November 14, 1775," in *Documents and Records Relating to the Province of New Hampshire . . . 1623–1776*, Vol. 7, 657.

81. Ibid., 658–60.

82. Chase, "Circular Instructions for the Seizure of Certain Royal Officials, Nov. 5–12, 1775," in *The Papers of George Washington, Revolutionary War Series*, Vol. 2, 301.

83. Davies, "Governor John Wentworth to the Earl of Dartmouth, December 3, 1775," in *Documents of the American Revolution*, Vol. 11, 200.

84. Ibid.

85. Bouton, "Provincial Congress Proceedings, November 15, 1775," in *Documents and Records Relating to the Province of New Hampshire . . . 1623–1776*, Vol. 7, 662.

86. Dexter, "October 9, 1775," in *The Literary Diary of Ezra Stiles, President of Yale College*, Vol. 1, 623–24.

87. Clark, "Captain James Wallace to Vice-Admiral Samuel Graves, October 14, 1775," in *Naval Documents of the American Revolution*, Vol. 2, 452.

88. Clark, "Nicholas Cooke to the Newport Town Council, October 21, 1775," in *Naval Documents of the American Revolution*, Vol. 2, 549.

89. Clark, "Journal of the Rhode Island General Assembly, October 31, 1775," in *Naval Documents of the American Revolution*, Vol. 2, 662.

90. Clark, "Captain James Wallace to the Inhabitants of Newport, November 14, 1775," in *Naval Documents of the American Revolution*, Vol. 2, 1023.

91. Bartlett, Proceedings of the Rhode Island General Assembly, October 31, 1775," in *Records of the Colony of Rhode Island and Providence Plantations in New England*, Vol. 7, 389.

92. Bartlett, Proceedings of the Rhode Island General Assembly, October 31, 1775," in *Records of the Colony of Rhode Island and Providence Plantations in New England*, Vol. 7, 390.

93. Hoadly, "At a Meeting of the Governor and Council of Safety, September 14, 1775," in *The Public Records of the Colony of Connecticut: From May 1775 to June 1776*, 128–29.

94. Ibid.

95. Hoadly, "An Act Providing for the Defence of the Sea Coasts of this Colony, October 11–25, 1775," in *The Public Records of the Colony of Connecticut: From May 1775 to June 1776*, 142.

CHAPTER FOUR: WINTER 1775–1776

1. Clark, "General Washington's Instructions to Captain Nicholson Broughton, September 3, 1775," in *Naval Documents of the American Revolution*, Vol. 1, 1287–88.

2. Chase, "General Orders, September 22, 1775," in *The Papers of George Washington, Revolutionary War Series*, Vol. 2, 35.

3. Chase, "General Washington to William Ramsay, December 4–11, 1775," in *The Papers of George Washington, Revolutionary War Series*, Vol. 2, 489–90.

4. B. Towne, "Philadelphia, December 12, 1775," *Pennsyvania Evening Post*, 4.

5. Clark, "Extract of a Letter from Boston, December 13, 1775," in *Naval Documents of the American Revolution*, Vol. 3, 84–85.

6. Ibid.

7. Clark, "Vice Admiral Graves to Major General Howe, December 13, 1775," in *Naval Documents of the American Revolution*, Vol. 3, 82.

8. Dexter, "December 10, 1775," in *The Literary Diary of Ezra Stiles, President of Yale College*, Vol.1, 642.

9. Clark, "Henry Babcock to Gurdon Saltonstall, December 13, 1775," in *Naval Documents of the American Revolution*, Vol. 3, 87.

10. Dexter, "December 13, 1775," in *The Literary Diary of Ezra Stiles, President of Yale College*, Vol.1, 643.

11. Dexter, "December 14–15, 1775," in *The Literary Diary of Ezra Stiles, President of Yale College*, Vol.1, 643–44.

12. Dexter, "December 16, 1775," in *The Literary Diary of Ezra Stiles, President of Yale College*, Vol.1, 644.

13. Chase, "Circular to the New England Governments, December 5, 1775," in *The Papers of George Washington, Revolutionary War Series*, Vol. 2, 492.

14. Chase, "General Washington to Governor Trumbull, December 2, 1775," in *The Papers of George Washington, Revolutionary War Series*, Vol. 2, 471–72.

15. Chase, "General Orders, December 3, 1775," in *The Papers of George Washington, Revolutionary War Series*, Vol. 2, 475.

16. Chase, "Circular Letter to the New England Governments, December 5, 1775," in *The Papers of George Washington, Revolutionary War Series*, Vol. 2, 492.

17. Chase, "General Washington to John Hancock, December 11, 1775," in *The Papers of George Washington, Revolutionary War Series*, Vol. 2, 533.

18. Force, ed., "General Sullivan to New Hampshire Committee of Safety, December 8, 1775," in *American Archives, Fourth Series*, Vol. 4, 221.

19. Force, ed., "General Greene to Governor Ward, December 10, 1775," in *American Archives, Fourth Series*, Vol. 4, 231–32.

20. Force, ed., "General Greene to Governor Ward, December 18, 1775," in *American Archives, Fourth Series*, Vol. 4, 311–12.

21. Roberts, "Journal of Abner Stocking," in *March to Quebec: Journals of the Members of Arnold's Expedition*, 564–65.

22. Henry B. Dawson, "General Daniel Morgan: An Autobiography," in *The Historical Magazine and Notes and Queries Concerning the Antiquities, History and Biography of America, Second Series*, Vol. 9 (Morrisania, NY: 1871), 379–80.

23. Charles Porterfied, "Diary of Colonel Charles Porterfield, *Magazine of American History*, Vol. 21 (April 1899), 319.

24. Roberts, "Journal of Abner Stocking," in *March to Quebec: Journals of the Members of Arnold's Expedition*, 565.

25. Force, ed., "Account of the Attempt on Quebeck, New York Gazette, January 17, 1776," in *American Archives, Fourth Series*, Vol. 5, 708.

26. Roberts, "Journal of George Morison," in *March to Quebec: Journals of the Members of Arnold's Expedition*, 537–38.

27. Ibid., 538.

28. Force, ed., "Account of the Attempt on Quebeck, *New York Gazette*, January 17, 1776," *American Archives, Fourth Series*, Vol. 5, 708.

29. Ford, "Proceedings of the Continental Congress, January 24, 1776," *Journals of the Continental Congress*, Vol. 4, 84.

30. Paul E. Smith, ed., "Oliver Wolcott to Philip Schuyler, January 24, 1776," in *Letters of Delegates to Congress: 1774–1789*, Vol. 3 (Washington, DC: Library of Congress, 1978), 130.

31. Smith, "Thomas Lynch to Philip Schuyler, January 20, 1776," in *Letters of Delegates to Congress: 1774–1789*, Vol. 3, 125.
32. Chase, "Council of War, January 18, 1776," in *The Papers of George Washington, Revolutionary War Series*, Vol. 3, 132–33.
33. Chase, "Council of War, January 16, 1776," in *The Papers of George Washington, Revolutionary War Series*, Vol. 3, 103.
34. Chase, "Council of War, January 18, 1776," in *The Papers of George Washington, Revolutionary War Series*, Vol. 3, 132–33.
35. Chase, "Circular to the Governments of Massachusetts, Connecticut, and New Hampshire, January 19, 1776," in *The Papers of George Washington, Revolutionary War Series*, Vol. 3, 145.
36. King George III, "His Majesty's most gracious speech to both houses of Parliament," October 27, 1775, Library of Congress, https://www.loc.gov/item/2005578060.
37. Ibid.
38. Ibid.
39. Chase, "General Washington to John Joseph Reed, January 4, 1776," in *The Papers of George Washington, Revolutionary War Series*, Vol. 4, 24.
40. Chase, "General Washington to John Hancock, January 4, 1776," in *The Papers of George Washington, Revolutionary War Series*, Vol. 4, 20.
41. Ibid.
42. Showman, "General Greene to Catharine Greene, January 13, 1776," in *The Papers of General Nathanael Greene*, Vol. 1, 182.
43. Clark, "Captain Francis Hutchinson to Major General Frederick Haldimand, December 23, 1775," in *Naval Documents of the American Revolution*, Vol. 3, 212–14.
44. Clark, "Journal of the Massachusetts Council, December 29, 1775," in *Naval Documents of the American Revolution*, Vol. 3, 291.
45. Clark, "Report of the Committee for Fitting Out Massachusetts Armed Vessels, January 12, 1776," in *Naval Documents of the American Revolution*, Vol. 3, 734.
46. Ibid.
47. Clark, "Journal of the Massachusetts House of Representatives, February 6, 1776," in *Naval Documents of the American Revolution*, Vol. 3, 1144.
48. Clark, "Journal of the Massachusetts House of Representatives, February 7, 1776," in *Naval Documents of the American Revolution*, Vol. 3, 1156.
49. "Proceedings of the Massachusetts House of Representatives, January 19, 1776," in *Journals of the House of Representatives of Massachusetts*, Vol. 51, part 2, 170–74.
50. Ibid., 175.
51. Force, ed., "Proceedings of the New Hampshire Provincial Congress, January 5, 1776," in *American Archives, Fourth Series*, Vol. 5, 1–2.
52. Ibid., 2.
53. Bouton, "Provincial Congress Proceedings, January 20, 1776," in *Documents and Records Relating to the Province of New Hampshire . . . 1623–1776*, Vol. 8, 44–45.

54. Bouton, "Letter from General John Sullivan, January 20, 1776," in *Documents and Records Relating to the Province of New Hampshire . . . 1623–1776*, Vol. 8, 55.

55. Bouton, The Council and Assembly of the Colony of New Hampshire to the Continental Congress, January 27, 1776," in *Documents and Records Relating to the Province of New Hampshire . . . 1623–1776*, Vol. 8, 67.

56. Ford, "Proceedings of the Continental Congress, May 14, 1775," in *Journals of the Continental Congress*, Vol. 4, 357.

57. Chase, "Governor Cooke to General Washington, December 19, 1775," in *The Papers of George Washington, Revolutionary War Series*, Vol. 2, 581.

58. Chase, "General Washington to Nicholas Cooke, December 20, 1775" and "General Washington to John Hancock, December 25, 1775," in *The Papers of George Washington, Revolutionary War Series*, Vol. 2, 585, 602.

59. Dexter, "December 25, 1775," in *The Literary Diary of Ezra Stiles, President of Yale College*, Vol. 1, 645.

60. Ibid., 645.

61. Dexter, "December 26, 1775," in *The Literary Diary of Ezra Stiles, President of Yale College*, Vol. 1, 646–47.

62. Clark, "Captain Wallace to Vice-Admiral Graves, December 28, 1775," in *Naval Documents of the American Revolution*, Vol. 3, 278–79.

63. Chase, "General Washington to Nicholas Cooke, January 6, 1776," in *The Papers of George Washington, Revolutionary War Series*, Vol. 3, 39.

64. Clark, "Journal of the Rhode Island General Assembly, January 8, 1776" and "Journal of the Committee Appointed to Build Two Continental Frigates, January 8, 1776," in *Naval Documents of the American Revolution*, Vol. 3, 676–77.

65. Clark, "Captain Wallace to Vice-Admiral Shuldham, January 14, 1775," in *Naval Documents of the American Revolution*, Vol. 3, 784.

66. Allen, "Providence, January 20, 1776," *Providence Gazette*, 3.

67. Ibid.

68. Clark, "Captain Wallace to Vice-Admiral Shuldham, January 14, 1775," in *Naval Documents of the American Revolution*, Vol. 3, 784.

69. Clark, "Journal of the Rhode Island General Assembly January 17, 1775," in *Naval Documents of the American Revolution*, Vol. 3, 835–36.

70. Chase, "Nicholas Cooke to General Washington, January 21, 1776," in *The Papers of George Washington, Revolutionary War Series*, Vol. 3, 159.

71. Force, ed., "Proceedings of the Connecticut General Assembly, December 14, 1775," in *American Archives, Fourth Series*, Vol. 4, 268–69.

72. Ibid.

73. Ibid.

74. Clark, "Journal of the Connecticut Assembly, December 15, 1775," in *Naval Documents of the American Revolution*, Vol. 3, 114.

75. Chase, "Governor Trumbull to General Washington, January 1, 1776," in *The Papers of George Washington, Revolutionary War Series*, Vol. 3, 8.

76. Chase, "Governor Trumbul to General Washington, January 22, 1776," in *The Papers of George Washington, Revolutionary War Series*, Vol. 3, 168.

77. Robert K. Wright Jr., *The Continental Army* (Washington, DC: Center of Military History, U.S. Army, 1989), 58.
78. Chase, "Governor Trumbull to General Washington, January 15, 1776," in *The Papers of George Washington, Revolutionary War Series*, Vol. 3, 97–98.
79. Chase, "Instructions to General Lee, January 8, 1776," in *The Papers of George Washington, Revolutionary War Series*, Vol. 3, 53.
80. Silas Deane, "Dr. Benjamin Gale to Silas Deane, November 9, 1775, Correspondence of Silas Deane . . . ," in *Collections of the Connecticut Historical Society*, Vol. 2 (Hartford, CT: 1860), 315–18.
81. Hoadly,"Meeting of the Council of Safety, February 2, 1776,"in *The Public Records of the Colony of Connecticut: From May 1775 to June 1776*, 233–34.
82. James Thacher, "February 10, 1776," in *Military Journal of the American Revolution* (Hartford, CT: American Subscription Publishing House, 1862), 62–63.
83. Chase, "General Washington to John Hancock, December 31, 1775," in *The Papers of George Washington, Revolutionary War Series*, Vol. 2, 625.
84. Force, ed.,"General Return of the Army of the United Colonies . . . January 8, 1776," in *American Archives, Fourth Series*, Vol. 4, 631–32.
85. Chase,"General Washington to John Hancock, January 4, 1776," in *The Papers of George Washington, Revolutionary War Series*, Vol. 3, 18–19.
86. Chase, "Circular to the New England Governments, December 23, 1775," in *The Papers of George Washington, Revolutionary War Series*, Vol. 2, 591–92.
87. Showman, "General Greene to Samuel Ward, December 31, 1775," in *The Papers of General Nathanel Greene*, Vol. 1, 173.
88. Chase, "General Washington to John Hancock, January 14, 1776," in *The Papers of George Washington, Revolutionary War Series*, Vol. 3, 84–85.
89. Chase, "General Washington to Joseph Reed, January 14, 1776," in *The Papers of George Washington, Revolutionary War Series*, Vol. 3, 89–90.
90. Chase, "Council of War, January 16, 1776," in *The Papers of George Washington, Revolutionary War Series*, Vol. 3, 103.
91. Chase, "General Washington to the Massachusetts General Court, February 10, 1776," in *The Papers of George Washington, Revolutionary War Series*, Vol. 3, 284.
92. Chase, "General Washington to Joseph Reed, February 10, 1776," in *The Papers of George Washington, Revolutionary War Series*, Vol. 3, 287.
93. Chase, "Council of War, February 16, 1776," in *The Papers of George Washington, Revolutionary War Series*, Vol. 3, 320–22.
94. Ibid.
95. Chase, "Plan for Attacking Boston, February 18–25, 1776," in *The Papers of George Washington, Revolutionary War Series*, Vol. 3, 332–33.
96. Chase, "General Washington to Joseph Reed, February 26, 1776," in *The Papers of George Washington, Revolutionary War Series*, Vol. 3, 370.

CHAPTER FIVE: SPRING 1776

1. Lesser, "General Return of the Army of the United Colonies . . . March 2, 1776," in *Sinews of Independence, Monthly Strength Reports of the Continental Army*, 16.

2. Rowena Buell, ed., *The Memoirs of Rufus Putnam* . . . , (Boston and New York: Houghton, Mifflin, and Co., 1903), 58.

3. Chase, "General Washington to John Hancock, March 7, 1776," in *The Papers of George Washington, Revolutionary War Series*, Vol. 3, 420.

4. Ibid.

5. Clark, "Diary of Captain Samuel Richards," in *Naval Documents of the American Revolution*, Vol. 4, 189.

6. Chase, "General Washington to John Hancock, March 7–9, 1776," n4, in *The Papers of George Washington, Revolutionary War Series*, Vol. 3, 426–27.

7. Heath, "March 4, 1776," in *Memoirs of Major-General William Heath*, 32–33.

8. Force, ed., "Extract of a Letter from an Officer of Distinction in the British Army, to a Person in London, March 5, 1776," in *American Archives, Fourth Series*, Vol. 4, 425–26.

9. Chase, "General Washington to John Hancock, March 7, 1776," in *The Papers of George Washington, Revolutionary War Series*, Vol. 3, 422.

10. Chase, "From the Boston Selectmen, March 8, 1776," in *The Papers of George Washington, Revolutionary War Series*, Vol. 3, 434.

11. Chase, "General Orders, March 9, 1776," in *The Papers of George Washington, Revolutionary War Series*, Vol. 3, 440.

12. Chase, "General Orders, March 13, Note 2 and General Orders, March 14, 1776," in *The Papers of George Washington, Revolutionary War Series*, Vol. 3, 459, 466.

13. Chase, "General Washington to John Hancock, March 19, 1776," in *The Papers of George Washington, Revolutionary War Series*, Vol. 3, 489–90.

14. Ibid., 490.

15. Chase, "General Washington to Lieutenant Colonel Joseph Reed, March 19, 1776," in *The Papers of George Washington, Revolutionary War Series*, Vol. 3, 493.

16. Chase, "General Orders, March 23, 1776," in *The Papers of George Washington, Revolutionary War Series*, Vol. 3, 516–17.

17. Chase, "Circular to Nicholas Cooke, Lord Stirling, Brigadier General William Thompson and Jonathan Trumbull Sr., March 27, 1776," in *The Papers of George Washington, Revolutionary War Series*, Vol. 3, 543; Lesser, "General Return of the Army of the United Colonies . . . April 28, 1776," in *Sinews of Independence*, 20.

18. Bouton, "Proceedings of the New Hampshire House of Representatives, March 11, 1776," in *Documents and Records Relating to the Province of New Hampshire . . . 1623–1776*, Vol. 8, 84.

19. Chase, "The New Hampshire General Court to General Washington, March 12, 1776," in *The Papers of George Washington, Revolutionary War Series*, Vol. 3, 454.

20. Chase, "General Washington to Meshech Weare, March 14, 1776," in *The Papers of George Washington, Revolutionary War Series*, Vol. 3, 472.

21. Chase, "Rhode Island General Assembly to General Washington, March 19, 1776," in *The Papers of George Washington, Revolutionary War Series*, Vol. 3, 494–95.

22. Chase, "General Washington to Governor Trumbull, March 14, 1776," in *The Papers of George Washington, Revolutionary War Series*, Vol. 3, 471.

23. Hoadly, "Meeting of the Governor and Council of Safety, March 18, 1776,"in *The Public Records of the Colony of Connecticut: From May 1775 to June 1776*, 250.

24. Hoadly, "Meeting of the Council of Safety, April 1, 1776," in *The Public Records of the Colony of Connecticut: From May 1775 to June 1776*, 256.

25. Clark, "Intelligence of Continental Navy, January 4, 1776" and "Commodore Esek Hopkins to John Hancock, April 9, 1776," in *Naval Documents of the American Revolution*, Vol. 4, 616, 735.

26. Clark, "Captain James Wallace, R. N. to Vice Admiral Molyneux Shuldham, April 10, 1776," in *Naval Documents of the American Revolution*, Vol. 4, 746–47.

27. Clark, "Remarks on Board His Majesty's Ship *Glasgow*, Saturday the 6th Day of April, 1776," in *Naval Documents of the American Revolution*, Vol. 4, 680–81.

28. Clark, "Extract of a Letter from the Captain of Marines (Samuel Nicholas) on Board the Ship Alfred, dated at New London, April 10, 1776," in *Naval Documents of the American Revolution*, Vol. 4, 751.

29. Clark, "Remarks on Board His Majesty's Ship Glasgow, Saturday the 6th Day of April, 1776," in *Naval Documents of the American Revolution*, Vol. 4, 681.

30. Clark, "Commodore Esek Hopkins to John Hancock, April 9, 1776," in *Naval Documents of the American Revolution*, Vol. 4, 736.

31. Southwick, "Newport, April 8, 1776," *Newport Mercury*, 2.

32. Ibid.

33. Ibid.

34. Clark, "Journal of HMS *Glasgow*, April 8, 1776," in *Naval Documents of the American Revolution*, Vol. 4, 710.

35. Clark, "Journal of HMS *Scarborough*, April 11–12, 1776," in *Naval Documents of the American Revolution*, Vol. 4, 768, 783.

36. John Anderson, "Newport, April 24, 1776," *Constitutional Gazette*, 2.

37. Clark, "Journal of HMS *Scarborough*, April 12-13, 1776," in *Naval Documents of the American Revolution*, Vol. 4, 783, 797.

38. Clark, "Journal of HMS *Scarborough*, April 13, 1776," in *Naval Documents of the American Revolution*, Vol. 4, 797.

39. Clark, "Journal of HMS *Scarborough*, April 14, 1776," in *Naval Documents of the American Revolution*, Vol. 4, 783, 814–15.

40. Ibid.

41. Chase, "General Washington to John Hancock, April 15, 1776," in *The Papers of George Washington, Revolutionary War Series*, Vol. 4, 69–70.

42. Robert Taylor, ed., "William Gordon to John Adams, May 1, 1776," in *Papers of John Adams*, Vol. 4, (Cambridge and London: Belknap Press, 1979), 159.

43. Powars and Willis, "May 23, 1775," *New England Chronicle*, 3.

44. Ibid., 216.

45. Ibid.

46. William J. Morgan, ed., "Thomas Cushing to John Hancock, May 17, 1776," in *Naval Documents of the American Revolution*, Vol. 5 (Washington, DC: U.S. Government Printing Office, 1970), 135.

47. Chase, "General Washington to General Ward, May 28, 1776," in *The Papers of George Washington, Revolutionary War Series*, Vol. 4, 403–4.

48. Ibid., 218.

49. Morgan, "Journal of HMS *Renown*, May 19, 1776," in *Naval Documents of the American Revolution*, Vol. 5, 149–50.

50. Powars and Willis, "May 23, 1776," *New England Chronicle*, May 23, 1776, 3.

51. Morgan, "Journal of HMS *Renown*, May 19, 1776," in *Naval Documents of the American Revolution*, Vol. 5, 149–50.

52. Morgan, "Journal of HMS *Experiment*, May 19, 1776," in *Naval Documents of the American Revolution*, Vol. 5, 164.

53. Chase, "General Artemas Ward to General Washington, May 21, 1776," in *The Papers of George Washington, Revolutionary War Series*, Vol. 4, 347.

54. Morgan, "David Cobb to Robert Treat Paine, May 20, 1776," in *Naval Documents of the American Revolution*, Vol. 5, 162.

55. Powars and Willis, "May 23, 1776," *New England Chronicle*, 3.

56. Chase, "General Washington to General Ward, June 16, 1776," in *The Papers of George Washington, Revolutionary War Series*, Vol. 5, 16.

57. Morgan, "Lieutenant Colonel Archibald Campbell to Major General William Howe, June 19, 1776," in *Naval Documents of the American Revolution*, Vol. 5, 619.

58. Ibid.

59. Ibid.

60. Ibid.

61. Morgan, "Captain Seth Harding to Governor Jonathan Trumbull, June 19, 1776," in *Naval Documents of the American Revolution*, Vol. 5, 618.

62. Morgan, "Lieutenant Colonel Archibald Campbell to Major General William Howe, June 19, 1776," in *Naval Documents of the American Revolution*, Vol. 5, 620.

63. Ibid.

64. Morgan, "Captain Seth Harding to Governor Jonathan Trumbull, June 19, 1776," in *Naval Documents of the American Revolution*, Vol. 5, 618.

65. Morgan, "Lieutenant Colonel Archibald Campbell to Major General William Howe, June 19, 1776," in *Naval Documents of the American Revolution*, Vol. 5, 620.

66. Morgan, "Lieutenant Colonel Archibald Campbell to Major General William Howe, June 19, 1776" and "John Bradford to John Hancock, June 20, 1776," in *Naval Documents of the American Revolution*, Vol. 5, 620, 636.

67. Morgan, "Levi Hollingsworth and Thomas Richardson to the Pennsylvania Committee of Safety, May 21, 1776," in *Naval Documents of the American Revolution*, Vol. 5, 186.

68. Ford, "Proceedings of the Continental Congress, May 7, 1776," in *Journals of the Continental Congress*, Vol. 4, 333.

69. Morgan, "Memorial of the Rhode Island Assembly to the Continental Congress, May 20, 1776," in *Naval Documents of the American Revolution*, Vol. 5, 165–66.

70. Ibid.

71. Ibid.

72. Ford, "Proceedings of the Continental Congress, May 30, 1776," in *Journals of the Continental Congress*, Vol. 4, 406.

73. Chase, "General Orders, April 15, 1776," in *The Papers of George Washington, Revolutionary War Series*, Vol. 4, 65.

74. Lesser, "General Return of the Troops of the United Colonies, Serving in Canada . . . May 11, 1776," in *Sinews of Independence, Monthly Strength Reports of the Continental Army*, 22.

75. Ibid.

76. Chase, "General Orders, April 27, 1776," in *The Papers of George Washington, Revolutionary War Series*, Vol. 4, 141.

77. Lesser, "General Return of the Troops of the United Colonies, Serving in Canada . . . May 11, 1776," in *Sinews of Independence, Monthly Strength Reports of the Continental Army*, 22.

78. Ibid.

CHAPTER SIX: SUMMER 1776

1. Force, ed., "A Return of the Troops before Quebec . . . March 30, 1776," in *American Archives, Fourth Series*, Vol. 5, 1100.

2. Mark R. Anderson, *The Battle for the Fourteenth Colony: America's War of Liberation in Canada, 1774–1776* (Lebanon, NH and London: University Press of New England, 2013), 285.

3. Chase, "General Thomas to General Washington, May 8, 1776," in *The Papers of George Washington, Revolutionary War Series*, Vol. 4, 231.

4. Force, ed., "General Thomas to the Commissioners in Canada, May 20, 1776," in *American Archives, Fourth Series*, Volume 6, 592.

5. Ibid.

6. Chase, "General Arnold to General Washington, May 8, 1776," in *The Papers of George Washington, Revolutionary War Series*, Vol. 4, 230.

7. Ibid.

8. Ford, "Proceedings of the Continental Congress, July 10, 1776," in *Journals of the Continental Congress*, Vol. 5, 534.

9. New Hampshire Historical Society, "Guide to the Timothy Bedel Papers, 1763–1787,", n.d., unpublished, 2.

10. Ibid.

11. Ford, "Proceedings of the Continental Congress, July 10, 17766," in *Journals of the Continental Congress*, Vol. 5, 534.

12. Ibid.

13. Ibid.

14. Force, ed., "An Account of the Unfortunate Affair at the Cedars, May 27, 1776," in *American Archives, Fourth Series*, Vol. 5, 599.

15. Ford, "Proceedings of the Continental Congress, July 10, 1776," in *Journals of the Continental Congress*, Vol. 5, 535.

16. Force, ed., "The Following Authentick Account is Communicated by an Officer of the Detachment it Principally Concerns, June 20, 1776," in *American Archives, Fourth Series*, Vol. 5, 598.

17. Ford, "Proceedings of the Continental Congress, July 10, 1776," in *Journals of the Continental Congress*, Vol. 5, 535.

18. Ibid.

19. Ibid.

20. Ibid.

21. Ibid.

22. Smith, "Commissioners to Canada to John Hancock, May 27, 1776," in *Letters of Delegates to Congress, 1774–1789*, Vol. 4, 83–84.

23. Ford, "Proceedings of the Continental Congress, July 10, 1776," in *Journals of the Continental Congress*, Vol. 5, 535.

24. National Archives, "Report of the Committee on the Cedars Cartel, June 17, 1776," Founders Online, https://www.founders.archives.gov/?q=Cedars%20Cartel&=1111311111&sa=&r=5&sr=.

25. Lesser, "Return of the Troops of the United Colonies, Serving in Canada . . . May 11, 1776," in *Sinews of Independence*, 22.

26. Chase, "General Thompson to General Washington, June 2, 1776," in *The Papers of George Washington, Revolutionary War Series*, Vol. 4, 428.

27. Chase, "General Thompson to Congress, June 3, 1776," n2 in *The Papers of George Washington, Revolutionary War Series*, Vol. 4, 433.

28. Chase,"General Sullivan to General Washington, June 6, 1776," in *The Papers of George Washington, Revolutionary War Series*, Vol. 4, 440–41.

29. Morgan, "General Thompson to General Sullivan, June 7, 1776," in *Naval Documents of the American Revolution*, Vol. 5, 408.

30. Anderson, *The Battle for the Fourteenth Colony: America's War of Liberation in Canada, 1774-1776*, 327.

31. Charles J. Stille, "Colonel Wayne to Dr. Franklin and Others," in *Major-General Anthony Wayne and the Pennsylvania Line in the Continental Army* (Port Washington, NY: Kennikat Press, 1968), 29; Force, ed., "Extract of a Letter from the Camp at the Mouth of the Sorel, June 12, 1776," in *American Archives, Fourth Series*, Vol. 6, 826.

32. Stille, "Colonel Wayne to Dr. Franklin and Others," in *Major-General Anthony Wayne and the Pennsylvania Line in the Continental Army*, 30.

33. Force, ed.,"Extract of a Letter from the Camp at the Mouth of the Sorel, dated June 12, 1776," in *American Archives, Fourth Series*, Vol. 6, 826–27.

34. Ibid., 827.

35. Anderson, *Battle for the Fourteenth Colony*, 329.

36. Force, ed., "Extract of a Letter from the Camp at the Mouth of the Sorel, dated June 12, 1776," in *American Archives, Fourth Series*, Vol. 6, 827.

37. Ibid.

38. Davies, "General Guy Carleton to Lord George Germain, June 20, 1776," in *Documents of the American Revolution*, Vol. 12, 152.

39. Force, ed., "A Return of the Continental Forces in Canada, June 12, 1776," in *American Archives, Fourth Series* Vol. 6, 915–16.

40. Ibid.

41. Chase, "General Washington to John Augustine Washington, April 29, 1776," in *The Papers of George Washington, Revolutionary War Series*, Vol. 4, 172–73.

42. Lesser, "General Return of the Army of the United Colonies Commanded by his Excellency General Washington, May 19, 1776," in *Sinews of Independence*, 22.

43. Ibid.

44. Ibid.

45. Ibid.

46. Ford, "Proceedings of the Continental Congress, May 14 and 16, 1776," in *Journals of the Continental Congress*, Vol. 4, 357, 360.

47. Ford, "Proceedings of the Continental Congress, June 1 and 3, 1776," in *Journals of the Continental Congress*, Vol. 4, 410–12.

48. Lesser, "Return of the Army . . . Under the Command of Major-General Horatio Gates, August 24, 1776," in *Sinews of Independence, Monthly Strength Reports of the Continental Army*, 30.

49. Chase, "Joseph Hawley to General Washington, June 21, 1776," in *The Papers of George Washington, Revolutionary War Series*, Vol. 5, 70–71.

50. Chase, "General Washington to John Hancock, July 4, 1776," in *The Papers of George Washington, Revolutionary War Series*, Vol. 5, 199–200; Ford, "Proceedings of the Continental Congress, July 5 and 8, 1776," in *Journals of the Continental Congress*, Vol. 5, 522, 527.

51. Chase, "General Washington to General Ward, July 9 and 11, 1776," in *The Papers of George Washington, Revolutionary War Series*, Vol. 5, 254–55, 276–77.

52. Smith, "George Washinton to Robert McKenzie, October 9, 1774," in *Letters of Delegates to Congress, 1774–1789*, Vol. 1, 166.

53. Smith, "Silas Deane to Elizabeth Deane, May 24, 1775," in *Letters of Delegates to Congress, 1774–1789*, Vol. 1, 403.

54. Showman, "General Greene to Samuel Ward, Sr., October 23, 1775," in *The Papers of General Nathanael Greene*, Vol. 1, 140–41.

55. Chase, "General Washington to Joseph Reed, February 10, 1776," in *The Papers of George Washington, Revolutionary War Series*, Vol. 4, 288.

56. Ibid.

57. Force, ed., "Proceedings of the Rhode Island General Assembly, May 6, 1776," in *American Archives, Fourth Series*, Vol. 5, 1215.

58. Force, ed., Stephen Hopkins to Governor Cooke, May 15, 1776," in *American Archives, Fourth Series*, Vol. 6, 467.

59. Force, ed., "Votes of Several Towns in Massachusetts Relating to Independence," in *American Archives, Fourth Series*, Vol. 6, 698–706.

60. Force, ed., Joseph Hawley to Elbridge Gerry, June 13, 1776," in *American Archives, Fourth Series*, Vol. 6, 844–45.

61. Force, ed., "Proceedings of the New Hampshire General Assembly, June 15, 1776," in *American Archives, Fourth Series*, Vol. 6, 1030.

62. Force, ed., "Proceedings of the Connecticut General Assembly, June 14, 1776," in *American Archives, Fourth Series*, Vol. 6, 868.

63. Thomas and Samuel Green, "Philadelphia, July 6," *The Connecticut Journal*, July 10, 1776, 2.

64. Timothy Green, "In Congress July 4, 1776," *The Connecticut Gazette and The Universal Intelligencer*, July 12, 1776, 2.

65. John Carter, "Providence, July 13," *The Providence Gazette and Country Journal*, July 13, 1776, 3.

66. Southwick, "In General Assembly, July Session, 1776," *The Newport Mercury*, July 22, 1776, 4.

67. Force, ed.,"Newport, July 22, 1776," in *American Archives, Fifth Series*, Vol. 1, 476.

68. Edward Powars and Nathaniel Willis, "Boston, Thursday, July 11," *The New-England Chronicle*, July 11, 1776, 3.

69. Force, ed., "Boston, Thursday July 18, 1776," in *American Archives, Fifth Series*, Vol. 1, 425.

70. Force, ed., "Portsmouth, New Hampshire, July 20, 1776," in *American Archives, Fifth Series*, Vol. 1, 427.

BIBLIOGRAPHY

Published Primary Sources

Abbott, William, ed. *Memoirs of Major-General Heath*. New York: William Abbott, 1901.

Ballagh, James C., ed. *Letters of Richard Henry Lee*, Vol. 1. New York: Macmillan Co., 1911.

Bartlett, John Russell, ed. *Records of the Colony of Rhode Island and Providence Plantations in New England*, Vol. 7. Providence, RI: A. Crawford Greene, State Printer, 1862.

Bouton, Nathaniel, ed. *Provincial Papers, Documents and Records Relating to the Province of New Hampshire*, Vol. 7. Nashua, NH: Orren C. Moore, State Printer, 1873.

Buell, Rowena, ed. *The Memoirs of Rufus Putnam*. Boston and New York: Houghton, Mifflin, and Co., 1903.

Chase, Philander D., ed. *The Papers of George Washington, Revolutionary War Series*, Vols. 1–5. Charlottesville: University Press of Virginia, 1985–1993.

Clark, William, ed. *Naval Documents of the American Revolution*, Vol. 1–4. Washington: US Government Printing Office: 1964–1969.

Commager, Henry S. and Richard B. Morris. *The Spirit of Seventy-Six: The Story of the American Revolution as Told by Its Participants*. New York: Harper & Row, 1967.

Davies, K. G. ed. *Documents of the American Revolution, 1770–1783*, Vols. 8–12. Shannon, Ireland: Irish University Press, 1975–1976.

Dawson, Henry B. "General Daniel Morgan: An Autobiography." In *The Historical Magazine and Notes and Queries Concerning the Antiquities, History and Biography of America, 2nd Series*, Vol. 9, 1871.

Deane, Silas. "Dr. Benjamin Gale to Silas Deane, November 9, 1775, Correspondence of Silas Deane," *Collections of the Connecticut Historical Society*, Vol. 2. Hartford, CT: 1860.

Dexter, Franklin B., ed. *The Literary Diary of Ezra Stiles*, Vol. 1. New York: Charles Scribner's Sons: 1901.

Farnsworth, Amos. *Amos Farnsworth Journal*. Massachusetts Historical Society, January 1898.

Force, Peter, ed. *American Archives, Fourth Series*, Vols. 1–5. Washington, DC: M. St. Clair and Peter Force: 1839–1843.

———. *American Archives, Fifth Series*, Vols. 1–3. Washington, DC: M. St. Clair and Peter Force: 1848–1853.

Ford, Worthington C., ed. *Journals of the Continental Congress, 1774-1789*, Vols. 2–5. Washington, DC: U.S. Government Printing Office, 1905–1907.

———. *Correspondence and Journals of Samuel Blachley Webb*. New York: Times & Arno Press, 1969.

Henshaw, William. *The Orderly Book of Colonel William Henshaw, of the American Army, April 20–Sept. 26, 1775*. Boston: A. Williams and Co., 1881.

Hoadly, Charles, ed. *The Public Records of the Colony of Connecticut: From October 1772 to April 1775*. Hartford, CT: Lockwood & Brainard Co., 1887.

The Lee Papers, Vols. 1–2. New York Historical Society, 1872.

LeMoine, J. M. *The Centenary Fete of the Literary and Historical Society of Quebec*, 1876.

Lesser, Charles H., ed. *The Sinews of Independence: Monthly Strength Reports of the Continental Army*. Chicago: University of Chicago Press, 1976.

Lincoln, William, ed. *Journals of each Provincial Congress of Massachusetts in 1774 and 1775, and of the Committee of Safety*. Boston: Dutton and Wentworth, Printers to the State, 1838.

Martin, Joseph Plum. *Private Yankee Doodle: Being a Narrative of Some of the Adventures, Dangers and Sufferings of a Revolutionary Soldier*. Eastern Acorn Press, 1962.

Mackenzie, Frederick. *The Diary of Frederick Mackenzie*, Vol. 1. Cambridge, MA: Harvard University Press, 1930.

Mevers, Frank C., ed. *The Papers of Josiah Bartlett*. Hanover, NH: University Press of New England, 1979.

Morgan, James, W., ed. *Naval Documents of the American Revolution*, Vol. 5. Washington, DC: U.S. Government Printing Office, 1970.

Porterfield, Charles. "Diary of Colonel Charles Porterfield." In *Magazine of American History*, Vol. 21, April 1889.

Reed, William. *The Life and Correspondence of Joseph Reed*. Philadelphia: Lindsay and Blakiston, 1847.

Roberts, Kenneth, ed. *March to Quebec: Journals of the Members of Arnold's Expedition*. Garden City, NY: Doubleday & Co., 1938.

Showman, Richard K. *The Papers of General Nathanael Greene*, Vol. 1. Chapel Hill: University of North Carolina Press, 1976.

Scott, Kenneth, ed. *Rivington's New York Newspaper: Excerpts from a Loyalist Press, 1773– 1783*. New York Historical Society, 1973.

Smith, Paul H., ed. *Letters of Delegates to Congress: 1774–1789*, Vols. 1-4. Washington, DC: Library of Congress, 1976.

Taylor, Robert J. *Papers of John Adams*, Vols. 3–4. Cambridge, MA: Belknap Press of Harvard University Press, 1979.

Thacher, James. *Military Journal of the American Revolution*. Gansevoort, New York: Corner House Historical Publications, 1998.

Tatum, Edward, Jr. *The American Journal of Ambrose Serle*. New York: Arno Press, 1969.

Taylor, Robert J., ed. *The Papers of John Adams*, Vol. 3, Cambridge, MA: Belknap Press, 1979.

Tomlinson, Abraham, ed. *The Military Journals of Two Private Soldiers, 1758–1775*. Poughkeepsie, NY: Abrahan Tomlinson, 1855.

Willard, Margaret Wheeler, ed. *Letters on the American Revolution, 1774–1776*. Boston and New York: Houghton Mifflin Co., 1925.

U.S. Census Bureau. "Estimated Population of American Colonies: 1610 to 1780." In *Historical Statistics of the United States: Colonial Times to 1970*, Part 2. U.S. Census Bureau.

UNPUBLISHED PRIMARY SOURCES

Guide to the Timothy Bedel Papers, 1763–1787," New Hampshire Historical Society.

King George III, "His Majesty's most gracious speech to both houses of Parliament, October 27, 1775, Library of Congress.

Letter from Peter Brown to his Mother, June 25, 1775, Massachusetts Historical Society.

Letter from William Prescott to John Adams, August 25, 1775, Massachusetts Historical Society.

Letter from Lt. J. Waller to a Friend, June 21, 1775, Massachusetts Historical Society.

"Report on the Committee on the Cedars Cartel, June 17, 1776," Founders Online, National Archives.

SECONDARY SOURCES

Ahlin, John Howard. *Maine Rubicon: Downeast Settlers during the American Revolution*. Camden, ME: Picton Press, 1966.

Anderson, Mark R. *The Battle for the Fourteenth Colony: America's War of Liberation in Canada, 1774–1776*. Lebanon, NH, and London: University Press of New England, 2013.

Atkinson, Rick. *The British Are Coming: The War for America, Lexington to Princeton, 1775–1777*. New York: Henry Holt & Co., 2019.

Beck, Derek W. "The First Naval Skirmish of the Revolution." *Journal of the American Revolution*, October 7, 2013, https://allthingsliberty.com/2013/10/first-naval-skirmish-revolution/.

Bell, J. L. *The Road to Concord: How Four Stolen Cannon Ignited the Revolutionary War*. Yardley, PA: Westholme Publishing, 2016.

Boatner, Mark M. *Encyclopedia of the American Revolution*. Essex, CT: Stackpole Books, 1966.

Brooks, Victor. *The Boston Campaign: April 1775–March 1776*. Cambridge, MA: De Capo Press, 1999.

Clark, Stephen. *Following Their Footsteps: A Travel Guide & History of the 1775 Secret Expedition to Capture Quebec*. Williamstown, MA: Clark Books, 2003.

Cutter, William. *The Life of Israel Putnam, Major-General of the Army of the American Revolution*, 3rd Edition. New York: George F. Cooledge & Brother, 1848.

Daniell, Jere R. *Colonial New Hampshire: A History*. Millwood, NY: KTO Press, 1981.

Desjardin, Thomas A. *Through A Howling Wilderness: Benedict Arnold's March to Quebec, 1775*. New York: St. Martin's Griffin, 2006.

Ellis, Joseph J. *Revolutionary Summer: The Birth of American Independence*. New York: Vintage Books, 2013.

Fischer, David Hackett. *Paul Revere's Ride*. New York and Oxford: Oxford University Press, 1994.

Flickinger, Floyd B. "Captain Morgan and His Riflemen." *Winchester-Frederick County Historical Society Journal*, Vol. 14 (2002).

Frothingham, Richard. *History of the Siege of Boston and of the Battles of Lexington, Concord, and Bunker Hill*. Boston: Little Brown & Co., 1896.

Gabriel, Michael P. *Major General Richard Montgomery: The Making of an American Hero*. Madison, NJ: Fairleigh Dickinson University Press, 2002.

Gavin, John R. *The Minute Men: The First Fight: Myths and Realities of the American Revolution*. Washington, DC: Potomac Books, 2006.

Gross, Robert A. *The Minutemen and Their World*. New York: Hill and Wang, 1976.

Hatch, Robert M. *Thrust for Canada: The American Attempt on Quebec in 1775–76*. Boston: Houghton Mifflin Co., 1979.

Humphreys, David. *An Essay on the Life of the Honourable Major-General Israel Putnam*. Indianapolis, IN: Liberty Fund, 2000.

James, Sydney V. *Colonial Rhode Island: A History*. New York: Charles Scribner's Sons, 1975.

Ketchum, Richard M. *Decisive Day: The Battle of Bunker Hill*. New York: John Macrae/Henry Holt & Co., 1974.

Labaree, Benjamin W. *Colonial Massachusetts: A History*. Millwood, NY: KTO Press, 1979.

Leamon, James S. *Revolution Downeast: The War for American Independence in Maine*. Amherst: University of Massachusetts Press, 1993.

Lefkowitz, Arthur S. *Benedict Arnold's Army: The 1775 American Invasion of Canada during the Revolutionary War*. New York and El Dorado Hills, CA: Savas Beatie, 2008.

Martyn, Charles. *The Life of Artemas Ward, the First Commander in Chief of the American Revolution.* New York: A Ward, 1921.

Matten, David B. *Benjamin Lincoln and the American Revolution.* Columbia: University of South Carolina Press, 1995.

Miller, Nathan. *Sea of Glory: The Continental Navy Fights for Independence, 1775–1783.* New York: David McKay Co., 1974.

National Park Service, Washington, DC. *The Siege of Boston, Part 1.* Historic Resource Study.

Nelson, James L. *George Washington's Secret Navy: How the American Revolution Went to Sea.* New York: McGraw Hill, 2008.

Nourse, Henry S. "A Forgotten Patriot." *American Antiquarian Society*, October 1890.

Patton, Robert H. *Patriot Pirates: The Privateer War for Freedom and Fortune in the American Revolution.* New York: Pantheon, 2008.

Paullin, Charles O. *The Navy of the American Revolution: Its Administration, its Policy and its Achievements.* New York: Haskell House Publishers, 1971.

Philbrick, Nathaniel. *Bunker Hill: A City, A Siege, A Revolution.* New York: Penguin Books, 2013.

Phillips, Kevin. *1775: A Good Year for Revolution.* New York: Viking, 2012.

Price, David. "Thomas Knowlton's Revolution." *Journal of the American Revolution.* September 2, 2021, https://allthingsliberty.com/2021/09/thomas-knowltons-revolution/.

Randall, Peter. *New Hampshire: Years of Revolution, 1774–1783.* New Hampshire Profiles, 1976.

Stille, Charles, J. *Major-General Anthony Wayne and the Pennsylvania Line in the Continental Army.* Port Washington, NY: Kennikat Press, 1968.

Strange, Lt. Col. "Historical Notes on the Defence of Quebec in 1775." *The Centenary Fete of the Literary and Historical Society of Quebec,* 1876.

Taylor, Robert J. *Colonial Connecticut: A History.* Millwood, NY: KTO Press, 1979.

Wilderson, Paul W. *Governor John Wentworth & the American Revolution.* Lebanon, NH, and London: University Press of New England, 1994.

Williamson, William. *The History of the State of Maine*, Vol. 2. Hallowell: Glazer, Masters & Smith, 1839.
Wright, Robert K. Jr. *The Continental Army*. Washington, DC: Center of Military History, U.S. Army, 1989.
Yerxa, Donald A. "The Burning of Falmouth 1775: A Case Study in British Imperial Pacification." *Maine Historical Society Quarterly* 14, no. 3, 1975.

NEWSPAPERS

New Hampshire
Fowle, *New Hampshire Gazette*, April 21, 1775.
Fowle, *New Hampshire Gazette*, May 5, 1775.
Fowle, New *Hampshire Gazette*, August 15, 1775.

Massachusetts
Hall, *The Essex Gazette*, February 28, 1775.
Powars and Willis, *New England Chronicle*, May 23, 1775.
Thomas, *Massachusetts Spy*, May 24, 1775.

Rhode Island
Southwick, *Newport Mercury*, April 24, 1775.
Allen, *Providence Gazette*, January 20, 1776.
Carter, *The Providence Gazette and Country Journal*, July 13, 1776.
Southwick, *The Newport Mercury*, July 22, 1776.

Connecticut
Watson, *Connecticut Courant*, April 24, 1775.
Green, *The Connecticut Gazette and The Universal Intelligencer*, September 1, 1775.
Green, *The Connecticut Journal*, July 10, 1776.
Green, *The Connecticut Gazette and The Universal Intelligencer*, July 12, 1776.

New York
Anderson, *Constitutional Gazette*, April 24, 1776.

Pennsylvania
Towne, *Pennsylvania Evening Post*, December 12, 1775.

ACKNOWLEDGMENTS

THIS TRILOGY ON THE FIRST MONTHS OF THE REVOLUTIONARY War across the colonies would not have been possible without the encouragement and support of my publisher, Bruce Franklin. It was he who suggested that I expand my focus from the southern colonies to the middle and northern colonies, and I am grateful for his vision. Tracy Dungan has once again done a fantastic job with the maps for this volume. Trudi Gershenov has produced another great looking cover, and Christine Florie worked diligently to correct my typos and mistakes. I appreciate everyone's effort and assistance.

My "go to" source for information remains the Rockefeller Library in Williamsburg, Virginia. It is my oasis of Revolutionary knowledge and I thank them for providing such a wonder resource to anyone interested in this time period. All of the folks at Colonial Williamsburg also deserve a nod of appreciation from me for their continued inspiration in teaching the American Revolution through living history.

INDEX